Ethnography, Linguistics, Narrative Inequality

To all with whom I have worked in education
and on behalf of narrative and voice

Ethnography, Linguistics, Narrative Inequality

Toward an Understanding of Voice

Dell Hymes

Taylor & Francis
Publishers since 1798

UK   Taylor and Francis Ltd, 1 Gunpowder Square, London EC4A 3DE
USA   Taylor & Francis Inc., 1900 Frost Road, Suite 101, Bristol, PA 19007

First published 1996

A catalogue record for this book is available from the British Library

ISBN 0 7484 0347 7
ISBN 0 7484 0348 5 (pbk)

Library of Congress Cataloging-in-Publication Data are available on request

Cover design by Hyberts Design & Type

Typeset in 10/12pt Baskerville
by Euroset, Alresford, Hampshire SO24 9PG.

Printed in Great Britain by SRP Ltd, Exeter.

Contents

Series Editor's Introduction

Dell Hymes's work has changed the way that we view language and the social world. *Ethnography, Linguistics, Narrative Inequality* is a powerful collection of essays that addresses theoretical, methodological and political issues about the study of language in social context. The contents are diverse, ranging from the critical discussion of American language planning and policy, to the study of the traditional narratives of Native Americans and stories written by African-American school children. At its heart is an analysis of the complex relationships between language, speech communities and social inequality.

This volume of essays spans the period from 1972 to the present. It begins from seminal discussions of the applications of ethnography and linguistics to education, with a focus on the contexts of American communities and schools. Given the current economic situations of many linguistic and cultural 'minority' communities in the US and elsewhere, it should not be surprising that Hymes's commentary on 'the origins and foundations of inequality among speakers' continues to ring true. Hymes asks how we can use theory and research in ethnography, linguistics and education to understand how particular discourses, languages and 'literacies' count and act in particular cultures' and communities' interests.

We see these questions at work in Hymes's 'ethnopoetic' analyses of the voices of Native American communities, school children, adolescents and university students. The section entitled 'Narrative and Inequality' includes discussions of work by Courtney Cazden, Amy Shuman, James Gee, Sarah Michaels, William Labov, and Nessa Wolfson. Many of these essays have been updated and revised, with additional theoretical comment and new text analyses. In addition to situating this work in relation to the broader histories of linguistics and ethnography, Hymes here provides a critical commentary o the contributions of Habermas, Bourdieu and, especially, Basil Bernstein (1996) to discussions of language and inequality.

For me, the key work in this volume is the essay entitled 'Speech and Language: On the Origins and Foundations of Inequality Among Speakers'. Originally published in 1973 in the journal *Daedalus*, this version features expanded discussions of the characteristics of writing systems and literacy, Bernstein's theory of codes, and the ideal speech situation. Beginning from Rousseau's 1756 essay on inequality, Hymes questions the 'principled schizophrenia [that] besets linguistics today' whereby 'the scientific and social goals of many practitioners are compartmentalized'. As an alternative, he proposes an ethnography of language that is a science of activism and intervention: 'The proper role of the scientist . . . should not be "extractive", but mediative. It should be to help communities be ethnographers of their own situations. . . .' He concludes that 'every form of human speech [has] gained the right, . . . to contribute on equal footing to what is known of human language.'

The tasks outlined by Hymes in this essay are a worthy guide for educational research language and literacy. He argues that we need to focus on, *inter alia*, the social and discursive relationships between and within speech communities, the linguistic and social differences between speech and writing, the institutional acquisition and use of 'linguistic resources', and, most importantly, the relationship between language and systems of domination and subordination. This is framed by his broader proposal for a science of 'mediative' practice, involving interventions with, on behalf of and along side of marginalized communities of speakers.

> In this way one can go beyond a liberal humanism that merely recognizes the abstract potentiality of all languages, to a humanism which can deal with concrete situations, with the inequalities that actually obtain, and help to transform them through knowledge of the ways in which language is actually organized as a human problem and resource.

For the past two decades, this challenge was pursued by John Gumperz and Hymes (1972/1986), and colleagues in the formation of an 'ethnography of communication', described across these chapters. Along with its companion piece 'Report from an Underdeveloped Country', 'Speech and Language' stands as a reminder that much current research that asks 'What counts as language?' and 'What counts as literacy?' also requires an analysis of language and social hegemony, which may act to cancel or 'write over' diversity and thereby mask the social origins of inequality:

> In Western civilization the dominant intellectual response to the existence of diversity has been to seek an original unity, either of

historical or psychological origin (sometimes of both). The dominant practical response has been to impose unity in the form of the hegemony of one language or standard.

These issues of linguistic and social inequality remain central to our work as teachers and researchers, particularly as we contend with the educational consequences of new economies and communities, hybrid voices and cultural identities. Hymes's ethnography of communication seems particularly appropriate for the study of how communities contend with the 'detraditionalization' brought on by demographic change, shifting relations of capital, communications technologies and systems of representation. Perhaps, sociologist Paul Heelas (1996, p. 3) cautions, the condition of 'postmodernity' has not marked as decisive and radical a shift from traditional and modernist beliefs and practices as many would have us believe. What Heelas terms a 'coexistence thesis' calls for a move away from 'before and after theorizing' towards the study of how communities and individuals reconfigure traditional values, practices and discourses in the face of new technologies, cultures and identities.

Narrative provide what Hymes called a textual 'architecture' where we can observe these residual and emergent cultural traditions brought into 'confluence' with each other. Hymes's analyses of the narratives of Zuni elders, African-American children and adults, and university studies here may provide evidence of 'social change and cultural loss' at work in the everyday acquisition and use of linguistic resources. We might view classroom narratives as evidence of diverse 'grammars of experience' brought to educational institutions. However, Hymes and Cazden signal that in institutions like universities, 'the right to think and express thought in narrative comes to be taken as a privilege, as a resource that is restricted' and, in instances, actively 'repressed'.

The matter of the 'uptake' of speakers' narratives by researchers, teachers and institutions is crucial. Our task is to understand how narratives work on behalf of cultural change, continuity and hybridity, and how the institutional uptake of children's narrative resources produces social inequality. Here Hymes emphasizes the importance of the work of Basil Bernstein in providing an analysis that links 'the cultural (communicative) nuts and bolts of exploitation and alienation' with larger patterns of reproduction that tend to be described in frustratingly abstract terms by sociologists.

Ethnography, Linguistics, Narrative Inequality brings together an analysis of language and the social, and a research practice that is committed to enabling communities of speakers to analyze and deal strategically with issues of voice, inequality and change. Hymes puts it this way:

Discourse ultimately cannot change the inequalities that make it rational for centers and margins of power alike to combine in ecological destruction . . ., nor change interests that find it reasonable to allow the destruction of habitat, even to continue to prepare for the destruction of us all; but discourse is everywhere, and scrutiny of our own and that of others is a lens that may sometimes focus light enough to illuminate and even to start a fire.

The perspectives and issues that Dell Hymes has raised for us over the past 20 years remain the key issues of language and literacy education: Whose narratives and whose literacies will count? In whose interests? In what kind of a society? In this book, we hear about the politics of voice and we hear the voices of many communities. Unlike the Trickster Coyote in the Zuni tale, Dell Hymes heard but didn't lose the song.

Allan Luke
February, 1996
Brisbane, Australia

References

BERNSTEIN, B. (1996) *Pedagogy, Symbolic Control and Identity*. London: Taylor & Francis.

Gumperz, J.J. and Hymes, D. (1972/1986) *Directions in Sociolinguistics: The Ethnography of Speaking*. New York: Holt, Rinehart & Winston. Rev. Ed. Oxford: Basil Blackwell.

HEELAS, P. (1996) 'Introduction: Detraditionalization and its Rituals', in HEELAS, P., LASH, S. and MORRIS, P. (Eds) *Detraditionalization*, Oxford: Basil Blackwell, pp. 1–20.

Prefaces

My efforts to think about language as part of life have been shaped by involvement with education and with people concerned about education, and I am grateful to Allan Luke for suggesting such a book and to the encouragement of Courtney Cazden.

I find myself with two prefaces, one rather personal, one rather general. I hope both have interest.

Much of my work has been concerned with the topics of the three parts: with ethnography as an approach, linguistics as a field, and narrative as a human accomplishment. The two chapters in Part I arose out of engagement with education, as the surprised dean of the Graduate School of Education at the University of Pennsylvania, and as an officer of the Council on Anthropology and Education, that part of the American Anthropological Association concerned with education. The first is an attempt to be explicit about what I understand the tradition and nature of ethnography to be – a cumulative coming to grips with local meanings and emergent configurations. When I think of the second chapter, I recall beside me as a chair of the meeting at which it was delivered someone for whom I had great respect, Eleanor Leacock, from whom I learned, as from her father, Kenneth Burke.

The two chapters in the second part each began with invitations to take part in general gatherings. Their themes are rooted in a constitutional inability to understand why students of language would not want to understand what goes on around them, and fail to accept that forms and meanings are part of social relationships, never wholly extricable from them, bearing on human life only insofar as such relationships are part of what is studied and understood. Those to whom this is obvious, and those to whom it is unimportant or invisible, mostly pass on opposite sides of the street these days, no longer bothering to dispute. The two chapters stem from a decade in which it seemed that the obvious might make a difference. To those in education, of course, it must. That no doubt is the reason that patterns of ability and competence are recognized as diverse and locally specific in education, and notions that permit their recognition cultivated there.

Probably I should apologize for length. As long as I can recall, I have been eager to gather in whatever seemed connected to a subject, a lover of terrain.

The six chapters of the third part have a good deal of original analysis. They take up and find inadequate some other approaches to narrative well known in education and elsewhere, and show, convincingly I hope, that aesthetic shape is normal, and probably universal, something that comes with language itself . . . that tellers make their points in culturally characteristic shapes . . . that writing may involve such shapes . . . that the possibility of narrative voice is given with the possibility of language, but at the same time, that its realization is partly at the mercy of others . . . that what happens to the potentiality of language is always at risk, often poignant.

Most of these chapters are technical in part, at least in the sense that linguistic training and analysis of poetry both lead one to notice verbal details and to explore relations among them. I hope enough is shown for others to use the approach and to explore and extend the little that is known.

The chapters arise out of various occasions, all connected with friends and colleagues concerned with education. The first two involve my concern over the years with Native American traditions, particularly those of the part of the world from which I come, Oregon. The others honor colleagues each in a different part of the world, Berkeley, Australia, London, Philadelphia. I thank them all.

This book's three parts represent three concerns necessary to an adequate grasp of what each of us has to say to each other and to ourselves. Each of us speaks (and writes) in a context of understandings and taken-for-granted conventions, a network of implication and form. If it matters to get these right, observation, asking, comparison, are needed – in short, ethnography. Without ourselves as subjects, those who observe and compare are likely to get things wrong. Without them, as observers and analysts, we are likely to be obscure to ourselves.

Probably everyone has views on languages, those they use themselves, those others use. Not many are in a position to pin down what goes on. In the United States it once seemed that the mission of modern linguistics was to share with everyone information and skills that could demystify the ways we speak and write, hear and read, their history and how they work now. That mission was overtaken by enthusiasm for fascinating aspects of language as an abstract formal device and visions of a kind of unity beyond. There are those who doubt that differences of language should be much of a problem. From a certain height or depth there seems to be so much in common, the potentiality of any variety of language so great. But differences remain, weighted with attitudes and evaluations, affecting life-chances, affecting self-respect.

A purpose of this book therefore is to argue for the obvious – at least to those whose *trained incapacity* permits (I take Veblen's term to apply to us all, if in different respects). That however much all language may be the same from certain standpoints, it does not count as the same in life. It is organized, not in grammars, but in styles, whose defining features and appropriate occasions require ethnographic linguistics, or linguistic ethnography, to discover.

A second purpose is to argue that theoretical goals are not the only worthwhile goals of the study of language. Education about language (not necessarily about theory) is as well. Elementary features of language should be known by everyone. It is shameful that fine poets and famous people publish books that make a mess of elementary facts as to the relations between English spellings and sounds. Ordinary people could do new and useful things with the language around them if elementary skill were provided, especially at an early age when it is easy and fun.

It is important to argue as well that the potential equality of languages, and of people with regard to language, is not actual equality. That inequality exacts a cost as to what people can convey, and what others will make of it. Some do much to address these things, but many more could help, not least by respecting and valuing the task.

Narrative is perhaps as old as language. It is at the heart of everyday life. Few live healthy lives with no one to tell what has happened. There is much about the rich possibilities of narrative not addressed in this book, but the part that is addressed is fundamental. Its recognition has arisen at the margins of culture and prestige, in concern for Native American traditions and young people not thought to speak appropriately. It would be fitting if recognition of the interest and richness of narratives from the margins should come to transform the whole.

Dell Hymes

Acknowledgments

'What is Ethnography?' (Chapter 1) first appeared as *Working Papers in Sociolinguistics* 45, distributed by the Southwest Educational Development Laboratory, Austin, Texas, 1978. It also appeared as Chapter 4 in my *Language in Education: Ethnolinguistic Essays* (1980) published in the Language and Ethnology Series of the Center for Applied Linguistics, Washington, DC. The book and series were available only briefly.

'Educational Ethnography' (Chapter 2) was my address (1979) as past president of the Council for Anthropology and Education, and appeared in the journal of the Council, *Anthropology and Education Quarterly* (1980) 11: pp. 3–8. It also appeared as Chapter 5 in *Language in Education: Ethnolinguistic Essays*.

'Speech and Language: On the Origins and Foundations of Inequality among Speakers' (Chapter 3) was written for a conference on Language as a Human Problem, organized by Einar Haugen and Morton Bloomfield, at the American Academy of Arts and Sciences in 1972. It appeared in *Daedalus* (Summer, 1973), pp. 59–86 (Proceedings of the American Academy of Arts and Sciences **102** (3). It also appeared as Chapter 2 in *Language in Education: Ethnolinguistic Essays*, expanded there, as here, in the discussion of writing, and of Bernstein and Habermas. This version has additional examples and references, and various revisions in details of writing.

'Report from an Underdeveloped Country: Linguistic Competence in the United States' (Chapter 4) began as a lecture, Toward Linguistic Competence, at the Festival of the Social Sciences, Amsterdam, April 1975. The lecture, somewhat edited, appeared in *Sociologische Gids* (1976) **76**(4): pp. 217–39. A substantially revised version appeared in *The Sociogenesis of Language and Human Conduct* (1983) (ed.) Bruce Bain, New York, Plenum, pp.

189–234. The present chapter has been augmented by a number of references, and the latter part has been reorganized and also rewritten at several points.

'Narrative Thinking and Storytelling Rights' (Chapter 5) joins reflections of my own and of Courtney Cazden. It first appeared in *Keystone Folklore* **22** (1978) 21–36, and then as Chapter 7 in *Language in Education: Ethnolinguistic Essays*, and Chapter 12 of Cazden (1992) *Whole Language Plus: Essays on Literacy in the United States and New Zealand*, New York: Teachers College Press.

'Narrative Form as a Grammar of Experience: Native Americans and a Glimpse of English' (Chapter 6) began as a transcript of an address at the Sixth Annual Boston University Conference on Language Development, Boston, October 1981, and appeared in Boston University's *Journal of Education*, **164**(2) (Spring 1982), pp. 121–42.

'Oral Patterns as a Resource in Children's Writing: An Ethnopoetic Notes' (Chapter 7) is a contribution to *Social Interaction, Social Context and Language: Essays in Honor of Susan Ervin-Tripp*, edited by Dan I. Slobin, Julie Gerhardt, Amy Kyratzis and Jiansheng Guo, and published by Lawrence Erlbaum Associates, Hillsdale, NJ. The analysis of the young boy's first writing there has been revised on one point, and analysis of writing by a teen-age girl has been added.

'Ethnopoetics and Sociolinguistics: Three Stories by African-American Children' (Chapter 8) appeared in *Linguistics in the Service of Society. Essays in Honour of Susan Kaldor* (1991) edited by Ian G. Malcolm, Perth, Institute of Applied Language Studies, Edith Cowan University, pp. 155–70. An earlier version appeared in *Working Papers in Educational Linguistics* **3**(2) (Fall 1987), pp. i–xxi, Graduate School of Education, University of Pennsylvania. The last section (Leona's story) has been corrected and revised.

'Bernstein and Poetics' (Chapter 9) appeared in *Discourse and Reproduction* (1994) edited by Paul Atkinson and Sara Delamont, Cresskill, NJ: Hampton Press. The analysis and discussion of the narrative by John L. has been somewhat revised.

'Inequality in Language: Taking for Granted' (Chapter 10) was given October 15, 1991 at the University of Pennsylvania, as a lecture in memory of Nessa Wolfson. It was the first of an annual series of lectures sponsored by the Wolfson family and the Graduate School of Education. The lecture appeared in the Graduate School's *Working Papers in Educational Linguistics* **8**(1) (1992). A somewhat revised version appeared in *Language, Communication, and Social Meaning*, Georgetown University Round Table on Languages and Linguistics (1992), edited by James E. Alatis, Washington, DC, Georgetown University Press, 1993, pp. 23–40, but unfortunately with the text discussed in the paper. The analysis and discussion of the text, She's a Widow, have been revised.

Part I
Ethnography

Chapter 1

What is Ethnography?[1]

Introduction

Ethnography has come to be much discussed in education. Often enough one hears some form of the question, 'What is ethnography?' The National Institute of Education commissioned a report to answer the question. All this might be puzzling to an anthropologist, especially to one with an interest in the history of the subject. If one traces the history of ethnography where it leads, one goes back centuries, indeed, to the ancient Mediterranean world, and the temporary rise and fall of ethnographic inquiry there, Herodotus being its most famous, but not only, exemplar. With regard just to the Americas, one can trace a fairly continuous history of ethnographic reports, interacting with the posing of ethnological questions, from the first discovery of the New World. There is a considerable modern literature on the practice of fieldwork, both in general and with regard to specific techniques, and more recently, ethics. A book addressed to ethnography in our own society (Spradley and McCurdy, 1972) has been used by teachers of composition to stimulate topics for their students. If ethnography is new to some in education, certainly it is not new to the world. When asked, 'What is ethnography?', would it not be enough to provide a short reading list, or to point to the discussion in some text of what research proposals often refer to as 'standard ethnographic method'?

I fear not. Anthropologists do not themselves have a unified conception of ethnography. In particular they do not have a unified conception of ethnography in relation to the study of institutions of our own society, such as education. And anthropologists are far from accepting or perfecting an integration of the mode of research they would consider ethnography with other modes of research into a society such as our own. The changing intellectual context of the human sciences as a whole introduces new questions and sources of diversity.

Educational research has been dominated by quantitative and experimental conceptions of research. It is easy for anthropologists of a variety of persuasions to criticize such methods. It is often harder for them to state concisely the alternatives. Ethnography cannot be assumed to be something already complete, ready to be inserted as a packaged unit in the practices and purposes of institutions whose conceptions of knowledge and research have long been different. If there is not careful thinking through of underlying conceptions and explicit attention to differences in them, 'ethnography' may be a brief-lived fad in educational research. Or worse, partial or superficial conceptions may be taken up.

The true opportunity of the current interest in ethnography is to enter into a mutual relation of interaction and adaptation between ethnographers and sponsors of educational research, a relation that will change both. Because of my conception of ethnography, I see in this prospect a gain for a democratic way of life. The following sketch is offered because I do not know of a similar attempt to consider the issues raised here in brief compass. Many others must contribute from their own experience and outlook.

The Ethnographic Tradition

One difficulty with the notion of ethnography is that it may seem a residual category. It is associated with the study of people not ourselves, and with the use of methods other than those of experimental design and quantitative measurement. Clearly not everything that is not experimental design and quantitative measurement should be considered ethnography, but a positive definition is not easy to provide. A major reason for the difficulty is that good ethnography has been produced under a great variety of conditions, by a great variety of persons, some of it before there was a profession to train such people, and professional training has been very much a matter of the transmission of a craft and of learning by doing – by personal experience.

It has not helped that some people talk as if the key to ethnography were a psychological experience, rather than the discovery of knowledge. It is clear that ethnography involves participation and observation. What should count as ethnography, what kinds of ethnography there are, may be more easily seen if we consider what makes participation and observation systematic – what, in short, counts as systematic ethnography.

The earliest work that we recognize as important ethnography has generally the quality of being systematic in the sense of being comprehensive. To be sure, any and all early accounts of travellers, missionaries, government officials and the like that may contribute information and insight about the culture of the peoples of the world have been welcomed and gleaned for what they could provide. But when Ibn Khaldun (1967 [1381]) or Father Sahagun (1956 [1840, composed 1547–1569]) are singled out, it is because they are both early and comprehensive. Their curiosity was not limited to curiosities. They had an interest in documenting and interpreting a wide range of a way of life.

4

Much of the early attempts to make ethnographic inquiry an explicit procedure reflect the desire to be comprehensive. These attempts are guides to inquiry, lists of questions, of observations to make. They bespeak a stage of history when much of the non-western world was little known to Europe, and when a variety of reasons, scientific, religious or practical, motivated some to seek more adequate knowledge. These guides to inquiry have in common a concern with all of a way of life (although their coverage may be unequal). What are the people of such and such a place like?

It was not long before there were explicit procedures that can be distinguished as *topic-oriented*. (Indeed, the Domesday Book and the inquiries of Sir William Petty[2] (1623–87) share in this lineage.) The great American example is Lewis Henry Morgan's questionnaires for recording kinship terminologies in the middle of the nineteenth century. It is worth pausing to consider the several aspects of Morgan's great work. First, he had a contrastive, or comparative insight: from his experience with the Iroquois Indians, together with his knowledge of classical Greece, he realized that there was a principle of kinship organization sharply contrasting with that familiar to contemporary Americans and Europeans. He sought then to determine the main types of kinship systems and their locations throughout the world. Second, he needed systematic information, information not available except as he sought it himself. Hence his own travels in the western United States and his relentless correspondence with those who could help. Third, he made use of his findings to formulate first a historical (*Systems of Consanguinity and Affinity*, 1870) and then evolutionary interpretation (*Ancient Society*, 1877) of the most general sort, of human development as a whole.

These three aspects of inquiry seem the essential ingredients of anthropological research proper, as distinct from inquiry that contributes to anthropology. Each aspect may exist independently – a contrastive insight, a seeking of specific information, a general interpretation. Anthropology proper exists insofar as the three are united in a common enterprise. Ethnography is more than a residual technique, but the name of an essential method, when all three are united.

With time there has come to be a certain body of ethnographic inquiry that can be said to be *hypothesis-oriented*. To be sure, Morgan had a general hypothesis. But it seems reasonable to distinguish the kind of ethnography organized and guided by John and Bea Whiting, for example, for inquiry into socialization in several contrasting societies. The Whitings had attempted to come to general conclusions, testing hypotheses on a theoretical base, from the ethnographic literature that existed at the time. They found, as so many find, that their questions were more specific than the literature could answer. The sources were not detailed enough for their purpose, and not comparable enough. Therefore they organized a project to provide the detailed, comparable information they needed. Ethnographic teams (generally, couples) were trained in terms of a guide to the field study of socialization, sent into the field in several different societies for an extended period of time, kept in touch with through correspondence throughout the field study, and brought back to write up their results. (Whiting, 1963, is a principal outcome.) Like Morgan, the Whitings had insight into contrasting types of society, a need for specific information, and a general theoretical frame (in this case, psychodynamic) to which contrast and specifics were relevant.

All three types of ethnographic inquiry continue to coexist in anthropology today. There may still be occasional discoveries of unrecognized peoples (as claimed in the Philippines a few years ago), for whom comprehensive information is to be provided from scratch. There are still many peoples, knowledge about whom has never been adequately systematized, and which has serious gaps. Fresh ethnography may be undertaken for first-hand knowledge as a basis from which to integrate all that is known, or to fill a gap in what is already known.

There are still discoveries of aspects of culture, or of perspectives on culture, such that the existing literature fails to provide much information. The 'ethnography of speaking' is a case in point. The Human Relations Area Files, although rich in ethnographic data, simply did not contain much information on cultural patterning of speech, let alone information at all on the fundamental question, the functions of speech in the society. (Anthropological theory had taken for granted that the functions of speech were everywhere the same.) When such a discovery or perspective comes to the fore, topic-oriented ethnography may be undertaken. One needs to find out something of the range of cultural patterning, once cultures are investigated from the new point of view.

Both comprehensive ethnography and topic-oriented ethnography lead to hypothesis-oriented ethnography. Given a substantial general knowledge of a culture, precise investigations can be planned. Indeed, hypothesis-oriented research depends on the existence of comprehensive ethnography, and can be fruitfully pursued only where the latter exists. Again, once something of the range of patterns for an aspect of culture is known, one begins to formulate more precise questions. Research may show the recurrence of a contrast in styles of speaking that can be called *direct* vs. *indirect* – but are the attributes of the two styles the same in each case? Are the functions the same? In the ethnography of speaking right now, one is aware of broad contrasts, usually presented as dichotomies (cf. Bernstein's *elaborated* and *restricted* codes). This fact is a sure sign, I think, of the topic-oriented stage and of the need to proceed to the hypothesis-oriented stage.

Schooling in Ethnographic Perspective

What might the subject of schooling in America be like in this context? Clearly there is a great deal of information already in hand. It is not so clear that the information is obtained and analysed in ways that permit all the insight possible into schooling. If schools were considered from the same standpoint as kinship systems or languages, the first question might be: what kinds of schools are there? It would not seem informative enough to know that test scores were up or down in general across all American schools, if in fact the country contains schools of many different types. The point would apply even within a single city or district. Are the schools of District 1 in Philadelphia all alike? If they are different, how many different kinds are there? Probably at any level of consideration, one would not want to say that all were alike, nor that all were incomparably unique. In sum, one would recognize a question of typology, as central to analysis.

A useful typology has to be designed in terms of a particular purpose. Kinship is important to social life, and central to many societies, but even so, a classification and analysis of societies according to kinship is not the same as a classification and analysis according to religion. There are strong connections, but not invariant bonds, among the various sectors of a way of life, and so also, among the various sectors of schools. A typology of schools in District 1 in terms of verbal skills or questions having to do with literacy would not necessarily be the right typology for some other purpose. Conversely, and here is an essential point, a typology for some other purpose is not necessarily right for a concern with verbal skills.

This essential point is an example of a general consideration that divides many ethnographers from an experimental model, at least as that model is understood by them. For many ethnographers, it is of the essence of the method that it is a dialectical, or feed-back (or interactive–adaptive) method. It is of the essence of the method that initial questions may change during the course of inquiry. One may begin with the assumption that every community must have a pattern for the residence of newly-married couples that can be of only one of four types, yet discover that the community one is studying actually determines the residence of newly-married couples on the basis of principles one had not foreseen. (The illustration is an actual one. See Goodenough, 1956).

The history of anthropology is replete with experiences of this sort. The general mission of anthropology in part can be said to be to help overcome the limitations of the categories and understandings of human life that are part of a single civilization's partial view. For many ethnographers, an essential characteristic of ethnography is that it is open-ended, subject to self-correction during the process of inquiry itself. All this is not to say that ethnography is open-minded to the extent of being empty-minded, that ignorance and naivete are wanted. The more the ethnographer knows on entering the field, the better the result is likely to be. Training for ethnography is only partly a matter of training for getting information and getting along. It is also a matter of providing a systematic knowledge of what is known so far about the subject. The more adequate this knowledge, the more likely the ethnographer will be able to avoid blind alleys and pursue fruitful directions, having a ground sense of what kinds of things are likely to go together, what kinds of phenomena need minimal verification, what most.

One conception of this process is that of Kenneth Pike. Pike (1965) generalized the experience of linguistic inquiry. In order to discover the system of sounds of a language one had to be trained to record the phenomena in question, and one had to know what types of sound were in general found in languages. Accurate observation and recording of the sounds, however, would not disclose the system. One had to test the relations among sounds for their functional relevance within the system in question. The result of this analysis of the system might in turn modify the general framework for such inquiry, disclosing a new type of sound or relation. Pike generalized the endings of the linguistic terms *phonetic* and *phonemic* to obtain names for these three moments of inquiry. The general framework with which one begins analysis of a given case he called $etic_1$. The analysis of the actual system he called *emic*. The reconsideration of the general framework in the light of the analysis he called $etic_2$.

When ethnographic and linguistic inquiry are described in such terms, it may be easy to see the connection with general scientific method and the exemplification of such method in the experimental sciences. For many ethnographers and linguists the spirit of inquiry is indeed the same. The scale and conditions of inquiry in ethnography, nevertheless, impose essential differences in tactics. Perhaps the key to these differences is meaning.

For ethnographic inquiry, *validity* is commonly dependent upon accurate knowledge of the meanings of behaviors and institutions to those who participate in them. To say this is not to reduce the subject matter of ethnography to meaning, let alone to native views of meaning. It is simply to say that accurate knowledge of meaning is a *sine qua non*. The problem is obvious enough in the case of a language and culture we do not know. It is less obvious in the case of communities around us. Yet even though one may live nearby, speak the same language, and be of the same ethnic background, a difference in experience may lead to misunderstanding the meanings, the terms and the world of another community. In Philadelphia, for example, a questionnaire was prepared by a central-office person generally qualified by training and ethnic background. The purpose of the questionnaire was to find out what parents thought of a community-relations policy and person. The questionnaire was duly administered. The student administering the questionnaire discovered, during informal conversations with parents, that they interpreted the questions differently than the designer and the school. The parents distinguished between a *playground* (having equipment designed for children to use) and a *playyard*, but the questionnaire did not. When asked if they had had a chance to meet their School-Community Coordinator, they answered 'no', because to them to *meet* would require having *talked*, and knowing by name, even first-name, not just having been introduced. In terms of the questionnaire their 'no's' were interpreted as *not having met*. The student administering the questionnaire was distressed, but the procedure of inquiry had no way for him to take account of what he had learned or to have what he had learned affect the presumed results (Abbot, 1968).

Experiences of this kind make ethnographers distrust questionnaires and quantitative results derived from them, if the meanings of the questions to those asked are taken for granted in advance. Many ethnographers do use questionnaires, but questionnaires devised after sufficient participation and observation to ensure their validity.

The validity of knowledge about persons, families, neighborhoods, schools, and communities in our country depends upon accurate and adequate knowledge of the meanings they find and impute to terms, events, persons, and institutions. To an important extent, such meanings cannot be taken for granted as uniform, even within a single city or school district, nor as known in advance. The overt forms may be familiar – the words, the attire, the buildings – but the interpretation given to them is subject to shift, to deepening, to fresh connecting up. (It has been found that within a single small factory in Pennsylvania, those who worked in different parts had different terms for the same things (see Tway, 1975).

It is in the nature of meanings to be subject to change, re-interpretation, re-creation. One has to think of people, not as the intersection of vectors of age, sex, race, class, income, and occupation alone, but also as beings making sense out of disparate experiences, using reason to maintain a sphere of integrity in an immediate world. All this is not to say that ethnography indulges in an infinite regress of personal subjectivity and idiosyncratic worlds. It has to be open to that dimension of social life, because that dimension affects the reality of social life, and the success or failure of social programs. The point is to stress the necessity of knowledge that comes from participation and observation, if what one thinks one knows is to be valid. And all this is not to say that members of a community themselves have an adequate model of it, much less an articulated adequate model. All of us are only partly able to articulate analyses of our lives and their contexts. The meanings which the ethnographer seeks to discover may be implicit, not explicit. They may not lie in individual items (words, objects, persons) that can be talked about, but in connections that can only gradually be discerned. The deepest meanings and patterns may not be talked about at all, because they are so fully taken for granted.

Here again the need to discover and validate in the given case is paramount. Our familiar categories of institutions, modes of communication or the like, are an indispensable starting point (Pike's *etic*$_1$), but are never to be equated with an analysis of the organization of a local way of life. We necessarily distinguish speech and song, and as polar opposites, there may be speech with no musical quality and singing without words. In our own musical traditions and in the cultures of the world, the interconnections and conceptions of these relationships of speaking and singing (and music generally) are various and diverse. Modern serious music includes such categories as

Sprechstimme introduced by Arnold Schoenberg. The Maori of New Zealand consider the playing of the flute a form of speaking. It is especially these local nodes of connection, these community-specific ways of putting the encyclopedia of culture together, that cannot be assumed in advance of inquiry, and that can only be discovered through participation and observation over time.

We know that Philadelphia has newspapers, radio stations, television stations, libraries, books, comic books, magazines, inscriptions and plaques, narrators and joke-tellers. Without ethnography we can collect statistics as to production and distribution. Only with ethnography can we discover the connections among these things in the lives of particular kinds of people. Even self-report cannot be relied upon – people are notoriously unable or unwilling to give accurate accounts of the amount of time they spend on various things, and a key to the significance of a type of television program may not be in the amount of time the family set is on, but in the family pattern of speaking around it. Is the set on, but ignored? Does someone insist on and get silence? Is the program essentially a resource for continuing conversation?

All that I have said is compatible with a generous view of scientific method. The subject-matter of ethnography – people and their worlds – imposes conditions such that validity and research design have a complexity and openness at the other end of the scale from the experimental design in many fields. Even so, there is a similarity to the problems of fields such as astronomy and geology in their observational aspects. In principle, a sufficient accumulation of valid knowledge about a particular society would make possible rather efficient, precise inquiries of an experimental or quasi-experimental sort. Indeed, there are some cases of this sort. My own experience is with languages. Given the accumulated knowledge of the Native American languages I have studied, it is possible to address many particular questions rapidly, systematically, precisely. If a new word is in question, it is a matter of minutes to establish its grammatical place in the system. One does know already just what questions must be asked, to establish that the word is a noun or a verb, say, and just what kind. If a newly discovered recording of a familiar word is in question, one knows exactly the possibilities of interpretation, how the facts of the language constrain the sounds that the letters may represent. (All of this presupposes a native speaker who has become accustomed to collaboration in work of this kind.) A social anthropologist can look at a newly collected schedule of kinship terms and place the system approximately quite quickly.

Ethnography and Openness

These examples illustrate two points made previously – that ethnographic training involves training in the accumulated comparative knowledge of the subject, and that the existence of comprehensive knowledge about a community makes more precise hypothesis-testing possible.

To leave matters here, however, might suggest that ethnography can become almost equivalent to laboratory work. The theoretical foundations on which it rests have yet to prove as certain as that. The social knowledge that ethnography serves is in the paradoxical position of becoming increasingly certain of more and more, and yet at the same time vulnerable to dispute about its very foundation. Our last example, that of kinship terms, is an excellent case in point. No one could deny the striking progress in our ability to recognize and describe the terms and behaviors relevant to kinship in the hundred years or so since Morgan's pioneering work. Descriptive technique, comparative typology, even mathematical modelling are well advanced. Yet it is possible to dispute the correct interpretation of particular findings (cf. Blu, 1967) and even the correct definition of the domain of *kinship* itself (Geertz and Geertz, 1975; cf. Schneider, 1972). Differences in analytic point of view can take different vantage points within a shared body of data (Blu, 1967) and even prescribe different definitional constructs for master-concepts such as the cultural and social, such as to require different placements of findings.

Notice that such disputes presuppose the success of ethnography. Ethnography has provided what there is to dispute. To be sure, new theory can bring out new aspects of old data, or point up its limitations, or require new kinds of data to develop adequately. Still, such disputes presuppose a great deal of valid first-order data, and they tacitly assume that valid first-order data is largely a matter of competence and talent, requiring perceptiveness and imaginative projection, to be sure, but not miracles of rapport and identification. The native's point of view can be grasped by someone who does not always like it or them (cf. Geertz, 1976).

In sum, ethnographers have available in many areas a first-order language of description that permits them to do work that can be judged for its competence, validity, richness, and the like. At the same time they work in a discipline whose second-order language of analysis is contested. A set of native terms may be accepted, but analysts argue as to the priority of one or another part of the data, or as to the scope of the data to be considered, or as to whether the case does or does not fit a certain concept or type. Some of these disputes can be resolved with increasing attention and precision. Others depend on conscious or unconscious commitments to what it means to be a scholar or scientist, and to what the world is or should be, such that resolution is unlikely. One can look at a schedule of kinship terms, then, and place it approximately quite quickly. But 'approximately' is a crucial term. Others may agree that that is a Crow system, and add, 'But . . .'. The ethnography of schooling and education no doubt will have the same experience. We can hope to reach the point at which anyone can look at a body of data and say quite quickly, 'Ah, that is a Henry Lea type of school', or the equivalent, or say that community or that family has a Hopi type of

11

educational process. We can probably not hope to reach the point at which no one will object, but you analyzed the school in isolation from X, or started the analysis from Y instead of Z.

There is a second question of language which may differentiate ethnography from the ideal conception of an experimental science. Some of what we believe we know about cultural patterns and worlds is interpretable in terms of structure, whether the ingredients of the structure be lines, graphs, numbers, letters or abstract terms. Some of what we believe we know resists interpretation in terms of structure. It seems to require, instead, *presentation.*

The need for presentation seems to cause no comment when the presentation is visual. 'A picture is worth a thousand words' and all that. Especially when the object of analysis is material culture, visual presentation is accepted as indeed essential. Even with social life, there is an increasing recognition of the value of visual presentation, through photographs and films. A telling account of necessity here was made by Frederick Barth, the Norwegian anthropologist, when he reported that in order to make good sense of a deceased colleague's field notes, he had to go to the place in question. He had worked ethnographically in the region (which is why he was asked to interpret the notes for publication), but still needed to see the land, the distances between a dwelling and its well, the heights and contours of the place – so much of the spatial configuration of life was taken for granted in the notes on behavior.

The difficulty with presentation seems to arise when the presentation is verbal. What is one to make, for example, of the relation between the two parts of Clifford Geertz's Balinese cock-fight – one part narrative, one part analytic (1972)? Geertz thinks that both parts are important.[3] I do also. Through his narrative skill, he is able to convey a sense (mediated by personal involvement) of the quality and texture of Balinese fascination with cockfighting. Evidence of the fascination is important. It supports taking the activity as a key to something essential about the Balinese; it helps us understand the analytic statements. A film might help too, but it would need something verbal from Geertz to teach us what we should learn from it. The narrative part of Geertz's article in effect points, as the narrator of film might do, and, also, in the absence of a film, shows. It does so through texture and proportion.

Many anthropologists agree that something of value can be learned from novels of certain sorts and even recommend certain novels. Clearly there is a sense in which narrative can be a source of knowledge. For some scientists and philosophers of science, it is a source of knowledge secondary to others, if not in principle reducible to others. Some ethnographers and philosophers of science hold the contrary. Narrative does not seem to them in principle entirely reducible to other forms of knowledge, but fundamental in its own right. Indeed, they may suspect that narrative accounts play a role in what scientists and administrators believe themselves to know, even though some of these may not acknowledge that role. It may be the case that structural forms of knowledge about social life are usually interpreted, even if covertly, in terms of images of kinds of person and situation, implicit or remembered narratives. If so (and I think it is so), the general problem of social knowledge is two-edged: both to increase the accumulated structural knowledge of social life, moving from narrative to structurally precise accounts, as we have commonly understood the progress of science, and to bring to light the ineradicable role of narrative accounts. Instead of thinking of narrative accounts as an early stage that in principle will be replaced, we may need to think of them as a permanent stage, whose principles are little understood, and whose role may increase. How often, one wonders, are decisions reached on the basis not only of numbers and experiments, but also on the basis of privileged personal accounts, fleshing out the data to make it intelligible? Sometimes these accounts may be provided by the investigator, sometimes by the audience ('I knew a case once. . .'). Sometimes they may not be articulated, yet influential nevertheless.

If narrative accounts have an ineradicable role, this need not be considered a flaw. The problem is not to try to eliminate them, but to discover how to assess them. What criteria can we provide equivalent to the criteria for assessing the significance and validity and reliability of statistical tests, and experimental designs?

The question of narrative brings us to another aspect of ethnography. It is continuous with ordinary life. Much of what we seek to find out in ethnography is knowledge that others already have. Our ability to learn ethnographically is an extension of what every human being must do, that is, learn the meanings, norms, patterns of a way of life. From a narrow view of science, this fact may be thought unfortunate. True objectivity may be thought to be undermined. But there is no way to avoid the fact that the ethnographer himself or herself is a factor in the inquiry. Without the general human capacity to learn culture, the inquiry would be impossible. The particular characteristics of the ethnographer are themselves an instrument of the inquiry, for both good and bad. For good, it is important to stress, because the age, sex, race or talents of the ethnographer may make some knowledge accessible that would be difficult of access to another. For bad, as we all recognize, because of partiality. Since partiality cannot be avoided, the only solution is to face up to it, to compensate for it as much as possible, to allow for it in interpretation. The conditions of trust and confidence that good ethnography requires (if it is to gain access to valid knowledge of meanings) make it impossible to take as a goal the role of impartial observer. The normal people from whom one has to learn will not put up with that. In principle, the answer lies in the view taken by Russell Ackoff, that scientific objectivity resides, not in the individual scientist, but in the community of scientists. That community has provided methods which to some degree, often a great degree, discipline the investigator and overcome partiality; the rest is a responsibility of critical analysis within the community.

The fact that good ethnography entails trust and confidence, that it requires some narrative accounting, and that it is an extension of a universal form of personal knowledge, make me think that ethnography is peculiarly appropriate to a democratic society. It could of course be reduced to a technique for the manipulation of masses by an élite. As envisioned here, ethnography has the potentiality for helping to overcome division of society into those who know and those who are known.

Such a vision of a democratic society would see ethnography as a general possession, although differentially cultivated. At one pole would be a certain number of persons trained in ethnography as a profession. At the other pole would be the general population, respected (on this view of ethnography) as having a knowledge of their worlds, intricate and subtle in many ways (consider the intricacy and subtlety of any normal person's knowledge of language), and as having necessarily come to this knowledge by a process ethnographic in character. In between – and one would seek to make this middle group as nearly coextensive with the whole as possible – would be those able to combine some disciplined understanding of ethnographic inquiry with the pursuit of their vocation, whatever that might be. From the standpoint of education, obviously one wants to consider the possibility of adding ethnographic inquiry to the competencies of principals, teachers and others involved with schools. But on the one hand, there is no reason not to seek to extend a knowledge of ethnographic inquiry to everyone. And, on the other hand, there is no reason to think professional ethnographers privileged. In their own lives they are in the same situation as the rest – needing to make sense out of a family situation, a departmental situation or a community situation, as best they can.

If this account sounds a little like a form of consciousness-raising, perhaps it is, but it is not the ordinary sort. In this sketch I have not brought out the sociocultural substantiality of ethnographic inquiry. It is a mode of inquiry that carries with it a substantial content. Whatever one's focus of inquiry, as a matter of course one takes into account the local form of general properties of social life – patterns of role and status, rights and duties, differential command of resources, transmitted values and environmental constraints. It locates the local situation in space, time and kind, and discovers its particular forms and center of gravity, as it were, for the maintenance of social order and the satisfaction of expressive impulse.

It is for this reason that much observational analysis of classrooms does not seem to me to merit the term *ethnography*. On the one hand, there is a kind of work which consists essentially of recurrent observations according to a pre-established system of coding. Such work violates the principle of being open to discovering meanings and patterns of behavior not foreseen. There is no provision for meanings, and patterns are excluded, since integral stretches of behavior are not observed. A superior kind of work analyzes intensively integral sequences of behavior. It contributes greatly to analytic control and to penetration to underlying meanings and connections. The limitation of the work is the lack of a comparative perspective. Thus, Ray McDermott (1977) interprets the difficulties, and projected failure, of one group of first-grade readers, in terms of the mode of interaction among them and the teacher (in contrast to the mode of interaction of another group with the teacher). Since his data is limited to the classroom, he is not able to consider differences in mode of interaction that the children may have brought with them to the classroom. A comprehensive ethnography would consider all the types of scenes in which the children (and teacher) participate, in order to assess validly the meaning of the behavior in one scene. From a larger point of view, the lack of a comparative ethnological perspective weakens the contribution the research might make. Suppose it is the case that what happens in the first-grade classroom is going to determine the success or failure of the children as readers, and ultimately, as adults. (This is McDermott's view.) We have to ask whether or not such a circum-stance is inevitable. Some Third World societies have had great success with literacy programs, through mobilization of the society to accomplish it. Is it impossible for the United States to give this kind of priority to universal literacy among its citizens, and mobilize to accomplish it? Is the fundamental question not this: how does it come about that one society, and not another, lets literacy depend on patterns of interaction in first-grade classrooms?

Such an interdependence between general and particular inquiry is essential to ethnography as a mode of inquiry – at least it is essential in my reading of the history of anthropology, and to what I would see as the contribution ethnography ought to make to education.

Notes

1 I want to thank Peggy Sanday for stimulus to write this paper, Richard Bauman and Joel Sherzer for including it in the series of Working Papers in Sociolinguistics, and Perry Gilmore for inviting its inclusion in a conference on education and ethnography that she coordinated for Research for Better Schools and the Graduate School of Education of the University of Pennsylvania.

2 Petty outlined 'A method of enquiring into the state of any country' and in 1686 a series of questions concerning 'The nature of the Indians of Pennsylvania' (Hodgen, 1964: 190; Slotkin, 1965: 481, n. 363, where the title is given as 'Quaeries concerning the nature of the natives of Pennsylvania'). Petty's questions were part demography – he has been called 'the greatest exponent of social statistics in the seventeenth century' (Slotkin, 1965: 139), part ethnology. He was a man who both recommended that the Royal Society admit only words that mark number, weight, or measure, and who was concerned with clearer definitions of ethnological entities – altogether a worthy forefather for any effort to integrate quantitative and qualitative methods today (cf Hymes, 1977). His program of ethnological investigation was similar to what Roger Williams (1643) had actually done some 40 years earlier among Indians, but still quite unusual for its time. By

the eighteenth century serious frames of reference for the collection and interpretation of cultural facts (*manners and customs*) were to become part of an established tradition, as in the Scottish work of Adam Ferguson, Lord Kames, James Millar, and William Robertson.

3   Geertz (1976) expresses superbly the dialectic between the two orders of analysis, the descriptive and the generalizing, that requires concern with adequacy of *presentation*. Thus, he writes (p. 223):

> Confinement to experience-near concepts leaves an ethnographer awash in immediacies, as well as entangled in vernacular. Confinement to experience-distant ones leaves him stranded in abstractions and smothered in jargon. The real question . . . is . . . how, in each case, ought one to deploy [the two sorts of concepts] . . . so as to produce an interpretation of the way a people lives which is neither imprisoned within their mental horizons . . . nor systematically deaf to the distinctive tonalities of their existence.

To be sure, a third part, comparative perspective (taken up in the next chapter) is desirable as well (cf. Dundes, 1994).

Chapter 2

Educational Ethnology[1]

One hears a good deal about ethnography in education today, but not about *ethnology*. I use ethnology in the title to call attention to issues that the use of ethnography alone might leave obscure. These issues have in common the theme: What would knowledge of schooling in the United States be like if anthropologists regarded it more like knowledge of kinship, chieftainship, religion, technology, and the like, in areas of the world in which anthropologists have worked long and intensively?

Two caveats: I do not wish to idealize anthropological study of Native American kinship, African chieftainship, South Asian religion, Oceanic economic life, and the like. In focusing on schooling, I do not wish to forget that an anthropological perspective on education is broader than schooling, and necessarily seeks to understand schooling as part of social life as a whole, and as one mode of learning and institutionalization among others.

It remains that educational research in the United States does focus on schooling, and that it would be different were an anthropological perspective to be thoroughly established. The difference would be a benefit, I think, to schools, to anthropology, and potentially, to democratization of knowledge and to the relations between academic centers of research and the communities of which they are part. The difference to research can be summarized in three words: *cumulative, comparative, cooperative*.

Understanding of individual schools is not now cumulative, but for the most part a matter of in and out. An individual school does not seem to count as a legitimate object of long-term study.[2] Boas is known for life-long study of the Kwakiutl, others are associated with other groups, but anthropologists do not seem to be associated with long-term involvement with particular schools or school systems. That makes the anthropology of schooling odd. One way to describe anthropology is to say that it has divided the world into names – names of peoples, languages, cultures – that it has made legitimate objects of knowledge. There are bibliographies of such knowledge, organized in terms of such names. If I discover an additional fact about such a unit, I can publish it as a legitimate addition to knowledge. My first publication, indeed, resulting from a first summer of field experience as a graduate student, was such: 'Two Wasco Motives' (Hymes, 1953). I had been able to record incidents missing from the texts collected a half-century earlier by Sapir, and a helpful professor encouraged me to write them up and send them off.

It is hard to imagine publishing 'Two Longstreth Classrooms' on the grounds that an earlier study had overlooked the two. (For Longstreth, the name of a school in West Philadelphia, substitute the name of any school near where you live.) Schools do not seem to be thought of as objects that it might take a long time, many hands, and even more than one generation, to come to understand. Individual schools do not seem to be thought of as individual in character. They are thought of, perhaps, as urban, inner-city, or the like, but mostly they seem to be thought of as equivalent settings for the interaction of certain recurrent variables – principals, teachers, pupils, curricula and methods of instruction. Comparative perspective seems to be a matter of differences on such variables, together with demographic data, test scores and the like. There does not seem to be a comparative perspective in terms of any of the integrative approaches to the little community that Redfield sketched years ago, or in terms of any other dimensions found in the anthropology of other areas.[3] Such comparative perspective, of course, would depend on knowledge of sociocultural context.

I do not claim to know educational research well, and apologize to those of you who do, but it is my impression, so far not corrected by any to whom it has been mentioned, that educational research does focus on the testing of relation among variables without much regard to sociocultural context. Specialists in educational research have been heard to lament its inconclusiveness on various points. Ten studies show a positive relationship between two variables, and 17 show a negative relationship. The obvious implication, it would seem, is that there may be two types of school, and that the variables under study were interacting in two different types of systematic contexts. That is a familiar anthropological point, from speech sounds to avoidance behavior and presence of belief in a supreme being. But, I am told, it is usually difficult to recover from educational studies the information about context that would enable one to characterize it.

If this impression is correct, then knowledge of schools in the United States is about 100 years behind knowledge of Native American kinship. The pioneer work of Lewis Henry Morgan brought together systematic information and proposed a broad typological dichotomy in 1871. Since that time, a galaxy of names – Kroeber, Lowie, Leslie Spier, George Peter Murdock, Driver, Lounsbury – have contributed to the more precise identification of relevant features, dimensions, processes and types. We seem nowhere near the identification of what would correspond to Omaha, Crow, Dakota, Iroquois, etc., types of school. Note that such types are not pigeonholes, but bases for analysis of particular structures and processes of change.

We do not have such bases for analysis of structure and change in American schools. Yet it cannot be the case that all schools in the United

States, or even in a single city, are the same. Nor, on the other hand, can it be the case that each is entirely unique. In a city or the country it seems a reasonable, fundamental question: What kinds of schools are there?

I suggest that we do not know because there has not been enough anthropology in educational research, and because educational anthropology has understandably been concerned with establishing its ethnographic mode of work. In education by and large, anthropology has come to mean ethnography, and ethnography has come to mean field work: participant observation, narrative description, and the like. I believe strongly in this mode of work, and will take it up briefly at the end. Here I want to stress the danger of letting the anthropological perspective on education become equated in other minds with just a mode of field work. The result will be dozens of people called 'ethnographers' because they have observed, although with little or no training in cultural analysis; attempts to insert 'ethnographic components' in helter-skelter research designs; a brief vogue for the name ethnography; and at the end a heightened immunity to the true challenge of an ethnographic, anthropological mode of thought.

Ethnography, as we know, is in fact an interface between specific inquiry and comparative generalization. It will serve us well, I think, to make prominent the term, 'ethnology', that explicitly invokes comparative generalization, and it will serve schooling in America well. An emphasis on the ethnological dimension takes one away from immediate problems and from attempts to offer immediate remedies, but it serves constructive change better in the long run. Emphasis on the ethnological dimension links anthropology of education with social history, through the ways in which larger forces for socialization, institutionalization, reproduction of an existing order, are expressed and interpreted in specific settings. The longer view seems a surer footing.

Let me come at the matter in terms of a map. If the ethnologists Alfred Kroeber or Harold Driver had tried to map North America in terms of what is known about its schools, would not most of the map be empty? If so vacant a map dealt with kinship, would there not be a demand for studies, an unwillingness to talk about 'Indian kinship' in the abstract until more were known in the concrete? The need for cumulative, comparative research would be obvious, as it has been obvious in the last generation in a less explored region such as New Guinea.

Some may object that such a call for an ethnological approach is based on a mistaken analogy. Schools and cultures, say, Longstreth in West Philadelphia, and Warm Springs Reservation in Oregon, are not alike. Schools are less autonomous and more subject to change, even manipulation, by external forces. An Indian community and an elementary school are not comparable units. I think the analogy holds, despite the differences. First, our sense of each named Indian community as a distinct entity is partly an artifact of our own profession. The academic requirement of contribution to knowledge through research, and the need to have a contribution of one's own, contributes to a tendency to differentiate the anthropological world into named entities that anthropologists can claim.

Second, the similarities among differently named Indian communities may be great; their contemporary circumstances on a reservation may be greatly shaped by external forces. Common ecological base, diffusion, pan-tribal movements, retention of elements of ancient tradition, and orientation common to many, all make the autonomy and distinctiveness of named Indian groups an empirical question, just as is the case with named schools. If one school has changed drastically in a decade, through change in the population served, another a mile or two away may have not. An essential dimension of comparative research might be the continuities that schools have, and are felt to have. Third, the issue of access to the research site may be very much the same today. With both schools and reservations one has to address suspicion rooted in past experience; concern about exposure and embarrassment; demands that research and the researcher be useful to those studied.

In regard to access, anthropology encounters the same problems with American schools that it encounters throughout the world, and has, perhaps, a better chance of solving them. Sustained cooperation can serve both parties, academics and schools. To say this is not to overlook the conflicts of interest that are latent; not everyone wants everything known, or even to know certain things at all. But the problems seem intrinsic to research, not to schools.

A leading element of sustained cooperation is the involvement of others in the research. Here a major anthropological tradition can be an essential asset. In the study of a language, a kinship system, or the like, one is to a great extent seeking to make explicit in a comparable framework what others, in a certain sense, already know. Speakers of a language, participants in a network of kinship, are not merely objects, but, as sources of information, partners in inquiry as well. This tradition suggests that the appropriate strategy for school personnel who seek advanced degrees is to capitalize on what they know where they are. Often enough they have been made to believe that a legitimate contribution to knowledge, and advanced degree, requires methodology and subject matter disconnected from their experience. Anthropological tradition suggests that they can capitalize on their experience, and make a far more valuable contribution to knowledge by doing so.

If the map of American schooling is to be made less empty, after all, it will require more than the anthropologists and anthropological funding available. Just so, knowledge of Native American traditions would be far less rich, given the small number of anthropological investigators, were it not for members of those cultures – George Hunt, William Beynon, and others – who became contributors of knowledge themselves.

At the Graduate School of Education at the University of Pennsylvania there has been such a program, now in its third year, involving a group of principals mainly, together with a few other school personnel. It is still too early to judge the research outcome, but indications are encouraging. It is clear that the program could not have begun, let along prospered, had the nature of degree requirements not been rethought in terms of principles of cooperation, indeed, partnership. Past experience, distrust, uncertainty of mutual benefit had to be overcome gradually. The anthropological principles were heard but only gradually believed. Had there been insistence on the model previously familiar to the principals, the isolated researcher carrying out an experimental design, the program would never have been possible. One essential aspect of the program has been training in observation and narrative reporting, concerned with better perceiving and expressing the process of implementing a reading program in each person's school. Another essential aspect has been grouping researchers in teams. The grouping provides moral support among people who are pursuing a degree above and beyond a full-time job. Ideally, rather than cheapening the degree, it provides for deeper insight. The grouping builds controlled comparison into the process. Finer perception of similarities and differences among schools can result.

These principals, and members of other school districts in the region, perceive the approach as taking their circumstances and needs into account. They see such a program as evidence that an Ivy League university, reputedly disinterested in less than élite affairs, is in fact responsive. Some in the faculty see such a program as a golden opportunity. There is little chance that one could find funding to study 15 or 30 schools simultaneously. Even given funding, there is little chance that the schools would let researchers in just because they knocked. The principle of cooperative ethnographic research leads to the schools and the University having investments in each other.[4]

This short account highlights the positive, ignoring the tremors, misunderstandings, partial understandings. It ignores the fragile dependence of the effort in the University itself on adjunct faculty. Yet it is fair to say that the effort has led to an atmosphere in which an anthropological approach is welcomed, indeed so welcome that interest outruns supply, an atmosphere in which the long-term questions of the role of anthropology in educational research can be addressed. Two long-term questions seem to me of especial importance: What will be the structure of knowledge of schooling? What will be its form? The importance of the questions lies in their implications for a democratic way of life. A mode of research that focuses on experimental design, quantitative techniques, and the impersonality of the investigator has its place, but, carried to its perfection, as the exclusive mode, would tend to divide society into those who know and those who are known. The anthropological recognition of the contribution of the practitioner as one who also knows counteracts that tendency. So does the legitimacy, indeed necessity, in ethnographic research of narrative. Good narrative accounting is not easy, and may be harder sometimes than quantitative analysis, but is more accessible to the citizens of society.

Moreover, it can be argued that even quantitative analysis invokes narrative models of social life at some point, and that meetings for the purpose of institutional decision-making certainly do. Explicit attention to narrative accounts and models can make an essential contribution. It can legitimate the form in which the knowledge of most citizens as to their circumstances is cast, and it can make apparent a hidden form of cultural hegemony. Of all the disciplines interested in schools, anthropology is best equipped to make that contribution.[5]

To sum up: I have argued that Native America and School America pose anthropological problems of the same kind. The question, 'What kinds of schools are there?', is naive, yet natural to an anthropological perspective. An answer draws on those aspects of anthropological tradition that regard research as cumulative, comparative, cooperative. A strategy that draws on such an answer, while looking to the long run, can hope to serve change and even immediate advantage.

Notes

1 This is the text of my address as outgoing presidential officer of the Council on Anthropology and Education, during the business meeting of the Council, at the annual meetings of the American Anthropological Association, December 1, 1979, in Cincinnati, Ohio.
2 An exception has been the ten-year involvement in three State of New York high schools on the part of Francis Ianni and others.
3 Gastil (1975) calls attention to regional cultural differences insofar as statistical indications permit, but notes the lack of explanatory power in such a preliminary approach. See his discussion of 'The relationship of regional cultures to educational performance,' pp. 116–27.
4 [Retrospective note] In the long run it did prove possible to instil a degree of ethnography in the principals, limited mainly by sensitivity to what they could say publicly in work that would be read by superiors. It proved difficult to install and sustain ethnology in the faculty.
5 See discussion of narrative in Hymes (1977) and in Cazden and Hymes (1978). On cognitive analysis of norms of interaction, embodied in an expressive genre, see Hymes (1979a) and the book to which it is a foreword.

Part II
Linguistics

Chapter 3

Speech and Language: On the Origins and Foundations of Inequality among Speakers

I conceive of two sorts of inequality in the human species; one, which I call natural or physical, because it is established by nature and consists in the difference of ages, health, bodily strengths, and qualities of mind or soul; the other, which may be called moral or political inequality, because it depends upon a sort of convention and is established, or at least authorized, by the consent of men. The latter consists in the different privileges that some men enjoy to the prejudice of others, such as to be richer, more honored, more powerful than they, or even to make themselves obeyed by them.

Rousseau (1964) [1756]

I use the second paragraph of Rousseau's second *Discourse* as an epigraph, and adapt its title, because I want to call attention to a link between his concerns and ours. Like him, we think knowledge of human nature essential and pursue it; like him, we think the present condition of mankind unjust, and seek to transform it. These two concerns, for example, provide the frame for Noam Chomsky's recent Russell lectures. Unlike Chomsky, but like Rousseau, moreover, some linguists are beginning to attend to a conception of linguistic structure as interdependent with social circumstances, and as subject to human needs and evolutionary adaptation. And like Rousseau, our image of the linguistic world, the standard by which we judge the present situation, harks back to an earlier stage of human society. Here Rosseau has the advantage over us. He knew he did this, and specified the limitations of it (see the end of note *h* to the *Discourse*). Many of us do it implicitly, falling back on a 'Herderian' conception of a world composed of traditional units of language-and-culture, for lack of another way of seeing the resources of language as an aspect of human groups, because we have not thought through new ways of seeing how linguistic resources do, in fact, come organized in the world. We have no accepted way of joining our understanding of inequality with our understanding of the nature of language.

Chomsky's Russell lectures (1971) are a case in point. The first lecture, 'On Interpreting the World', presents implications of a certain conception of the nature of language and of the goals of linguistic research, leading to a humanistic, libertarian conception of man. The second lecture, 'On Changing the World', is about injustice, its roots in inequality of power, and the failure of scholars and governments to deal with the true issues in these respects.

There is little or no linguistics in the second lecture, just as there is little or nothing of social reality in the first. Such principled schizophrenia besets linguistics today; the scientific and social goals of many practitioners are compartmentalized. Edward Sapir warned years ago against such an alienation from experience and social reality on the part of 'the many kinds of segmental scientists of man' (1939, cited from Mandelbaum (1949): 578). It mirrors neither the true nature of language nor its relation to social life; it reflects, rather, a certain ideological conception of that nature and that relation, one which diverts and divorces linguistics from the contribution, desperately needed, that it might make to the understanding of language as a human problem.

The heart of the matter is this. A dominant conception of the goals of 'linguistic theory'[1] encourages one to think of language exclusively in terms of the vast potentiality of formal grammar, and to think of that potentiality exclusively in terms of its universality. A perspective which treats language only as an attribute of *man* leaves language as an attribute of *men* unintelligible. In actuality language is in large part what users have made of it. Navajo is what it is partly because it is a human language, partly because it is the language of the Navajo. The generic potentiality of the human faculty for language is realized differently, as to direction and as to degree, in different human communities, and is useless except insofar as it is so realized. The thrust of Chomskian linguistics has been to depreciate the actuality of language under the guise of rejecting an outmoded philosophy of science. We must see beyond the ideological effect of such a thrust and recognize that one cannot change a world on which one's theory permits no purchase. One of the problems to be overcome with regard to language is a widespread linguist's conception of it. A conception of how we encounter and use language in the world, a notion which I call that of *ways of speaking*, is needed.

Let me consider now four broad dimensions of language and of sources of inequality with regard to them. Throughout I shall try to indicate the place of a conception of ways of speaking. Linguistics as part of the problem will be addressed again at the end of the chapter, and as well in the chapter that follows, and in the final chapter of the book.

Some Dimensions of Language as a Human Problem

It is striking that we have no general perspective on language as a human problem, not even an integrated body of works in search of one. Salient problems, such as translation, multilingualism, literacy and language development, have long attracted attention, but mostly as practical matters, constituting applications of linguistics, rather than as proper, theoretically pertinent parts of it. There have been notable exceptions, as in the work of Einar Haugen and Uriel Weinreich, but for about a generation most linguistic thought in the United States has seen the role of language in human life only as something to praise, not as something to question and study. Perhaps this situation reflects a phase in the alternation of 'high' and 'low' evaluations of language to which the philosopher Urban (1939: 23) called attention. The skeptical period after the First World War did see leading American theorists of language devote themselves to language problems, such as those involving new vehicles for international communication (Jespersen, Sapir), the teaching of reading (Bloomfield), literacy (Swadesh), language as an instrument and hence a shaper of thought (Sapir, Whorf), and linguistic aspects of psychiatric and other interpersonal communication (Trager, Hockett, in the early 1950s). Perhaps this issue of *Daedalus* (see Acknowledgments, p. xiii) is a sign that the climate of opinion is shifting once again toward a balanced recognition of language as 'at one and the same time helping and retarding us', as Sapir put it in one context ((1933), cited from Mandelbaum, 1949:11).

In any case, it is unusual today to think of language as something to overcome, yet four broad dimensions of language can usefully be considered in just that way: *diversity* of language, *medium* of language (spoken, written), *structure* of language, and *functioning* of language. Of each we can ask,

- when, where, and how it came to be seen as a problem;
- from what vantage point it is seen as a problem (in relation to other vantage points from which it may not be so seen);
- in what ways the problem has been approached or overcome as a practical task and also as an intellectual, conceptual task;
- what its consequences for the study of language itself have been;
- what kinds of study, to which linguists might contribute, are now needed.

I cannot do more than raise such questions; limitations of knowledge would prevent my doing more, if limitations of space did not. To raise such questions may help, I hope, to stimulate development of a general perspective.

Overcoming Diversity of Language

This problem may be the most familiar, and the historical solutions to it form an important part of the subject matter of linguistics itself: lingua francas, koines, pidgins and creoles, standardized languages, diffusion and areal as in India convergence, multilingual repertoires, and constructed auxiliary languages. The myths and lexicons of many cultures show a widespread and presumably ancient recognition of diversity of language, although not uniformly in the mold of the Tower of Babel. The Busama of New Guinea and the Quileute of the State of Washington believed that originally each person had a separate language, and that community of language was a subsequent development created by a culture hero or transformer. Thus it is an interesting question whether it is unity or diversity, within or between speech communities, that has seemed the thing requiring an explanation.

In Western civilization the dominant intellectual response to the existence of diversity has been to seek an original unity, either of historical or of psychological origin (sometimes of both). The dominant practical response has been to impose unity in the form of the hegemony of one language or standard. The presence of the Tower of Babel story in the civilization's sacred book legitimated, and perhaps stimulated, efforts to relate languages in terms of an original unity and played a great part in the development of linguistic research. Indeed, some rather sophisticated work and criticism on the subject can be found from the Renaissance onward. The dating of the origin of linguistic science with the comparative–historical work of the early nineteenth century reflects institutionalization as much as or more than intellectual originality (Diderichsen, 1974; Metcalf, 1974). Christian and humanitarian concern to establish the monogenesis of man through the monogenesis of language was felt strongly well through the nineteenth century, from the dominance of the 'ethnological question' in the first part through controversies involving Max Müller, Darwin, Broca, and others (discussed in Hymes, 1971a). The special interest of Europeans in Indo-European origins became increasingly important in the century, the idea of a common linguistic origin stimulating and legitimating studies of common cultural origins and developments. Humanitarian motives played a part as well – Matthew Arnold appealed to Indo-European brotherhood as a reason for the English to respect Celtic (Irish) culture and perhaps the Irish, and Sir Henry Maine made a similar appeal on behalf of the peoples of India. Sheer intellectual curiosity and satisfaction must also always be assigned a part in motivating work in comparative–historical linguistics, and humanistic concern probably played a part in a major contemporary effort to establish a common historical origin for all languages, that of the late Morris Swadesh (1971). (For other aspects of the history of linguistic anthropology see Hymes, 1983a).

The most salient effort toward a conceptual unity of human languages today is linked, of course, with the views of Noam Chomsky. Concern for such a unity is itself old and continuous – the appearance of disinterest among part of a generation of US linguists before and after the Second World War was a local aberration whose importance is primarily due to Chomsky's reaction against it. He has reached back to the seventeenth and eighteenth centuries for an ancestral tradition (1966), when he had only to take up the tradition in this country of Boas and Sapir, or the European tradition, partially transplanted to this country, of Trubetzkoy and Jakobson. In both of these traditions some significant things were being said about universals of language in the 1930s and early 1940s. It is true, however, that the history of the tradition of general linguistics stretching back through the nineteenth century (and, Jakobson would argue, continuing through the Enlightenment to origins in medieval speculative grammar), had been lost from sight in American linguistics, and a sense of it is only now being recovered. It is true, too, that the tradition since Herder and von Humboldt did not much appeal to Chomsky, since its universalism is combined with an intense interest in typology, understood as characterizing the configurations of specific languages as well as characterizing general features of language.

Here we touch on the inescapable limitation of either kind of effort to conceive the unity of human language. Although one used to speak of the discovery of a genetic relationship as *reducing* the number of linguistic groups, the word and the thought were both badly misleading. Languages may disappear through the destruction of their speakers, but not through the publication of linguistic papers and maps. Related languages remain to be accounted for as to their differences and developments as well as to the portion (often quite small) of their makeup that shows a common origin. Likewise, the discovery of putative universals in linguistic structure does not erase the differences. Indeed, the more one emphasizes universals, in association with a powerful, self-developing faculty of language, the more mysterious actual languages become. Why are there more than one, or two or three? And if the internal faculty of language is so constraining, must not social, historical, adaptive forces have been even *more* constraining, in order to produce the plenitude of languages actually found? For Chinookan is not Sahaptin is not Klamath is not Takelma is not Coos is not Siuslaw is not Tsimshian is not Wintu is not Maidu is not Miwok is not Yokuts is not Costanoan. . .(is not Tonkawa, is not Zuni, is not Mixe, is not Zoque, is not any of the numerous Mayan languages, or affiliates of Mayan, if one extends the horizon). The differences do not disappear, and the likenesses, indeed, are far from all Chomskian universals. Some likenesses exist because of a genetic common origin (Penutian), some because of areal adaptations (Northwest Coast for some, California for others), some because of diffusion, some because of limited possibilities and implications (à la Greenberg's typology). Franz Boas once argued (1920) against exclusive concentration on genetic classification, calling the true historical problem the development of languages in all their aspects. A similar point can be made today as against concentration on putative universals. Most of language begins where universals leave off. In the tradition from Herder and von Humboldt through Boas and Sapir, languages are 'concrete universals', and most of language as a human problem is bound up with the adjective of that term.

As modes of overcoming diversity of language intellectually, both genetic classification and putative universals locate their solutions in time. There is a past reference, a historical origin of languages or an evolutionary origin of the faculty of language, and there is a present and future reference, one which draws the moral of the unity that is found. Neither speaks to the present and future in terms of processes actually shaping the place of language in human life, for the faculty of language presumably is a constant and genetic diversification of languages is mostly a thing of the past. For the present and foreseeable future the major process is the adaptation of languages and varieties to one another, and their integration into special roles and complex speech communities. Understanding this process is the true problem that diversity of language poses, both to humankind and to those who study humankind's languages.

The essence of the problem appears as communication, intelligibility. Some are concerned with the problem at the level of the world as a whole, and efforts to choose or shape a world language continue.[2] Some project this concern on to the past, speaking of a 'stubborn mystery' in the ' "profoundly startling", "anti-economic" multiplicity of languages spoken on this crowded planet' (Steiner, 1971:70). Such a view is anachronistic, for the diversity was not 'anti-economic' when it came into being; it was just as much a 'naturally selected, maximalized efficiency of adjustment to local need and ecology' as the great variety of fauna and flora to which Steiner refers in the passage just quoted. Universal processes of change inherent in language, its transmission and use, together with separation and separate adaptation of communities over the course of many centuries, suffice to explain the diversity. Simply the accumulation of unshared changes would in time make the languages of separate groups mutually unintelligible. There is of course more to it than physical and temporal distance (as Steiner insightfully suggests); there is social distance as well. Boundaries are deliberately created and maintained, as well as given by default. Some aspects of the structures of languages are likely due to this. If the surface form of a means of communication is simplified greatly when there is need to overcome barriers, as it is in the formation of pidgin languages, then the surface form of means of communication may be complicated when there is a desire to raise or maintain barriers (Hymes, 1971b: 73). This latter process may have something to do with the fact that the surface structures of languages spoken in small, cheek-by-jowl communities so often are markedly complex, and the surface structures of languages spoken over wide ranges less so. (The observation would seem to apply at least to North American Indian languages and Oceania).

Speech Communities

In any case, the problem is one of more than languages. It is one of speech communities. Here the inadequacy of concepts and methods is most painfully apparent. The great triumph of linguistic science in the nineteenth century, the comparative–historical method, deals with speech communities as the source and result of genetic diversification. The great triumph of linguistic science in the twentieth century, structural method, deals with speech communities as equivalent to language.[3] Genetic diversification can seldom be said to occur any longer, and a speech community comprising a single language hardly exists. The study of complex speech communities must benefit mightily from the tools and results both of historical linguistics, for the unraveling and interpretation of change, and of structural linguistics, for the explicit analysis of linguistic form. But it cannot simply apply them, it must extend them and develop new tools.

The needs can be expressed in terms of what is between speech communities and what is within them. Despite their well-known differences as to psychology, both Bloomfield and Chomsky reduce the concept of speech community to that of a language (Bloomfield, 1933, Ch. 3; Chomsky, 1965: 3). This will not do. The boundaries between speech communities are thought of first of all as boundaries of communication, but communication, or mutual intelligibility as it is often phrased, is not solely a function of a certain objective degree of difference between two languages or some series of related languages. One and the same degree of objective linguistic differentiation may be taken to demarcate boundaries in one case, and be depreciated in another, depending on the social and political circumstances.[4] And intelligibility itself is a function not only of features of linguistic form (phonological, lexical, syntactic), but also of norms of interaction and conduct in conversation, and of attitudes towards differences in all these respects. In Nigeria one linguist found that as soon as members of a certain community recognized a related hinterland dialect, they refused to understand it (Wolff, 1959). Other communities are noted for the effort they make to understand despite great difference.

Such considerations cut across language boundaries. One may be at a loss to understand fellow speakers of his own language if his assumptions as to appropriate topics, what follows what, and the functions of speech are different (as happens often enough in classrooms between teachers of one background and students of another), while many of us have had the experience of following a discussion in a language of which we have little grasp, when the topics, technical terminology, and norms of conduct are professionally shared.

To repeat, communication cannot be equated with a *common* language. A term such as *the English language* comprises all linguistic varieties that owe their basic resources to the historical tradition known as English. That language is no longer an exclusive possession of the English, or even of the English and the Americans – there are perhaps more users of English in the Third World (just as there are more Christians), and they have their own rights to its resources and future. Many varieties of 'English' are not mutually intelligible within Great Britain and the United States as well as elsewhere. In fact, it is an important clarification if we can agree to restrict the term *language* (and the term *dialect*) to just this sort of meaning: identification of a historically derived set of resources whose social functioning – organization into used varieties, mutual intelligibility etc. – is not given by the fact of historical derivation itself, but is problematic, needing to be determined, and calling for other concepts and terms.

We are in poorly explored territory here. Even with consideration restricted to groups which can communicate, there is a gamut from 'I can make myself understood' at one end, to 'she talks the same language' at the other. Probably it is best to employ terms such as *field* and *network* for the larger spheres within which a person operates communicatively. One's *language field* would be the sphere within which one has knowledge (or command) of languages as such; one's *speech field* would be the sphere within which one has knowledge (or command) of patterns of use (implicating competence in speaking, hearing, writing, reading); one's *network* would be the sphere of relationships in which the two kinds of knowledge (or command) are joined. The term *community* is best reserved for units with some degree of self-reproduction and support.

Clearly the boundary (and the internal organization) of a speech community is not a question solely of degree of interaction among persons (as Bloomfield said, and others have continued to say), but a question equally of attributed and achieved membership, of identity and identification. If interaction were enough, school children would speak the TV and teacher English they constantly hear. Some indeed can so speak, but do not necessarily choose to do so. Some years ago I was asked by teachers then at Columbia Point (Boston) why the children in the school did not show the influence of TV, or, more pointedly, of daily exposure to the talk of the teachers. A mother present made a telling observation: she had indeed heard children talk that way, but on the playground, playing school. When playing school stopped, that way of talking stopped, too.

Community, in this sense, is a dynamic, complex, and sometimes subtle thing. There are latent or obsolescent speech communities on some Indian reservations in this country, brought into being principally by the visit of a linguist or anthropologist who also can use the language and shows respect for uses to which it can be put. There are emergent communities, such as New York City would appear to be, in the sense that they share norms for the evaluation of certain variables (such as post-vocalic *r*), that have developed in this century. There are other communities whose stigmata are variable and signs of severe insecurity, like those of New York, or the community of *porteños* in Buenos Aires, composed principally of immigrants concerned to maintain their distance and prestige *vis-à-vis* speakers from the provinces (who, ironically enough, have lived in the country much longer). There can be multiple membership, and there is much scope for false perception; authorities, both governmental and educational, are often ignorant of the existence of varieties of language and communication under their noses. An unsuspected variety of creolized English was discovered recently on an island off Australia by the chance of a tape recorder being left on in a room where two children were playing. When the linguist heard the tape and could not understand it, he came to realize what it was. That such a language was known by the children was entirely unknown to the school. Indians who have been beaten as children for using their Indian tongue or blacks who have been shamed for using deep Creole will not necessarily trot the language out for an idle enquirer.

In general, when we recognize that this diversity of speech communities involves social as well as linguistic realities, we must face the fact that there are different vantage points from which diversity may be viewed. One person's obstacle may be someone else's source of identity. In the United States and Canada today one can find Indians seeking to learn the Indian language they did not acquire as children. Leveling of language seems neither inevitable nor desirable in the world today. It is common to mock efforts at preservation and revitalization of languages as outmoded romanticism, but the mockery may express a view of human nature and human needs whose shallowness bodes ill.

What is within a speech community in linguistic terms has begun to be understood better through recent work in sociolinguistics. Empirical and theoretical work has begun to provide a way of seeing the subject steadily as a whole. It suggests that one think of a community (or any group, or person) in terms, not of a single language, but of a *repertoire*. A repertoire comprises a set of ways of speaking. Ways of speaking, in turn, comprise *speech styles*, on the one hand, and *contexts of discourse*, on the other, together with *relations of appropriateness* obtaining between styles and contexts.

Membership in a speech community consists in sharing one or more of its ways of speaking – that is, not in knowledge of a speech style (or any other purely linguistic entity, such as a language) alone, but in terms of knowledge of appropriate use as well. There are rules of use without which rules of syntax are useless. Moreover, the linguistic features that enter into speech styles are not only the 'referentially-based' features usually dealt with in linguistics today, but also the 'stylistic' features that are complementary to them, and inseparable from them in communication. Just as social meaning is an integral part of the definition and demarcation of speech communities, so it is an integral part of the organization of linguistic features within them. (Cf. Bernstein's concept of 'restricted' and 'elaborated' code, classical diglossia, liturgy.) The sphere adequate to the description of speech communities, of linguistic diversity as a human problem, can be said to be: *means of speech, and their meanings to those who use them*. (This concept is dealt with in more detail in Hymes (1972b; 1973a)).

No one has ever denied the facts of multilingualism and heterogeneity of speech community in the world, but little has been done to enable us to comprehend and deal with them. Until now a 'Herderian' conception of a world of independent one language–one culture units, a conception appropriate enough, perhaps, to a world pristinely peopled by hunters and gatherers and small-scale horticulturalists, has been tacitly fallen back upon.

There has begun to be work to characterize complex linguistic communities and to describe speech communities adequately. Such description must extend to the value of speech itself in the life of a community: whether it is a resource to be hoarded or something freely expended, whether it is essential or not to public roles, whether it is conceived as intrinsically good or dangerous, what its proper role in socialization and demonstration of competence is conceived to be, and so forth.[5] Through such work one can hope to provide adequate foundations for assessing diversity of language as both a human problem and a human resource.

Diversity could stand as the heading for all of the problems connected with speech and language, once our focus is enlarged from languages as such to speech communities – existing diversity as an obstacle, and sometimes diversity that it is desired to maintain or achieve. Nevertheless, it is worthwhile to comment separately on three topics that have been singled out for attention in their own right. These are problems connected with the media, the structures, and the functions of language.

Overcoming the Medium of Language

Not long ago one might have said that most of the world was attempting to overcome the spokenness of language through programs of literacy, while some of the advanced sectors of civilization – the advertising and communications industries, and the university – were hailing the approaching transcendence of language in graphic form. McLuhan is not prominent now, but polarization of spoken and written language remain very much with us. A good deal has been said about speaking and writing, about oral and literate cultures (Wade, 1972), and I have no new generalization to add, but I do have a bit of skepticism to advance. We really know very little as to the role of the medium of language. Technological determinism is not generally popular, for good reason, so it is puzzling to find it avidly welcomed in the sphere of communication. There is no more reason to regard it as gospel there than elsewhere. Certainly, it is impossible to generalize validly about oral vs. literate cultures as uniform types. Popular social science does seem to thrive on three-stage evolutionary sequences – David Riesman, Margaret Mead, Charles Reich have all, like McLuhan, employed them – but if dogmatic Marxism is not to be allowed such schemes, for good reason, it seems a little unfair to tolerate them in dogmatic McLuhanism, Ongism e.g. that primary oral narrative is always prolix (Ong, 1988 [1982] – see the examples in Chapter 6), and the like.

In such theses, nevertheless, lies a major threat and fascination of media. Is use of one medium of communication rather than another simply transfer of an underlying competence that remains constant? Or is there more to it than that? Is the communicative medium itself partly constitutive of meaning, even of reality, even perhaps of language itself?[6]

Undoubtedly the adaptation of communication to an oral–auditory channel – to mouth, throat, air and ear – has helped shape human language, for example, as to the range in number of phonological units in languages (a medium with different properties might have facilitated more or permitted less), and as to relation among units (sequences, kinds of change) conditioned by the physical characteristics of the sounds. So much has become a matter of considerable interest to linguists. Not so the adaptation of verbal communication to a manual–visual channel, to hand, things scripturable and eye. The origin and history of writing systems has sometimes attracted interest, but as a separate specialty; linguists do not usually think of the written channel as shaping, hence partly explaining, their object of study.[7] Writing is usually seen as a record of something already existing. Interest in the history of writing has to do with the nature of different modes of representation of language, their evolution, diffusion, and effect on what one can know about languages represented by them. Debates about writing have to do with adequacy of different representations (past or present), and, more generally, with the adequacy of any written norm as basis for linguistic analysis.

Many modern linguists, reacting against the inadequacies of conventional writing systems, and the role of conventional writing systems as symbols of cultural domination, have indeed insisted that written forms are entirely derivative of speech, entirely secondary, arbitrary, not, as so often thought in traditional cultures, intrinsic to what is expressed in them. (Hall, 1975, for example, maintains such a view vigorously.) Many linguists associated with Chomsky's approach have looked more kindly upon conventional English orthography, perhaps reacting against a preceding generation's reaction against tradition, and certainly on general principle. Whereas the preceding generation emphasized study of the spoken form of language, Chomsky and others deprecate the spoken form as a highly imperfect, even degenerate, manifestation of structure. The net effect is the same. The issue is the accuracy of a system of writing in representing something else, the something else being primary. As a secondary realization of the structure of language (whether in speech or in the mind), writing has had little or no theoretical interest of its own. Independent linguists, such as Dwight Bolinger, 1946; H. J. Uldall, 1944; and Josef Vachek, 1944–49, have defended the partial autonomy of writing, as requiring investigation, but their lead has been little followed.

The views of American linguists have perhaps been unduly influenced by the situation of English. The patent discrepancy between conventional spelling and actual pronunciation helped one approach dismiss writing; reaction has led others (Chomsky and Halle, 1968) to impute to speakers of English today a feature of conventional spelling that others cite as a salient example of how pronunciation has left spelling behind. Conventional spelling of course does often fit earlier stages of pronunciation, for example, the 'gh' in 'right', 'night', 'light' once was pronounced as in Scots and in German *recht, nacht, licht.* But to claim that analysis shows that speakers have in their linguistic structure today a sound they do not know, may never have heard, and cannot pronounce is rather a tour de force, *épater les bourgeois.*

In any case, no general principle about writing is at stake, only an analysis of English. There are languages whose written form is not a spelling at all (Chinese), and there are languages whose conventional written form matches spoken phonology well (Spanish). Wherever English belongs between these two poles, it is inadequate as a basis for thinking about the relation between speech and writing.

The point is this: the general issue is not the degree to which one mode is an accurate equivalent of the other, or of underlying structure. Such a formulation limits the relation between speech and writing to one of representation. The true general issue is the relation between speech and writing as *modes of action.* It is as modes of action that speech and writing are fundamentally related to each other. Diversity and inequality are not manifest in matters of representation alone; they are manifest in what it means to speak, to write (or hear and read), at all, and of course in what it means to do so in one or another way. In sum, the fundamental relation between speech and writing is not between successive, or correlative levels of linguistic structure. The fundamental relation is that of choice of means within communicative repertoires. (Clearly my use of 'speech', 'speaker', etc., in much of this chapter must be understood as surrogate for all communicative modes, wherever speech is not specifically contrasted with others.)

This perspective, choices of means embedded in acts, helps keep in view two considerations essential to study of writing: a) graphic means (including electronic – cf. Murray, 1988) are not neutral, but have social meaning; b) graphic means have scope and organization of their own.

As to the first: linguists involved in practical work, such as literacy, standard language planning and education, have long had reason to know that to choose what form of language is to be written, and to choose how it is to be written, are never purely technical matters. Cultural values and social hierarchies are involved. A notable consequence for the situation of language in the world is that many languages, and varieties of language, have not been thought worth writing, or even capable of being written; their written forms, and what exists in them in writing, has come largely from outsiders with a religious or scientific mission. The efforts of outsiders have not always been welcome, and in any case, the sheer fact of the existence of a written form has not been sufficient reason for it to be used. A social interest must be mobilized, as many missionaries have found, (such facts show that it is silly to explain writing by appeal to its obvious advantages, as if the advantages were self-realizing; more is said on the cultural role of writing below) or a social interest may have to be overcome. A technically advantageous form of writing may be rejected because of the prestige of some alternative or to protect some interest. [Thus, the Korean *hangul* had to wait several centuries and a change of social order to be generally adopted; the government of Somali had to resolve an orthographic impasse by fiat (the solution was indeed in the interest of the country as a whole); Chinese plans for Romanization seem to have been shelved].

Such questions occur within the United States with regard to the place of varieties of language other than standard English in classrooms, and modes of writing English dialects and Indian languages. A linguist's concern for the efficiency and universality of a phonetic orthography may encounter a Native American's preference for something emblematically different from English symbols, while a linguist taking the standard orthography for granted in his work may unwittingly reinforce social prejudice.

African-American parents may react strongly against the suggestion that their children be taught with materials that represent the speech of their community, as something distinct from standard English, while African-American college students may protest against being penalized for departures from standard orthographic practice.

Social meaning is not limited to ethnic, regional, or dialect differences. Joseph Jaquith (1983) has pointed out a contrast between conventional and vernacular spellings, particularly in signs and advertisements, associated with the durability, cost, prestige of a product or service. Vernacular spellings employ phonetic and quasi-phonetic approximations and substitutions ('rite', 'kwik', 'Andy's Chee-pees'), syllabary-like uses of alphabet letters (E-Z), etc. (The vernacular spellings of words such as 'rite', 'nite', 'lite', incidentally, are evidence against imputed psychological reality and phonological fit for the 'gh' in the conventional spelling.) Quite within the scope of the standard language, then, graphic competence in American English embraces more than one variety of spelling. The relation between speech and writing has to be discussed in terms of styles of writing, as well as of speech.

The above examples have dwelt on the representational relation of writing to speech, but of course scriptorial competence is not limited to knowledge of how to represent speech or structures strictly common to writing and speech alike. In keeping with a tendency that might be called 'communicative plenitude' – meaningfulness expands to fill available means – the significance of graphic signs is not restricted to representation of phonic ones or of an element of structure indicated by both. Nor, of course, is the significance of a phonic sign restricted to manifestation of a graphic one, or of an element indicated by both. Users notice not only the respect in which such signs convey the referentially-based relationships of grammar, but also the respects in which such signs, and some of their referentially indifferent details, are associated with persons, places, purposes, and styles, are susceptible to play and aesthetic patterning, etc., and elaborate these possibilities. Such elaboration gives rise to devices and relationships that are specific to each medium, having no exact counterpart in the other, but being part of what one can do with language only when language is being used in the medium of question. Within the field of language, of competence in language, styles of speech and styles of writing become partly autonomous families of symbolic form. Such growth in the range of means is one respect in which the resources of languages change in scope in the course of history. Part of the competence in language of many people is shaped by, must be partly explained by, the availability and characteristics of graphic channels.

We are often reminded of how much is missed when linguistic analysis is based on examples that omit essential features of speech, such as intonation and voice quality. This is indeed a crucial obstacle to be overcome by linguistics if it is to deal adequately with language. One seldom thinks of the converse, of how much is missed when one neglects features specific to writing and print. It is as if the field of competence in language had the shape of a butterfly, one wing specific to speaking, one to writing, the body common to both. Linguistic analysis has focused on the body, as it were, and while that is vital, so are the wings.

Put another way: sometimes to speak is to read aloud, sometimes to write is to transcribe. Such cases of close equivalence are special cases, interesting just because of that. Unfortunately, linguistic analysis has proceeded as if such cases were general.

Having emphasized that speech and writing are not isomorphic, but have autonomy, I do not want to suggest that they are wholly disjunct. It would be a mistake to postulate a universal, absolute contrast between styles of speaking and styles of writing. We need instead to broach the more general topic of *communicative styles*. The organization of communicative means may follow lines dictated by modalities, but need not. A style may integrate features from different components of structure, so that a style of graphic English might select and group together features of orthography, morphology, syntax, diction, discourse. With regard to any one component, it may select some and not other features (e.g., one spelling, alternate, or construction rather than another); may have features uniquely its own (as in a specialized typography); may integrate features from more than one medium.

The integration of spoken and gestural signs within a communicative paradigm should be well known (for an excellent analysis of a case, see Sherzer (1973) cf. Hymes (1974): 102). Integration of spoken and graphic signs should not be surprising. The metalinguistic use of finger-indication of written characters in the midst of conversation is well enough known from Japan. *Ad hoc* hand depiction of letters does occur in interactions in the United States (quite independently of sign language). The relation between spoken presentation and styles associated with print (what might be called scriptive styles) has undergone great change in the last generation or so, both in lectures and public talk generally. There has also been a marked rise of engaged performance, as distinct from prudent reading, by poets. Identification of the social meaning of styles and analysis of their appropriateness and effect must deal with such shifting and mingling.[8]

In sum, the point of view from which to grasp the relation between speech and writing, as media or modalities of language, is function. How are the features of modalities organized for the purposes of those who employ them?

Having emphasized that speech and writing are to be seen as modes of action, I do not want to seem to suggest that they are everywhere the same modes of action. Their degree of autonomy from each other, their relative hierarchy, their integration into communicative styles, all these are problematic and to be determined ethnographically.

As a general principle, one may assume that difference of means will condition differences in what is accomplished. That would seem to hold for all symbolic forms. That speech and writing are not simply equivalent, but have been developed historically in at least partly autonomous ways; that choice of a style specific to speech, or specific to writing, or mingling both, may affect meaning and outcome, all this seems obvious. There is little systematic knowledge, however, as to repertoires of choice and strategies for choosing, as to the degree of autonomy and the consequences of it.

One thing we do know is that a given society may define the role of any one medium quite differently from another society, as to scope and as to purpose. I have elaborated this point with regard to speaking elsewhere. Here, let me illustrate it briefly with regard to writing.[9] For one thing, new writing systems continue to be independently invented – one was devised in 1904 by Silas John Edwards, a Western Apache shaman and leader of a nativistic religious movement. The sole purpose of the writing system is to record the 62 prayers Silas John received in his vision and to provide for their ritual performance. Competence in the system has been restricted to a small number of specialists. Discovery and study of this system by Keith Basso (Basso and Anderson, 1973) has shown that existing schemes for the analysis of writing systems fail to characterize it adequately, and probably fail as well for many other systems, having been devised with evolutionary, *a priori* aims, rather than with the aim of understanding individual systems in their own terms. The development of an ethnography of writing, such as Basso (1974) has proposed is long overdue.[10] Here belongs also study of the many surrogate codes found round the world – drum-language, whistle-talk, horn-language, and the like. Their relation to speech is analytically the same as that of writing (Stern, 1957), and they go together with the various modalities of graphic communication (handwriting, handprinting, typing, typographic printing, electronic mail, etc.), as well as the various modalities of oral communication (chanting, singing, declamation, whispering, etc.) in an account of the relations between linguistic means and ends.

As to ends, the Hanunoo of the Philippines are literate – they have a system of writing derivative of the Indian Devanagari – but they use it exclusively for love-letters, just as the Buan of New Guinea use their writing. In central Oregon the town of Madras has many signs, but the nearby Indian reservation, Warm Springs, has almost none, and those only where strangers impinge – the residents of Warm Springs do not need the information signs give (Philips, 1974). At one time Vista workers tried to help prepare Warm Springs children for school by asking Indian parents to read to them in preschool years. US schools tend to presuppose that sort of preparation, and middle-class families provide it, showing attention and affection by reading bedtime stories and the like, but Warm Springs parents show attention and affection in quite other ways, had no need of reading to do so, and the effort got nowhere. The general question of the consequences of literacy has been forcefully raised for contemporary European society by Richard Hoggart in a seminal book (Hoggart, 1957; note also Hoggart, 1971).

Many generalizations about the consequences of writing and the properties of speaking make necessities out of possibilities. Writing, for example, can preserve information, but need not be used to do so (recall IBM's shredder, Auden's 'Better Burn This'), and we ought to beware of a possible ethnocentrism in this regard. Classical Indian civilization committed vital texts to memory, through careful training in sutras, for fear of the perishability of material things. Classical Chinese calligraphy, the cuneiform of Assyrian merchants, and the style of hand taught to generations of Reed students by Lloyd J. Reynolds, are rather different kinds of things. Television may have great impact, but one cannot tell from what is on the screen alone. In any given household, does the set run on unattended? Is the picture even on? Is silence enforced when a favorite program or the news comes on, or is a program treated as a resource for family interaction?

We have had a great deal more study of means than of meanings. There appear to be many more books on the alphabet than on the role of writing as actually observed in a community; many more pronouncements on speech than ethnographies of speaking; many more debates about television and content-analysis of programs than first-hand accounts of what happens in the rooms in which sets are turned on. The perspective broached above with regard to speech communities applies here, since media are a constituent of the organization of ways of speaking (i.e., ways of communication). We need particularly to know the meanings of media relative to one another within the context of given roles, settings and purposes, for the etiquette of these things enters into whatever constitutive role a medium may have, including the opportunity or lack of it that persons and groups may have to use the medium. In England and France a typed letter is not acceptable in some contexts in which it would be taken for granted in the United States; the family Christmas letter in the United States is a genre that can be socially located; subgroups in the United States differ dramatically in their assumptions as to what should be photographed and by whom (Chalfen, 1987; Worth, 1972).

At Warm Springs reservation in central Oregon, at the burial of a young boy killed in a car accident, his team-mates from the Madras High School spoke haltingly in turn beside the grave and presented the parents with a photograph of the boy in athletic uniform, 'as we would like to remember him' – a shocking thing, which the parents stoically let pass – for them the last sight of the dead person, which bears the greatest emotional distress, had already been endured in the church before coming to the cemetery. When the rites were complete, Baptist and Longhouse, when all the men, then all the women, had filed past the gravesite, taking each in turn a handful of dirt from a shovel held out by the uncle of the boy, and dropping it on the half-visible coffin within the site, when the burial mound had been raised over the coffin, the old women's singing ended, and the many flowers and the toy deer fixed round the mound, then, as people began to leave, the bereaved parents were stood at one end of the mound, facing the other, where their friends gathered to photograph them across it. That picture, of the manifestation of solidarity and concern on the part of so many, evident in the flowers, might be welcome.

The several media, of course, may occur together in several mixes and hierarchies, in relation to each other and in relation to modalities such as touch. Communities seem to differ as to whether tactile or vocal acts, or both together, are the indispensable or ultimate components of rituals of curing, for example. In some parts of Africa, languages are evaluated partly in terms of their greeting systems, and the Haya of northern Tanzania, who are acquiring Swahili, find it less satisfying than their own language, for in a Haya greeting one touches as well as talks.[11]

Finally, the use of media and modalities needs to be related to the norms by which a community takes responsibility for performance and inter-pretation of kinds of communication. My stress here obviously is on the qualitative basis of assessing media as a human problem. Statistics on radios and newspapers and the like barely scratch the surface. I think it entirely possible that a medium may have a constitutive effect in one community and not in another, due to its qualitative role, its social meaning and function, even though frequencies of occurrence may be the same in both. We have to do here with the question of identities and identifications, mentioned earlier with regard to varieties of language in schools. We need, in short, a great deal of ethnography.

Overcoming the Structure of Language

Concern to overcome the structure of language seems to have centered around the function of naming, either to achieve a uniform relation between language and meaning as a semantic ideal, or to avoid it as a spiritual desert or death. Early in the development of Indo-European studies, when modern languages were thought degenerate in form, the great pioneer of recon-struction, Franz Bopp, sought to infer an original Indo-European structure in which meanings and morphemes went hand in hand, reflecting perhaps an original, necessary relationship. Others have sought to realize a semantic ideal in the present, by constructing an artificial language, or by reconstructing an existing one to convey the universal meanings required by science and philosophy. One thinks especially of the late seventeenth century (Dalgarno, Bishop Wilkes, Leibniz) and the early twentieth century (Russell, the early Wittgenstein, Carnap, Bergmann, and others). Still others have thought that the ideal relationship between meaning and form might be glimpsed in the future, once linguists had worked through the diverse structures of existing languages to the higher level of structure beyond them. Such was Whorf's vision (Whorf, 1942).

At an opposite extreme would be a philosopher like Brice Parain (1969) who despairs of the adequacy of language, and, of course, adherents of the Zen tradition that regards language's inveterate distinguishing of things as a trap to be transcended. Intermediate would be the conscious defense of other modes of meaning than that envisioned in the semantic ideal, in particular, the defenses of poetry and of religious language (Burke, 1941). And here would belong conceptions of literary and religious use of language as necessarily in defiance of other, conventional modes of use (Mascall, 1968; Ramsey, 1957). Much of philosophy and some of linguistics seem to have found their way back to an open-ended conception of the modes of meaning in language; and are experiencing great surges of interest in poetics and rhetoric.

Such work is of the greatest importance, but it does leave the general question of the adequacy of language, or of a particular language, in abeyance. It would seem that the structures of languages have never been wholly satisfactory to their users, for they have never let them rest. Shifts in the obligatory grammatical categories of languages over time, like the shift from aspect to tense in Indo-European, bespeak shifts in what was deemed essential to convey. Conscious reports of such concerns may have appeared first in classical Greece, when Plato complained that the processual character of Greek verbs favored his philosophical opponents, although, at the time, devices such as the suffix -*itos* for forming abstract nouns were growing in productivity. When in the fourth century AD Marius Victorinus tried to translate Plotinus from Greek into Latin, there was no adequate abstract terminology in his contemporary Latin, and his clumsy efforts to coin one met with little acceptance, thus inhibiting the spread of the Neo-Platonic philosophy in that period. Some centuries later 'theologisms' had evolved in Latin which quite matched the terms of the Greek fathers in precision and maneuverability.[12] In the early modern period, English writers lamented the inadequacies of English and set out to remedy them (Blackall, 1959; Brunot, 1947; Jones, 1953).

At Warm Springs, some fifteen years ago, a speaker of Wasco (a Chinookan language), acknowledging Wasco's lack of a term for a contemporary object, said that when he was a boy, if one of the old men had come out of his house and seen such a thing, he would have coined a word for it, 'just like that' (with a sharp gesture). There are no such old men anymore to coin words or shape experience into the discourse of myth (Sapir, 1909: 48, lines 1–2).

Such fates are common, though not much attended to by linguists. The official preference is to stress the potentiality of a language and to ignore the circumstances and consequences of its limitations. Yet every language is an instrument shaped by its history and patterns of use, such that for a given speaker and setting it can do some things well, some clumsily, and others not intelligibly at all. The cost, as between expressing things easily and concisely, and expressing them with difficulty and at great length, is a real cost, commonly operative and a constraint on the theoretical potentiality of language in daily life. Here is the irreducible element of truth in what is known as the 'Whorf hypothesis': means condition what can be done with them, and in the case of languages, the meanings that can be created and conveyed.

The Chomskian image of human creativity in language is a partial truth whose partiality can be dangerous if it leads us to think of any constraints on linguistic communication either as nugatory or as wholly negative. As to the force of such constraints, the testimony of writers[13] and the comparative history of literary languages should, perhaps, suffice here. As to their positive side, we seem to need to repeat the development of thought discerned by Cassirer (1961: 24–5) in Goethe, Herder, and W. von Humboldt:

> To them, the Spinozistic thesis, that definition is limitation, is valid only where it applies to external limitation, such as the form given to an object by a force not its own. But within the free sphere of one's personality such checking heightens personality; it truly acquires form only by forming itself . . . Every universal in the sphere of culture, whether discovered in language, art, religion, or philosophy, is as individual as it is universal. For in this sphere we perceive the universal only within the actuality of the particular; only in it can the cultural universal find its actualization, its realization as a cultural universal.

We need ethnography to discover the specific forms which the realization of universality takes in particular communities, and, where the question is one of speech, we need ethnographies of speaking.

Whorf (1941) himself led in describing the organization of linguistic features pertinent to cultural values and world views as cutting across the usual sectors of linguistic description, and as involving 'concatenations that run across . . . departmental lines' (that is, the lines of the usual rubrics of linguistic, ethnographic, or sociological description that divide the study of a culture and language as a whole). Whorf referred to the required organization of features as *a fashion of speaking*, and one can see in his notion an anticipation, though not developed by him, of the sociolinguistic concept of *ways of speaking*. The crucial difference is that to the notion of speech styles, the sociolinguistic approach adds the notion of contexts of situation and patterns relating style and context to each other.

Here, as before, the great interest is not merely in diversity or uniformity, but in the possibility that such differences shape or constitute worlds. Do semantic-syntactic structures do so? Sapir and Whorf thought that for the naive speaker they did, although contrastive study of language structures was a way to overcome the effect. What Chomsky describes as the seemingly untrammeled creative aspect of language use was treated by Sapir as true, but not true in the same way for speakers of different languages. Each language has a formal completeness (i.e., it shares fully in the generic potentiality of human language), but does so in terms of an orientation, a 'form-feeling' of its own, so as to constitute quite a unique frame of reference toward being in the world. A monolingual's sense of unlimited adequacy is founded on universality, not of form or meaning, but of function, and that very sense, being unreflecting, may confine him all the more. The particular strengths of a given language are inseparable from its limitations. This is what Sapir (1924) (in Mandelbaum, 1949: 153, 157), preceding and giving the lead to Whorf, called

> a kind of relativity that is generally hidden from us by our naive acceptance of fixed habits of speech as guides to an objective under- standing of the nature of experience. This is the relativity of concepts, or, as it might be called, the relativity of the form of thought . . . It is the appreciation of the relativity of the form of thought which results from linguistic study that is perhaps the most liberalizing thing about it. What fetters the mind and benumbs the spirit is ever the dogged acceptance of absolutes.

I think this is as fair a statement of the evidence and parameters of the situation today as it was more than a half-century ago when Sapir wrote it. I cite Sapir here partly because linguistics in the United States, having worked its way through a decade or so of superficial positivism, shows some sign of having worked its way through another decade or so of superficial rationalism, and a readiness to pick up the thread of the complexly adequate approach that began to emerge in the years just before the Second World War in the work of men like Sapir, Firth, Trubetzkoy, and Jakobson.

Multilingualism

To return to relativity: the type associated with Sapir and Whorf in any case is underlain by a more fundamental kind. The consequences of the relativity of the structure of language depend upon the relativity of the function of language. Take, for example, the common case of multilingualism. Inference as to the shaping effect of some one language on thought and the world must be qualified immediately in terms of the place of the speaker's languages in his biography and mode of life. Moreover, communities differ in the roles they assign to language itself in socialization, acquisition of cultural knowledge and performance.

Community differences extend to the role of languages in naming the worlds they help to shape or constitute. In central Oregon, for example, English speakers typically go up a level in taxonomy when asked to name a plant for which they lack a term: 'some kind of bush'; Sahaptin speakers analogize: 'sort of an A', or 'between an A and a B' (A and B being specific plants); Wasco speakers demur: 'No, no name for that,' in keeping with a cultural preference for precision and certainty of reference.[14]

This second type of linguistic relativity, concerned with the functions of languages, has more than a critical, cautionary import. As a sociolinguistic approach, it calls attention to the organization of linguistic features in social interaction. Work has begun to show that description of fashions of speaking can reveal basic cultural values and orientations. The worlds so revealed are not the ontological and epistemological worlds of physical relationships, of concern to Whorf, but worlds of social relationships. What are disclosed are not orientations toward space, time, vibratory phenomena, and the like, but orientations towards persons, roles, statuses, rights and duties, deference and demeanor (cf. Bauman and Sherzer, 1974; Darnell, 1972; Hogan, H.M. 1971). Such an approach obviously requires an ethnographic base.[15]

Overcoming the Function of Language

Diversity is a rubric under which the phenomena of language as a human problem can be grasped; the questions which underlie our concern with diversity can be summed up in the term, *function*. What differences do language diversities make through their role in human lives? Some of these differences have been touched upon, and I want to take space for only general consideration here. Linguists have mostly taken the functions of language for granted, but it is necessary to investigate them. Such investigation is indeed going on, but mostly not in linguistics. It is a striking fact that problems of overcoming some of the ordinary functioning of language in modern life attract increased attention from philosophers, writers, and sociological analysts of the condition of communication in society, while many linguists proceed as if mankind became more unified each time they used the word *universal*, freer and more capable of solving its problems each time they invoked linguistic competence and creativity. (This is what I mean by superficial rationalism.)

Serious analysis of the functioning of language has been found in England and the continent much more than in the United States. Let me merely mention here Merleau-Ponty on the 'prose of the world', Heidegger on speaking as 'showing', Brice Parain (already cited) on the inadequacy of language, Barthes on *l'écriture*, LeFebvre on *discours*, Sartre on precoded interpretations of events such as the Hungarian uprising, and Ricoeur on hermeneutics, and state briefly the significance of two approaches, those of Bernstein and of Habermas.

Bernstein

Bernstein's work has a significance apart from how one assesses particular studies, which have been considerably shaped by the exigencies of support for practical concerns. His theoretical views, which precede the studies, are rooted in belief that the role of language in constituting social reality is crucial to any general sociological theory, and that that role has not yet been understood, because it has been approached in terms of an unexamined concept of language. For Bernstein, linguistic features affect the transmission and transformation of social realities through their organization into what he calls *codes*; that is, through selective organization of linguistic features, not through the agency of a language, such as English, as such. He is noted for his twin notions of *restricted* and *elaborated* codes. This dichotomy has not always done the texture of his thought good service, for the two notions have had to subsume a series of dimensions that ought analytically to be separated, dimensions that may combine differently in different communities. (See discussion in Hymes, 1974, Ch. 4, and discussion below.)[16] Nevertheless, one dimension essential to his work is essential to understanding any language as a human problem in the contemporary world. It is the dimension of a contrast between more implicit and more explicit styles.

Let me interpret Bernstein's view of a major importance of the contrast. It is not that one of the styles is *good*, the other *bad*. Each has its place. The more implicit style, in which many understandings can be taken for granted, is essential to efficient communications in some circumstances, and to ways of life in others. But, and this is an aspect of Bernstein's view that has sometimes been overlooked, the more explicit style is associated with predominantly universalistic or context-free meanings, while the more implicit style is associated with particularistic or context-specific meanings. And, argues Bernstein, the universalistic meanings possible to the more explicit style are essential, if one is to be able to analyze means of communication themselves, to describe the ways in which meanings come organized in a community in the service of particular interests and cultural hegemony, and so gain the knowledge and leverage necessary for the transformation of social relationships.

Bernstein has surely put his finger on a crucial issue. There is difference in command of verbal resources, and in access to them, and it is not the case that inequality would be overcome by ending prejudice and discrimination against all forms of speech. Some discrimination among verbal abilities and products is not prejudice, but accurate judgment. The transformation of society to a juster, more equal way of life requires transformation of genuine inequalities in verbal resource. But – here is the crux – we know very little about the actual distribution of verbal resource and ability in our society. We know too little to be able to specify the complex ways in which such a distribution becomes a source of inequality. We must be thankful to Bernstein for the courage to insist on an essential truth – with one and the same language, there are socially shaped contrasts in way of speaking and verbal resource – but we must go beyond his analytic scheme.

The implication of Bernstein's argument is that command of the more explicit style ('elaborated code') should be common to all. To apply such a remedy, one would have to enable others to identify reliably the more explicit style, on the one hand, and the desired kind of cognitive power, on the other, and assume a necessary link between them. Let me suggest some of the difficulties. It would hardly suffice to equate the style with the proprieties of the standard language, although some (not Bernstein) would be tempted to do so; nor can one equate cognitive power with profusion of words. Certain kinds of analysis of social life no doubt require certain kinds of verbal resource, but we are far from knowing how much of the verbal style in which we now couch such analysis is necessary, how much merely customary. There are verbal repertoires without something of what is necessary – in this I agree with Bernstein. But is the problem merely a matter of lack of certain concepts and terms? of certain modes of analytic statement (together with verbal means that facilitate them)? or of an entire orientation toward meanings, as Bernstein suggests?

There is further difficulty in linking the one style to universalistic, context-free meanings. No use of language is ever wholly context-free. The indexical function, as C.S. Peirce called it, is ever-present and ever essential to interpretation (as Harold Garfinkel has stressed in developing the perspective known as *ethnomethodology*). Certainly there are differences in degree of dependence and independence, but their relationship to forms of social life and cognitive power is not self-evident. We may think of science and scholarship as dealing in universalistic, context-free meanings, but such work can be highly particularistic and context-dependent, if one thinks in terms of ability and opportunity to share in it. There are large elements of faith and authority, both for those outside these fields and for those within them (as studies in the sociology of science and knowledge show). If public communicability of analytic knowledge is considered, then adaptation to particular contexts of understanding may have an essential role. Some forms of knowledge, indeed, may require literary rather than scientific methods for their effective transmission, and it is not clear where such verbal methods fit within the contrast in question. The understanding of the perspective of others that is necessary to desired forms of change requires uses of language with narrative and expressive qualities; these qualities often partake of particularistic, context-dependent meanings. It may be that some who would be said to have an 'elaborated code' need greater command of such qualities, and the devices that convey them, to make effective their effort to change ideas and practices. It may be that some who would be said to have a 'restricted code' have sufficient analytic power, but need command of certain of such qualities and devices in order to be heard by some they seek to reach. Finally, we tend to think of explicitness as frankness, as egalitarian and democratic (at least in public communication), yet in some societies (cf. Rosaldo, 1973) explicitness is experienced authoritarian, whereas implicitness, allusion, and indirectness is essential to traditional, reciprocal, consensual modes of resolving issues.

It seems that Bernstein's analytic scheme has inherited a longstanding tendency to dichotomize kinds of meaning and communication and to consider kinds primarily in terms of a cognitive ideal, whereas the actual fabric of relationships among kinds of meaning, communicative style, and social consequences is more intricate.

This is not to depreciate Bernstein's work. More than anyone else in sociolinguistics, he has called attention forcefully to essential dimensions of the organization of ways of speaking and styles of speech. A contrast or polarity of explicitness and implicitness is probably a universal dimension of means and speech. The same is true of simplification and complication of message-form, another dimension associated prominently with the notions of restricted and elaborated codes. One or the other is frequently the salient feature of an important, institutionalized use of language. There is need for analytic clarification of these dimensions, as elements of general linguistic theory, and for a wide range of descriptive and comparative studies. Contemporary linguistics has given attention to simplification and complication as aspects of pidginization and creolization, but their universal relevance has been neglected (cf. Hymes, 1971b).

Bernstein himself does not claim validity for his analysis beyond the English situation. The fact that his work attracts international attention indicates that it corresponds to something real in other situations. The proper use of the stimulus of his work is not to impose its categories, or conjure with them, but to discover how the dimensions to which he calls attention do come organized in the given case.

In doing so, it is necessary to differentiate dimensions from one another, for example, explicitness/implicitness, and complication/simplification. Explicitness may be found with either a complex or simplified message-form; so may implicitness. It is necessary to disentangle three factors of communicative events, message-form, content, and context. A broad dichotomy, such as restricted vs. elaborated, may seem to subsume them – to posit restriction (or elaboration), in all three. The three factors are analytically, and often empirically, distinct. One needs to discover the relationships among them.

In applying the global contrast, or a contrast of dimension, then, one must not begin with a simple two-fold choice (as many have done and continue to do). There may be restriction or elaboration in respect to each factor. Such a contrast (symbolized here R/E) generates eight possible types of relationship, as the following table shows.

	Message-form	Content	Context
(1)	R	R	R
(2)	R	R	E
(3)	R	E	R
(4)	R	E	E
(5)	E	R	R
(6)	E	R	E
(7)	E	E	R
(8)	E	E	E

The eight-fold framework provides a more adequate, because more differentiated, starting point, but chiefly it simply illustrates the need of differentiation and needs to be superseded in the light of empirical work.

Bernstein himself has elaborated his initial dichotomy in different respects, and it is instructive to consider each critically. One kind of elaboration develops additional distinctions of content and application (cf. Bernstein 1972; 1973; 1977a; 1977b; 1990). These distinctions have their own interest. The critical observation to be made is that the basis of elaboration remains binary contrast as to the range of alternatives. At each point, one category has greater, one lesser, range.

Here is the source of a limitation of Bernstein's development of his initial insight, and of applications of such ideas. First, binary contrasts may be inadequate to the actual organization of ranges of alternatives. The locally relevant, valid categorization may not be binary, but quantitatively variable along a scale, may be ternary, etc. If one discovers local norms, there may be a contrast between two styles, one more and one less explicit, or complex. There may also be an unmarked norm, from which a second and third style are distinguished, as markedly more and less explicit, or simple and complex, respectively. Binary categories, however suggestive, prejudge.

Second, there is a persistent tendency to interpret the wider range of alternatives (the 'elaborated' category) as more valuable, even though Bernstein himself sometimes cautions against this. It is hard to avoid such interpretation, especially if one thinks in terms of a cognitive ideal. 'More' suggests more information, more precision, etc. Yet in actual life, forms of message with the widest range of contexts open to them may be the least valued, others with a narrower range valued the most. A message more elaborated in form may be considered more trivial in content. Evaluation cannot be built into the descriptive framework. Local orientations toward meaning or values must be discovered.

Consider an illustration of rows (5, 6) above. Within institutions and circles of high prestige, most of the elaboration of form of a genre of message may be treated as incidental reaffirmation, even if not predictable in detail, and the key to interpretation, found in manner or nuance of expression; such an orientation is very similar to the orientation described for restricted code use in Bernstein's initial formulations and identified there with lower social status.

Again, consider an illustration of rows (3, 4). A message may be restricted in form, highly predictable, context-determined, yet considered rich and open in content. Men and women of high status, commanding what their community considers valued elaborated forms, may give much of themselves to repeated experience of a message, a piece of music, ritual sequence, literary or religious text, finding not increase of information so much as increase of connection, resonance, depth.

Spareness, predictability, context-dependence or form may go with either shallowness or with depth, with poverty or with richness of meaning, and so may prolixity, unpredictability, context-independent of form. The value of the meaning is analytically independent of the code-characteristics. There may be a tight connection in particular cases, but one cannot prejudge what will be connected to what.

It is indeed an important step toward an adequate basis of research just to transect the initial dichotomy with this one of valued meaning, so as to be able to speak of 'deep elaborated/shallow elaborated' and 'deep restricted /shallow restricted' codes, variants, or styles. (Nothing of course depends on the particular adjectives 'deep 'and 'shallow'; another pair, such as 'thick' and 'thin', would serve.)

This four-fold distinction resembles, but seems different from, an elaboration that Bernstein himself has made. He has come to distinguish 'codes' from 'variants' (Bernstein, 1973). Earlier, some persons had been said to have both elaborated and restricted codes, and others only restricted codes. Now each code is considered to have both restricted and elaborated variants. Obviously this is not to reduce the two codes to equivalence. Code continues to designate an underlying, selective orientation toward kinds and possibilities of meaning. And it seems that a person is still considered to come to have essentially one code-orientation or the other.

Now, recognition of parallel variants in both codes does mean that one cannot readily determine the presence of a code from the form of messages. Much of Bernstein's earlier work sought to identify codes from features of message-form, and is called into question by the change. If the implications of the change are pursued, then future research must concentrate on communicative strategies in natural settings and employ participant observation fully. Operative orientations toward meanings cannot be assessed adequately from text apart from context. An apparently restricted utterance may be merely practical in a context in which something is known to one's hearer; an apparently elaborated utterance may be elaborated from pedantic habit, not cognitive force.

To adapt and revise an assumption formulated by Joos, 1961, by and large 'text does not signal its own strategy'. Much of what is needed for assessment of orientations is accessible only in persons, not in transcripts. And it becomes essential to speak in the first instance, not of codes, but of styles, as I have done earlier in interpreting Bernstein's view of the implicit/explicit dimension. To speak of a style leaves open the meaning of the style to those who use it; code, in Bernstein's work, does not.

As noted, Bernstein seems to consider that a person comes to have essentially either one code-orientation or the other. The restricted variant of the elaborated code seems intended to account mainly for predictable aspects of social interaction, greetings, casual conversation, and the like (as did the earlier attribution of a restricted code to elaborated code users), rather than for the experience, say, of a middle-class Christian Scientist hearing the Bible and Mary Baker Eddy in fixed text, Sunday after Sunday – and finding new meaning. Bernstein sometimes attends to such situations, but the thrust of his analysis continues to be that the distribution of code orientations in the society is tantamount to a distribution of people. (Else why distinguish distinct codes as underlying parallel variants?)

I want to suggest that there is something answering to the two types of code-orientation, but not, on that basis alone, two types of people. I want to suggest that persons *in fact have alternative code-orientations,* that such indeed is the common state of affairs in modern society, and that *the central problem is not that some people have one and others do not* (as most users of Bernstein's ideas have assumed). *The central problem is the management of the relation between the two.*

If people differ as types in terms of code-orientations, it is in terms of types of management of the relation. There may be many types of management; there is no reason to assume in advance that there are just two. (For an account of an analogous situation at a national level, cf. Neustupny [1974].)

In sum, each ideal type of code-orientation identified by Bernstein has a necessary part in the life of a person, whatever the person's social origin and experience. Each person must, to some extent, project an analysis of the social life and change in which he or she is caught up, and each must to some extent 'traditionalize' some sphere of experience and relationships. Both orientations are to some degree inevitable for all. To understand people in this regard, one must think of them as having repertoires of code-orientation, and as having to adapt to a communicative ecology that favors now one, now another, element of the repertoire, there being often enough serious tension between person and niche. Many people can be thought of as having to spend much of their waking life in 'verbal passing', employing a style constrained by job or group, and unable to satisfy felt needs for use of language in other ways.

Such ecological deprivation may involve lack of others with whom to pursue certain kinds of cognitive elaboration and play, or lack of others with whom to have certain meanings taken for granted. Many life choices are made for the sake of 'someone to talk to' in these senses. The problem, then, is not absence of the orientation in the person, nor absolute absence of contexts for an orientation, but a specific network of relations between orientations, contents and contexts.

Habermas

This analysis brings us to the way in which problems of modern society have been interpreted as problems of contrasting code-orientation by Jurgen Habermas (see Habermas, 1970a,b; 1971; Schroyer, 1970; 1971).

Habermas develops a contrast analogous to Bernstein's. His starting point is not observation of class and family differences in communication, but analysis of theories of knowledge and communication in science and everyday life. Starting from the neo-Marxian tradition of the Frankfurt School, with its attention to the Hegelian roots and cultural problems of Marxist thought, Habermas has turned to the positive contributions of a psychoanalytic perspective and the possibilities of grounding a theory that is critical of society and emancipatory in aim in the nature of language and communication. He may be said to give a reinterpretation of Marxian categories of analysis in communicative and linguistic terms.

Like Bernstein, Habermas contrasts two orientations toward communication. One is a technical cognitive interest, and has to do with activity guided by technical rules based on empirical knowledge; such activity comprises 'instrumental action systems' or, generally, 'purposive rational action systems'. Scientific, technological, and to some extent bureaucratic modes of rationality and communication are based on this interest. There is, however, an equally fundamental and valid orientation, a practical cognitive interest, which has to do with activity guided by the symbolic processes of everyday life. It is typically dialogic and narrative in its forms of verification and explanation and involves interpretive understanding and indeed reflexive self-understanding. It cannot be reduced to the models and formalizations of instrumental action.

It is Habermas' view that whereas the free market was the dominant ideological rationalization of the capitalist order in the nineteenth century, the notion of technological progress serves that role today, and that a great threat to human life in modern society is the invasion of spheres of practical symbolic interaction by the technological orientation. Value preferences and special interests masquerade in the idiom of instrumental necessity; personal and expressive dimensions of meaning become inadmissible over a greater and greater range of activity. Official social science in its positivistic interpretation of its task actually aids in the maintenance and establishment of technological control, in contrast to those trends in social science concerned with understanding socio-cultural life-worlds and with extending intersubjective understanding (what may loosely be called a family of interpretive approaches), and those trends concerned with analyzing received modes of authority in the interest of emancipating people from them. Whereas the criterion of critical evaluation advanced by Marx stressed material inequality, and the contradiction between production for use and production for profit (use-values vs. exchange-values), Habermas stresses communicative inequality and the conflict between an ideal speech situation and communication distorted and repressed by actual patterns of socialization and interaction. To quote him:[17]

> We name a speaking-situation ideal where the communication is not
> only not hindered by external, contingent influences, but also not
> hindered by forces which result from the structure of
> communication itself. Only then does the peculiarly unforced
> compulsion of a better argument dominate.

This conception has left Marxism and much of social science behind.
Habermas' ideal adds an invaluable dimension, necessary to critical analysis
of social appearances, but there is no adequate link to ongoing social
processes and projected states of affairs. Real situations can be criticized in
terms of the ideal. No means of progressing toward the ideal, other than
criticism, is given. This is why Schroyer (1973) in a sympathetic account
considers Habermas only to complement, not to replace, a Marxian analysis
of inequality and change. One can go further and suggest that Habermas'
analysis contributes only the generic notion of the ideal communicative
situation, as a notion that must be integrated into the foundations of a
linguistic theory adequate to social life. He does not contribute a satisfactory
formulation of the notion.

Notice that the ideal, as formulated by Habermas, is in the end
analogous to the ideal implicit in Bernstein's treatment of the 'elaborated
code'. The need for a complementary orientation is sympathetically
recognized by both, and Habermas gives it foundation in a thorough-going
critique of narrow conceptions of knowledge. But in the end, the role of the
mode of symbolic interaction, for Habermas, is to permit complete
explicitness. The explicitness is rooted, not in a code as such, but in the
dialogic relations of the participants in a communicative situation, and that is
a decisive advance. But the possibility of a positive role for restrictions within
symbolic interaction is forgotten. In the light of the ideal (quoted above), all
restrictions fall short.

This, I submit, is utopian, not in the good sense of an imagined ideal,
but in the bad sense of an ideal whose unrealizability may distort evaluation
of situations and efforts toward change. The ideal of unrestricted speech is
said to be inherent in human communication, and it seems to be assumed
that the logic of historical development moves toward its realization. An
ethnographically informed analysis of ideals of communication suggests
otherwise.

The ideal of unrestricted speech is not the sole ideal inherent in attested
ways of speaking. In some societies, indeed, unrestricted speech is viewed as
dangerous, and the view is pervasively institutionalized (e.g., traditional
Ashanti society, Hogan, 1971; Burundi, Albert, 1972; Malagasy, Keenan,
1973). Speech as a source of mischief and evil is a recurrent theme in cultural
wisdom. Such cases might be said to represent a stage of human history to be
transcended, and the particular practices may indeed yield to change (they
tend to go with dichtomization of sex roles, for example). Still, there are
particulars that express functions that appear to be perennial requisites of
social life.

Habermas' ideal of unrestricted communication is specifically a cognitive ideal of colloquy. It is an ideal of the right and contribution of every member of a group in the resolution of problems. As such, it is an advance over a purely scientific ideal, for it comprises political decision as well. (It resembles the ideal of persuasion long advocated by Kenneth Burke, and taken by many to be regulative for science and democracy). But the ideal does not speak to the perennial requisite of structure. What may appear as restriction is, from another point of view, simply the existence of structure. And it is not possible to envisage viable social life without structure in the sense at least of shared understandings of rights and duties, norms of inter-actions, grounds of authority, and the like. Even the most free conversational situation, in norms about turns, inherently shows elements of restrictive structure. Habermas presumably is concerned simply that no structure prevent a member of a group from having a right to participate in decision. But if one considers the possibility of an obligation to contribute what one knows and wants, the lack of a right to remain silent or to refuse commitment to a consensus – real enough issues – one has again a matter of constraint. In general, the universality of *appropriateness* as a meaning and ideal of speech situations is equivalent to the inherent presence of a principle of structure.

Moreover, not all social life is problem-solving and decision-making in the intended sense. There are everywhere satisfactions in uses of language that embody play, employ unequally shared performance abilities, accept ritual-life repetitions of words accepted as authoritative. One cannot envisage a viable form of life in which every point is open to dialogic determination at every point – in which everyone can say everything to everyone in every way at every moment in every place.

It can be objected that this is an unfair *reductio ad absurdum*, but Habermas does not show how to avoid such reduction. Such a reduction can be avoided only by a theory of communicative competence based on more than rational reflection alone, but built up through patient study and comparison of ideals of communication developed in actual communities.

In sum, every community embodies alternatives to the unique cognitive ideal, and any community (such as a revolutionary group) that could bring closer approximation to the ideal would have to embody alternatives.[18] The theory can only criticize communicative structure in the light of its absence; it cannot address real structures and choices among them. Yet therein lies the true problem for any community and person, revolutionary or not.

The problem can be phrased in terms of Habermas' ideal: What costs in communicative inequality should be accepted in order to gain the benefit of greater equality than now obtains? It could be more adequate to say: What kinds of communicative inequality are acceptable, what unacceptable, in the light of the historical situation and aspirations of a given community? (I say 'given community', for if a community wished to maintain certain forms of communicative structure, Habermas' ideal would not condone its being 'forced to be free'.)

The psychiatrically informed ideal of the ending of repressed communication seems faulty on similar grounds. The cognitive ideal, presumably, is to overcome repression that prevents solution of life-problems. From this it does not follow that no repression is permissible, that life should be lived in terms of an ideal of access to all unconsciously held knowledge. One could not play tennis that way – but to be serious, such a prescription would resemble a Christian ideal of a life without hidden sin, and might entail neurasthenia if rigorously observed. A healthy view of the relation between conscious and unconscious knowledge seems to me to be found in a statement by Sapir and its gloss by Harris (Sapir, 1927, cited from Mandelbaum, 1949: 559; Harris, 1951: 330):

'Complete analysis and the conscious control that comes with a complete analysis are at best but the medicine of society, not its food.' Which means: Don't take it as food; but also: Do take it as medicine.

Bernstein and Habermas are important in their pioneering efforts to analyze the problems of linguistic and communicative inequality. Both fall back on a cognitive ideal to which the absence of restriction, hence 'more is better', is intrinsic. Such an ideal is essential to certain aspects of social problems, but not sufficient to all. Both scholars are able to criticize cultural situations, but not to articulate alternative situations that answer the cultural nature of human life, that give a legitimate place to the practicalities of ordinary life and the full range of needs of human nature.

Both have a sense of a range of needs, to be sure, and other contemporary theorists have hardly addressed the issues at all. Bernstein and Habermas are representative particularly in the fact that the analysis of each revolves around a dichotomy. The influence of each indicates that the dichotomy touches something real in our experience and also that the realities involved have only begun to be analyzed. Dichotomies are symptoms of recognition of an issue; first approximations in addressing it. Adequate knowledge and successful change require linking the insights in such dichotomies to actual situations. Such linkage depends on ethnography, and ethnography leads to reconstruction of initial theories in more articulated, diversified form. Communicative theory, as a foundation of social theory and practice, will be informed by cases, and dichotomies will give way to sets of dimensions, diversely ranked and apportioned, in justice to the experience and aspirations of specific communities.

In sum, overcoming the function of language is first of all a problem of discovering the functions language does have. It is valuable to conceive ideal states of affairs, but the imagining and, equally, implementing of ideal situations should be, as Habermas implies and Bernstein would agree, open and dialogic. If diverse communities and traditions are among the voices, the outcome is likely to be a plurality of conceptions of what should be. For many communities, the goal of transformation will be not only to overcome obstacles to openness, but also to overcome threats to patterns interwoven with the meaning of a way of life.

If we seek to evaluate such things critically, comparative ethnographic perspective is essential, in order to overcome the obstacle of unwitting ethnocentrism in efforts to think about principles and premises of verbal interaction. We are likely to extrapolate and project ideal notions of our own tradition, unwittingly misrepresenting the realities of our own conduct and the ideals of others. For example, many would be likely to link Habermas' speaker-situation ideal of unforced compulsion with the explicitness of Bernstein's ideal-type 'elaborated code', and think of explicitness (in public communication at least) as frank, direct, egalitarian. As noted earlier, however, explicitness and directness may be experienced as authoritarian, and associated with imposed decisions (cf. Darnell and Foster, 1988; Hymes, 1986; 1990; Rosaldo, 1973; Rushforth, 1981).

Thinking About Linguistic Inequality

Occasionally linguists have been so carried away by ideological certitude as to state that all languages are equally complex. This is of course not so. It is known that languages differ in sheer number of lexical elements by a ratio of about two to one as between world languages and local languages. They differ in number and in proportion of abstract, superordinate terms. They differ in elaboration of expressive and stylistic devices – lexical, grammatical and phonological. Languages differ in number of phoneme-like units, in complexity of morphophonemics, in complexity of word-structure (both phonological and morphological), in utilization of morphophonemically permitted morpheme-shapes, etc.

The usual view is that such things are distinctions without a difference, that all languages are equally adapted to the needs of those who use them. Leaving aside that such equality might be an equality of imperfect adaptations, speech communities round the world simply do not find this to be the case. They are found to prefer one language for a purpose as against another, to acquire some languages and give up others because of their suitability for certain purposes. No government can afford to assume the equality of all the languages in its domain.

The usual answer to this objection is that languages are potentially equal. This is so in one vital respect: all languages are capable of adaptive growth, and it is a victory of anthropologically-oriented linguistic work, particularly, to have established this point. The difficulty with the usual answer is twofold. First, each language constitutes an already formed starting point, so it is not clear that expansion of resources, however far, would result in two languages being interchangeable, let alone identical. Limiting consideration to world languages, we find that many who command more than one prefer one to another for one or more purposes, and that this is often enough a function of the resources of the languages themselves. Second, the realization of potentiality entails costs. The image of a child acquiring mastery of language by an immanent unfolding misleads us here. It has an element of truth to which the world should hearken, but it omits the costs and the constitutive role of social factors. Most languages of the world will not be developed, as was Anglo-Saxon, into world languages over the course of centuries. (It is speculated that Japanese may be the last language to join that particular club.)

I regret to differ from so many colleagues on this issue, but if linguistic work is to make its contribution to solution of human problems, it is necessary not to blink realities. How could languages be other than different, if languages have any role in human life? To a great extent, languages, as said, are what has been made of them. There is a truth in the thesis of potentiality and a truth in the thesis of equivalent adaptation across communities, but both truths fall short of contemporary reality, where languages are not found unmolested, as it were, one to a community, each working out its destiny autonomously. Not to start from that reality is to fall back on the Herderian image, a falling back that is all too common. If the image were a reality, then analysis of linguistic inequality would perhaps be only an exercise for some who take pleasure in languages the way one may take pleasure in kinds of music. Given our world, analysis of linguistic inequality is of practical import.

What, then, are the sources and consequences of linguistic inequality? The kinds of diversity discussed above contribute, of course, but having hardly raised the question, we have no clear notion of the answer. Four categories articulated by the sociologist Talcott Parsons can serve as an initial guide.

First, languages differ in their makeup as *adaptive resources*; the linguistic resources of speech communities differ in what can be done with them, as has been indicated. A generation ago some kinds of difference were regarded with a spirit of relativistic tolerance, as special virtues of the languages that had them, and so one got at least some account of their lexical and grammatical strengths. A present temper treats mention of differences as grounds for suspicion of prejudice, if not racism, so that Whorf, who believed fervently in the universal grounding of language, and extolled the superiority of Hopi, has become, like Machiavelli, a perjorative symbol for unpleasant facts to which he called attention. Such a temper discourages learning much about this fundamental aspect of language.

Second, linguistic resources differ as an aspect of *persons* (agents) and personalities. In addition to variability inevitable on genetic grounds, there is variability due to cultural pattern. Conceptions of male and female roles, or of specialized roles, including that of leadership, may differ markedly among speech communities, so that eloquence or other verbal skills may be necessary for normal adult roles in one society (commonly for men, not women), and essential to no important role at all in another. The requirements of a speaking role may be simple, or subtle and difficult, as in the special bind of a traditional Quaker minister who had to speak out of spiritual silence and, desirably, after periods of doubting his calling (Bauman, 1974). Differences in desired skills, of course, feed back upon the ways in which the linguistic resources of a community are elaborated.

Third, linguistic resources differ according to the *institutions* of a community. So far as I know, comparative analysis of institutions has not much considered the ways in which they do or do not require or foster particular developments of verbal skill and resource, or at least has not phrased its findings as contributions to the understanding of language. There are indeed some analyses of the development of the verbal style and resources of particular sciences, of science as a social movement and of religious and political movements. My impression is that there are case studies, but not coordinated efforts toward a comparative analysis.

Fourth, linguistic resources differ according to the *values and beliefs* of a community. Infants' vocalizations, for example, may be postulated as a special language, one with serious consequences, such that special interpreters are required, so that a child's wishes can be known and its soul kept from returning whence it came. The shaping of linguistic resources by religious concerns appears to be attracting interest (cf. Samarin, 1976). A community's values and beliefs may implicitly identify spontaneous speech as a danger to the cultural order, as among the traditional Ashanti, or they may treat speaking, and especially elaborate speaking, as a badge of inferiority, both between persons and among the orders of a social hierarchy, as is the case with the Wolof of Senegal. The normal condition of a community may be constant chatter on the one hand, or pervasive quiet on the other, according to how speech is valued.

Such a fourfold guide to differences does not in itself go beyond a Herderian perspective of discrete speech communities, each part of the cultural plenitude of the world. Such description bears on inequality, however, when speech communities are viewed in a larger context. Differences by themselves would constitute inequality only in the sense of lack of equivalence, not in the sense of inadequacy. But just as the resources of a speech community must be described as speech styles in relation to contexts of situation, when the community is being described, so also must they be assessed in relation to contexts of human problems.

The essential thing seems to me to be to assess a speech community in terms of the relation between its abilities and its opportunities. Every speech community is to some degree caught up in a changing relationship with a larger context, in which opportunities for the meaningful use of traditionally fostered abilities may be declining, and novel opportunities (or requirements) may be impinging – for which members have not been prepared. The term *competence* should be employed within just such a perspective. It should not be a synonym for ideal grammatical knowledge, as it has been used by Chomsky, or extended to a speech community collectively, as used by David De Camp, or extended to ideal communicative knowledge as by Habermas, or done away with, as Labov has seemed to prefer. Rather, *competence* should retain its normal sense of actual ability. Just such a term is needed to address the processes at work in actual communities and their consequences for persons. As a term for ideal knowledge, competence may overcome inequality conceptually, but only as a term for actual abilities, assessed in relation to contexts of use, can it help to overcome inequality practically. (On the development of the idea of communicative competence, see Hymes 1967d, 1971c, 1979b, 1984, 1985c, 1987e, 1992d. Habermas took up the term but changed the direction.)

Conclusion

To sum up: from one standpoint the history of human society can be seen as a history of diversity of language – diversity of languages as such, diversity as to their media, structures, and functions and of diversity as a problem. From another standpoint, diversity has been a resource and an opportunity – for scholars to understand the potentialities of language and for speakers to develop the potentialities of forms of life and identities.

From antiquity it has been the mark of a true science of humanity, of greatness, to attempt to comprehend the known diversity of cultures and history. Herodotus did so in a narrative of his age's great conflict between East and West, incorporating his world's ethnology. The Enlightenment, while recognizing a debt to antiquity, was conscious of the superiority and the challenge of a new horizon provided by knowledge of manners and customs from the New World and from remoter Africa and Asia. The Victorian evolutionists, while recognizing Enlightenment precedent, were conscious of superiority and challenge in a horizon provided by recognition of humanity's great prehistoric antiquity. In this century there has been no brand-new horizon of data in space or time to vivify the whole, but sheer expansion of numbers of scholars and studies, a new depth as well in primate studies and finds of fossil man, gradual establishment of a principle of methodological relativism, and now increasing participation in the study of one's own society, can count as equivalent.

Now we are at a juncture where only the future, not the scope of the past or the present, offers the possibility of a new horizon. The choices appear to be retrenchment and irrelevance, the service of domination or the service of liberation through universalization. The sciences of humankind have developed in the matrix of a certain relationship between one part of the world and the rest. Anthropology has been fairly described as the study of colored people by whites.[19] That matrix has changed irreversibly. A science limited to certain societies or interests was always implicitly a contradiction in terms; increasingly, it has become an impossibility or a monstrosity.

Knowledge about people is a resource, just as control of oil and armies. Peoples cannot accept permanent inferiority in this regard.

For the scholar, the problem is complicated by relations not only between his or her own country and others, but by relations between the governments of other countries and their own peoples. Usually any knowledge worth having, that he or she can gain, entails a relationship of mutuality and trust with people being studied. Thus universalization of the science must mean extension not only to all countries of participation, but to all communities. The proper role of the scientist, and the goal of his and her efforts, should not be 'extractive', but mediative. It should be to help communities be ethnographers of their own situations, to relate their knowledge usefully to general knowledge, not merely to test and document. Such a role could be the safeguard of both the intellectual and the ethical purposes of the science itself.

The study of language has had a checkered career in the history just sketched. It became a self-conscious activity, and to a great extent has developed, as an instrument of exclusion and domination. The analysis of Sanskrit in ancient India, of classical songs and writings in ancient China, of Greek and then Latin in the ancient Mediterranean, of nascent national languages in the Renaissance (e.g., Nebrija's grammar of Castilian), were in the interest of cultural hegemony. Only in our own century, through the decisive work of Boas, Sapir, and other anthropologically oriented linguists (as components of the general triumph of methodological relativism in the human sciences), has every form of human speech gained the right, as it were, to contribute on equal footing to what is known of human language.

The present situation of linguistics in the United States is mixed, if not obscure. A Chomskian perspective holds out the liberation of mankind as an aspiration, but its practice can contribute only conceptually at best, if it is not in fact an obstacle to work that is needed. This chapter has argued for understanding speech communities as actual communities of speakers. In this way one can go beyond a liberal humanism which merely recognizes the abstract potentiality of languages, toward a humanism which can deal with concrete situations, with the inequalities that obtain and can help to transform them through knowledge of the ways in which language is organized as a human problem and resource.

Notes

1   The phrase 'Linguistic Theory' ought to refer to a general theory of language, or at least a general theory of the aspects of language dealt with by linguists, but it has been appropriated for just those aspects of language dealt with in transformational generative grammar – or by competing forms of formal grammar – another consequence of Chomsky's skill as a polemicist. Hence the quotation marks.

2   For example, discussion of 'The Problem of Linguistic Communication in the Modern World', *La Monda Lingvo-Problemo*, **3**, 9 (1971): 129–76.

3   There are noble exceptions – Schuchardt in the nineteenth century, for one, and the Prague School and J. R. Firth in the twentieth century, but the main thrust of successive developments has been as described. Transformational grammar is included under structural method here because it shares the same assumptions when contrasted to a functional approach. Cf. the contrast drawn in Hymes (1967a).

4   Assumptions as to the bases of mutual intelligibility, and as to relations among linguistic boundaries, ethnic boundaries, and communication are analyzed in Hymes (1968).

5   On complex linguistic communities, see Ferguson (1966; 1991). On comparative study of the role of speaking, see Hymes (1966; 1970a; 1972b) . The work of John Gumperz and William Labov and their students has been of special importance to the understanding of the problems dealt with in this section.

6   Fourteen paragraphs were added to the original article at this point.

7   The possibility is considered by Greenberg, 1968: 133, in the course of a lucid account of approaches to language classification. He suggests the semantic features of richness in quasi-synonymity as a possible example of a characteristic that would permit one to treat languages that exist in written form as a class from the standpoint of linguistics proper.

   Greenberg's requirement is that the external fact of a functional role go together with linguistically internal facts of structure. In what follows I argue that the fact of written form does not itself uniquely determine functional role; there is need for a typology within the category, 'language with a written form'. Greenberg's requirement would still hold for several types within the category, provided that the notion of 'internal facts of structure' is interpreted in the broad sense of the organization of means of speech (and writing), not in the narrow sense of grammar proper.

8   Both plenitude and integration are perhaps illustrated by traditional and vernacular styles pointed out by Jaquith. Each may entail something in speech. A sign in one spelling may perhaps be read aloud in one way, a sign in the other in another. If so, if 'right', *et al.*, go with one spoken style, 'rite', *et al.*, with another, the differences cannot be in the sounds the letters are considered to spell. The spelled sounds are the same. The differences would be in sub-phonemic detail, tempo, voice quality, intonation, and perhaps other aspects of manner.

   Other examples of interacting styles:

-   Allen (1992) describes a common, complex interplay of speech characters drawn by hand in the air by users of Chinese.
-   Smith and Schmidt (1994) explore the social and stylistic meanings associated with the several styles of Japanese writing, (*kanji, hiragana, katakana rômaji*).

   Ronald Scollon – responding (personal communication) to an observation that about thirty years ago American academics began not to read prepared texts, but speak to or from them, so much so that to read now may make a presentation seem boring, however cogent the material – points out that in overseas and international settings speaking in English to one's audience in a less formal manner (as has come to be expected in many situations in the United States) can be prejudicial to non-native users of English. People who have assiduously studied written English discourse for years can follow a condensed, written essay read out loud more easily than a more audience-sensitive talk with nuances of intonation, irony, and jokes. Scollon suggests that the oral features that make a talk more effective than reading a written text may work against those not part of the speaker's community of oral style. Having learned to be chatty and jokey to humanize presentations, one may not include, but exclude people whose competence is in formal written style.

9   See works cited in Note 5, and, on writing, Hymes, 1964: 24–5.

10   For steps toward a much needed ethnography of reading, see Boyarin (1992) and Heath (1983); note especially Boyarin, p. 3.

11   I owe this information to Sheila Dauer.

12   From a comment by G. E. von Grunebaum, in Hoijer, 1954: 228–9.

13   For example, T. S. Eliot, 1943: 16:

> one has only learnt to get the better of words
> For the thing one no longer has to say, or the way in which
> one is no longer disposed to say it.

The question of Herderian standpoint and the mixed standing of linguistic resources as determinants is reviewed in Hymes (1970a)

14   From work of David French. On the general issue, see Hymes (1966; 1972b).

15   Cole, Gay, Glick, Sharp (1971) is an excellent demonstration of the necessity of ethnography for assessment of linguistic and cognitive abilities, even though, unfortunately, the authors do not disclose the linguistic characteristics of the material on which their work rests.

16   Thirty-four paragraphs were added to the original article at this point. For more on the significance of Bernstein's work, see Chapter 9.

17   From an article, 'Summation and Response', *Continuum*, Spring–Summer 1970: 131, as cited in Schroyer, 1973: 161.

18   Cf. these lines from a conscientious-objector camp in Oregon in World War II ('Chronicle of Division', Part v) (Everson, 1968: 199–20):

> The pacifist speaks,
> Face to face with his own kind, And seeks to fashion a common course
> That all may mark.
> But whatever he offers,
> Finds already framed in another's thought
> A divergent approach.
> The binding belief that each allows
> Is cruxed on rejection:
> Thou shalt not kill.

> But for all the rest,
> What Voice shall speak from the burning bush,
> In the worksite noons,
> When the loaf is broken,
> And brief and rebuttal countercross,
> And no one wins?

19   Cf. Willis (1973). This discussion draws on my introduction to the book in which his paper appears (Hymes, 1973b).

Chapter 4

Report from an Underdeveloped Country: Toward Linguistic Competence in the United States[1]

There is nothing new in the goal of understanding language as a part of social life. What is new, as we near the end of the century, is the proliferation of activity toward that goal. Forty-odd years ago a paper on the meanings of kinship terms could count as a bridge between formal linguistics and social life and have a special designation, 'ethnolinguistic', in its title (Garvin and Riesenberg, 1952). Today the scholarly world abounds with bridges and designations – 'sociolinguistic', 'ethnography of speaking' 'ethnography of communication', 'pragmatics', 'conversational analysis', 'sociology of language', 'social psychology of language', together with 'communication', 'intercultural' and 'cross-cultural communication', 'semiotics)' ethno-methodology', 'discourse'. Yet work that has useful bearing on the situation of particular communities and groups is not as commonplace as one might hope, nor is work that builds a truly social study of language that is concrete, yet comparative, cumulative, yet critical, as normal as one might expect. More such work is appearing, yet, with regard to knowledge of itself in terms of language the United States remains a largely underdeveloped country. There is more authority about language in linguistics and among savants of the media, than knowledge to explain, and even transform, the role that language has in our lives.

It would be useful to compare the United States with other countries in regard to the connection of established disciplines, practical situations, and the life of language. What is taken for granted in the United States might come into focus as something particular, the result of a certain social history and certain valuations. The United States might come into focus as one kind of place, or series of places, alongside China, Denmark, India, Nigeria, and other countries (cf. Berry, 1983).

We are not far enough along to be able to ask 'Why is the United States the way it is?' because we have yet to realize that the United States is a certain way. One way we are, I suspect, is due to an interaction of subtle forms of hegemony with a widespread belief that aesthetic and expressive elaborations in language are feminine, not masculine, a certain equation of masculinity for boys with a good heart, open hand and willing back. Be that as it may, let me broach some aspects of the present situation in terms of tasks that connect the social sciences, linguistics and sociopolitical trends.

The sociopolitical trends are of concern in terms of linguistic discrimination and inequality. These trends simmer, and sometimes may boil, and in any case directly affect the degree to which our society achieves its professed goals. Prediction is risky – neither the left nor the right foresaw the realities of the 1960s, and the 1970s did not much foresee the offensives mounted by the Reagan administration and the Gingrich ascendancy. The best guess may be simply that the situation will change. If so, language practices and language rights may become central to the ideology of the society. Language may be given a further part in explaining the persistence and growth of a large underclass (white as well as black); repression of an immigrant work force that does not immediately abandon its original languages may increase; tensions with reality may be felt in a society that sometimes idealizes equality in interaction, an absence of verbal airs, while at the same time separating those with a secure place within the economy from those without. Ideals of verbal equality as a goal may even be abandoned; social inequality be verbally masked in new ways; new modes of verbal marking and displacement arise through tacit decisions as to who is part of society after all. As I write there is more of revenge than hope in the air, more of a war on the dark and poor than an ingathering of the meek.

Even if the country remains, so far as the media detect, linguistically simply some sort of mush, those who believe in a society better than we now have should develop a well-grounded critique. What ideal or vision can we entertain in terms of language?

Two ingredients of a vision are longstanding. One is a kind of negative freedom, freedom from denial of opportunity due to something linguistic, whether in speaking or reading or writing. One is a kind of positive freedom, freedom for satisfaction in the use of language, for language to be a source of imaginative life and satisfying form. In my own mind I would unite the two kinds of freedom in the notion of *voice*: freedom to have one's voice heard, freedom to develop a voice worth hearing. One way to think of the society in which one would like to live is to think of the kinds of voices it would have.

If issues couched in terms of language may come to the fore in ways not expected, now is the time to build knowledge needed to understand them when they arise. If the condition of American society is not satisfactory, language may be a sphere in which to raise consciousness and direct critique.

Something of the sort has made a difference in connection with women's issues. Claims of connection between certain features and kinds of oppression may have sometimes been overstated, or have implied wholescale assumptions about the relation of language to thought and social life that overreach. Language use, nonetheless, is inseparable from everyday life, and contentions about it cannot be ignored. One can identify a pronoun more easily than a controller of corporate policy. Turns at talk are more easily observed than musical chairs among government agencies and interests the agencies ostensibly regulate.

Discourse ultimately cannot change the inequities that make it rational for centers and margins of power alike to combine in ecological destruction (Anderson, 1973), nor change interests that find it reasonable to allow the destruction of habitat, even to continue to prepare for the destruction of us all; but discourse is everywhere, and scrutiny of our own and that of others is a lens that may sometimes focus light enough to illuminate and even to start a fire.

Such a thought may seem like clutching at a straw, as against analysis of modern society in terms of the state, multinational financial institutions, and the like. Perhaps it is. Still, no other likely lever of change is evident except immiserization. Rather than wait for the worst to get worse and then perhaps turn better, we may find scrutiny of language, literacy, and discourse productive of both knowledge and change.

Five Tasks

If one were to try to do something about the language situation of the United States, how to proceed? Five tasks can be singled out:

1   Remedy the degree to which the United States is *terra incognita* with regard to information as to varieties of language and values as to their use.
2   Analyze the processes by which something linguistic comes to be recognized as a problem.
3   Analyze the development of cultural hegemony through language in the United States, historically and in comparative perspective.
4   Criticize the assumptions and practices of linguistics and the social sciences with regard to language.
5   Shape the study of language in accord with such critique, not only as to what is done, but also as to who does it and for what ends.

Somewhat crudely reduced to parallel formulations:

- What counts as a language?
- What counts as a language problem?
- What counts as proper use of language?
- What counts as a contribution (about language) to linguistics, to sociology, etc.?
- What will count in changing the above?

Let me suggest something about each of these five tasks in the following sections.

Task 1: *Terra Incognita*

Most people are likely to think of issues of language in terms of languages. There is much to be brought to attention simply as to the actual heterogeneity of the United States in this regard. Many may think of Montana as a state of big sky and few people, but Beltramo (1981) has identified some 37 or so languages in varying degrees of use among its population: Cree, Chippewa, Atsina, Blackfoot, Crow, Teton, Assiniboine Flathead, Kalispel, Kutenai, of American Indian languages; the French-Indian creole, Metis; French, English, Gaelic, German, Norwegian, Danish, Swedish, Finnish, Dutch, Polish, Czech (and Slovak), Serbo-Croatian, possibly Russian, Hungarian, Greek, Italian, Spanish, Basque, Hebrew, and Yiddish, of languages from Europe; Arabic; Chinese, Japanese, Korean, Miao (spoken by the recent immigrant Hmong), Vietnamese, and Lao (used as a *lingua communis* by Vietnamese with some other Asians).

The book to which Beltramo contributes, *Language in the USA* (Ferguson and Heath, 1981), is a major step toward making our language situation intelligible to researchers. Here I want to call attention to two considerations often overlooked in thinking about named languages. One concerns the repertoire of language varieties present in a situation and the other that aspect of language that has to do with attitudes and practices in its use. Understanding of each requires a mode of work that is ethnographic.

Varieties of Language

Communities and Ethnic Groups

In a situation involving English and another language, most schools and scholars would assume that the number of elements (varieties of language) is two. Often the true number is at least four.

In Native American communities, where the native language survives in a traditional form, there may be also a more widely used vernacular variety. A local vernacular English will be found besides a local standard English. The vernacular may have a socially significant role. Someone who has been away and returns may have to take up the 'Indian English' again or be judged snobbish. This vernacular variety may show distinctive, creative adaptations of English material to phonological, syntactic, and semantic patterns that are Indian.

There are various varieties of Indian English in the United States, but only recently have there come to be published analyses. A pioneer work is Leap (1974). In it he shows that a double negative in the English of the people of Isleta Pueblo on the Rio Grande in New Mexico is not an error, nor the borrowing of an error, but a way of maintaining a difference between two kinds of negation (negation of predicate: negation of object) present in

66

Isleta. (The difference is equivalent to 'The fire is not burning' vs. 'There is no fire.') (Cf. also Leap, 1993).

Varieties of English are distinguished not only by phonological and grammatical traits, but also by patterns that are poetic, or rhetorical, in nature. The characteristic voices of the older people of an Indian community may be colored by the native language not only in a narrowly linguistic sense, but also in modes of expressing and replaying experience. Relations in discourse, ways of segmenting and sequencing events, may maintain something of the centrality of the narrative logic of the traditional way of life. Such characteristics of Indian use of English have mostly gone unnoticed.

A fourfold situation as to varieties of English and Indian language is usefully depicted for the Cree in the Canadian province of Alberta by Darnell (1971). A brief, clear picture of a situation involving three languages (Indian, English, and Spanish) is given by Brandt (1970). As is often the case in the Southwest, degrees of command differ rather markedly across four generations (each approximately 20 years). Voegelin, Voegelin, and Schutz (1967) pioneered in an overview of a state (Arizona) as a language situation with special concern for Indian languages. See, especially now, Kroskrity (1993).

The importance of getting beyond language names to varieties is shown by a prize-winning study of the language development of Pima Indian children in Arizona. Their speech was analyzed in relation to norms from English-speaking children in Maryland. No information was given as to English spoken by the Pima, or indeed, around them in Arizona.

Again, some years ago, a comparison of Choctaw, an Indian language of the Southeast, and English, was prepared. The study was intended to be useful in schools with Choctaw children, by pointing to differences between the languages that might present special difficulties in learning English. The comparison was between traditional standard Choctaw and standard English. The varieties of Choctaw and English actually known and used by the children were ignored.

This kind of question arises with particular force with regard to Spanish. Major groups of Spanish speakers in the United States, Puerto Ricans, Dominicans, Cubans, and Chicanos, are organizationally and linguistically distinct. There is indeed a distinction to be observed between *Chicanos*, resident for some time in the United States, and *Mexicans*, recently arrived. The differences pose problems for practical programs. Not the least problem is attitude toward a standard language on the part of many users of Spanish and many Anglos. Some Puerto Ricans sympathetic to working-class problems may question whether maintenance of standard Spanish is in their interest or that of someone else. Teachers of Colombian origin may indict the Spanish of their Puerto Rican students. Native speakers of Spanish may do poorly in (standard) Spanish class in comparison with Anglo students. Anglo teachers who may have excused students in the past on the grounds of their being Spanish may be heard to tell Chicano children, 'I used to think your trouble was that your language was Spanish. Now I see that you don't have any language at all.' (I owe this to Eduardo Hernandez-Che; cf. Ruskin and Varenne, 1983).

The fact is that Chicanos may experience as many as four varieties of Spanish alone. In Austin, Texas, there is a local standard, *northern Mexican*, also called *Español formal, Español correcto, Español politico* (polite), *Español bueno, Español bonito*, or *straight Spanish*. There are also *popular Spanish* (called also *Mejicano, everyday Spanish, Español, Español de East Austin*, or *Español mocho*), so-called *Spanglish* (also called *Tex-Mex, Español mocho, Español revelto*, or *Español mixtureado*), and *Calo* (also called *Pachuco talk, Barrio language, pachuquismos, Hablar al modo loco*, or *vato language*). (I owe this information to Lucia Elias Olivares.) A teacher may not accept the local standard as deserving classroom recognition, but instead consider Castilian, Colombian, or some other nonlocal variety the norm. If the local standard is accepted, the other varieties of the children's language experience still are likely to be ignored or condemned.

There is a great deal still to be learned about the diverse and changing situation of Spanish. The state of sociolinguistic research into New World Spanish has been surveyed by Lavandera (1974) with critical observations. Hernandez-Chavez, Cohen and Beltramo have provided an overview of Chicano language (1975). Craddock (1981) gives a useful introduction to New World Spanish generally, and Zentella (1981) to the specific situation of Puerto Rican Spanish. See now also Bergen (1990) and Roca and Lipski (1993).

The vernacular varieties of English used by African-Americans have come to be better known, but the state of knowledge about language among them is perhaps not much better. The full range remains obscure. Some African-American scholars have asked why there has been so much attention to the variety associated with the street and young adolescent males and so little to others. Why so much fascination with the ritual insults and obscenities of 'playing the dozens', and so little attention to the eloquence of the preacher and minister or to the subtle use of 'black' features by many of the middle class? (cf. the review articles by Mitchell-Kernan, 1972, and Wright, 1975). The impetus given by the civil rights movement and the turbulence of the 1960s has not been sustained by systematic study, apart from a few individuals. (Studies of black English have been surveyed by Abrahams and Szwed, 1975; cf. Baugh, 1983).

The decision of a suit about education in Ann Arbor on the basis of language brought judicial recognition of a variety, black English, that could be defined linguistically, but the case is often misinterpreted. What was ordered was not instruction in black English, but workshops for teachers about the nature of Black English. The plaintiffs had not sought to base a case on language, but the judge found that language was the only grounds legally available to him. The law stated that equal opportunity could not be denied for reasons that included language. It said nothing about denial of equal opportunity on grounds of class or economic status.

The decision was widely misinterpreted because of a division of opinion among African-Americans themselves as to the status of black English. Its general stigmatization has led many to reject it themselves. The common anthropological attitude of using the language of the community led some linguists in the 1960s to pioneer use of Black English forms in written materials for classrooms; by many African-Americans the effort was taken as a threat. In Philadelphia some unions threatened to strike if such materials were introduced. In the wake of the Ann Arbor decision, classrooms in the school district in Philadelphia in which I lived were forbidden to represent on the blackboard the nonstandard forms actually used by children in relating their experiences. All this indicates, of course, that educated African-Americans may share with other educated Americans a view of writing as almost something sacred (cf. Illich, 1983). What may be tolerable in speech may become a symbolic issue if visible in chalk or print.

For every language situation, there is a need to know not only the range of varieties in terms of linguistic characteristics, but also the range of varieties in terms of modes or channels. 'Speech' and 'writing' name the obvious contrast, but reality is more complex. Speech and writing are not each homogeneous things, but modalities whose use is diversely shaped. One must discover the routines, genres, and functions of each. As work in urban classrooms by Susan Fiering and Susan Florio has shown, what counts as official writing for a teacher may be only a portion of the kinds of actual writing in which children engage. A variety of uses for social interaction and personal expression can be seen if one looks.

In general, we have little accurate knowledge of where and what literacy is in our society. We may have an image of what it should be, but it would be hard to find a careful profile of the actual life of literacy in a community. For a child acquiring a way of life, the literacy of the school comes after encounter with street signs, delivered newspapers and magazines, hubcap names that distinguish cars, Sunday school perhaps, brand names and advertisements on the breakfast table, and so on. A child would become literate to some degree without school, simply as a part of walking, eating, playing, being a Methodist, and the like.

It would be useful to imagine the school as a trading post or mission, offering goods and practices to a community that already has something of the kind and would have, even if the school enclave were not there. Classrooms add to experiences of literacy that children have before they come to school and to those they develop as they grow, play, attend church, work, and become involved otherwise apart from school. It is important to know what the rest of life outside school tells children as to the nature and value of literacy. (See the important work of Heath, 1982; 1983, contrasting three groups in a region of South Carolina, and Fishman, 1988, and Galindo, 1994, on the special case of the Amish).

The Ann Arbor decision might have opened an opportunity so far missed. Scholars and public may associate language with the contents of a grammar, but not with the ways in which the contents are organized for use. If language is legally protected, if equality of opportunity cannot be denied on grounds of language, then it matters very much to the future of the country how comprehensively language is defined. A conception of participation in a speech community as more than knowledge of a grammar, as consisting of knowledge of appropriate use as well, has been advanced (Hymes, 1967c, 1972b, 1974). If this conception of what it means to know a language were adopted, then the cultural and social aspects of life of concern to many African-Americans, Hispanics, and others would be brought within the scope of the stated law. The place of language in the life of the community would be understood as more than a matter of sounds, spellings, grammatical categories and constructions. It would be properly understood as involving varieties and modalities, styles and genres, ways of using language as a resource.

Black English itself, of course, is a matter of all these things. Studies show how important are certain ways of using language (cf. Whatley, 1981, as an introduction; the important book by Smitherman, 1977; Kochman, 1972; Mitchell-Kernan, 1972), and norms and mastery for contexts of use (cf. Abrahams, 1972; Hoover, 1978; Baugh,1983; Hinson, 1995, and for an English case, Hewitt 1986).

Black English also points up a phenomenon for which the depiction of a language situation in terms of just a set of languages, dialects, varieties, or levels of usage is inadequate. On the one hand, much the same linguistic features may be prejudicial to a working-class African-American speaker but not to a middle-class white. Lyndon Johnson became President with marked dialect features that might have disqualified a black. On the other hand, distinctive African-American style is acceptable, even applauded, in a case such as that of A. D. King, Sr's participation as a minister at the 1980 Democratic National Convention.

There is a phenomenon here connected with the notion of *voice.*. Certain voices are acceptable, even valued, in certain roles, but not others. A black minister, a British actor, an aged Native American leader, and perhaps some others, have a niche of acceptability distinct from a linear two-dimensional model of levels of class-based norms, vertically, and situational styles varying with degree of self-consciousness, horizontally. The two-dimensional model is important to the study of community-wide change, but is too gross to catch evaluations of speech and speakers that involve special personifications and roles.

Varieties of language are intimately involved with attitudes and values related to their use, and discussion of black English inevitably broaches such questions. Before continuing, however, let me say something more about the United States from the standpoint of language varieties of European origin. Criteria for describing national language situations have identified the United States as having six major languages: English, German, Italian, Spanish, Polish, and Yiddish (Ferguson, 1966: 321). (Immigration in recent decades may put Asian and Pacific languages in such a list, especially if one focuses on a region, such as California.) Most work with regard to these and other immigrant languages (apart from English) has been concerned with their relation to their Old World counterparts. Studies have focused on survival and change of Old World features and on adoption of English features in adaptation to the New World environment. Relatively little has been done to identify the uses of varieties of these languages as part of the general verbal repertoires of the communities. Even the history of the use of German and other languages in bilingual schools and in churches in earlier generations is little known to the public at large, which falsely imagines past immigrants from Europe to have invariably adopted English promptly. Knowledge of such European-origin languages was well surveyed four decades ago by Haugen (1956), who is the source as well of the richest study of a single language (1953). Efforts to develop knowledge of the German language situation are reflected in Gilbert (1971), who has made an interesting comparison between German and French as well (1981).

The maintenance of a number of languages through schools, newspapers, and churches has been surveyed by Fishman (1966). There is perhaps an increase in interest in maintenance now on the part of a good many. In some urban centers and in some institutional contexts, at least, there is considerable bilingualism and multilingualism. New York City television stations offer programs in Spanish, Chinese, Korean, Japanese, Greek, Portuguese, and Italian, and there are at least five Spanish language stations in the country as a whole (*New York Times*, April 21, 1975, p. 59), as well as one Navajo one. The four-day 61st annual convention of the Apostolic Church of America at George Fox College in Newberg, Oregon, in July 1975 had dual sessions in English and Finnish for its 1000 delegates from 52 churches across the country (*The Portland Oregonian*, July 5, 1975, p. B7). A multilingualism clipping service would accumulate a great many such facts.

Despite all that has been done to Native American cultures and languages, 50 or 60 remain viable and are used in homes. Some 44 attract the efforts of missionary linguists as having a 'justified need for Bible translation' (*Washington Star-News*, December 21, 1974, citing the *Conference on American Indian Languages Clearinghouse Newsletter*, March 1975, **3**(2): 3) Information of this kind becomes known to residents of a locality, members of an organization, and specialists in a subject, but seldom goes further. Because of the isolation of such facts from one another the public allows us to continue to think of the country as blanketed by English, our particular bit of information being the odd exception. Even where extinction is likely in the near future, as has become the case at the end of the century, it is risky to assume that no speaker is left at all. Cultural values may keep someone with knowledge from putting him or herself forward while another, older speaker lives.

We are pretty ignorant, by and large, of the sum to which the odd exceptions add up. Probably few are aware that Hawaiian Creole English may emerge as a literary language (Romaine, 1994). Official statistics are of little use. According to the 1960 census, for example, there were only 1200 native speakers of French in Louisiana, because it was presumed that any native-born American was a native speaker of English. Only the foreign-born were recorded as having a different mother tongue. The actual situation and the range of styles are indicated in Tentchoff (1975). The 1960 census was discussed by McDavid, 1966: 321. It would be one mark of success for a language-oriented movement if it succeeded in deepening the knowledge that the census and other government agencies provide and publish. There are, of course, considerable constraints of time, expense, and training governing what census takers themselves can do. Their inquiries and other records could be supplemented by detailed study in selected areas. (On the present situation, and improvements motivated by bilingual education, see the valuable overview of Waggoner, 1981. For English generally, cf. now Horvath and Vaughan, 1991).

It is all too common, unfortunately, for official records and scholarly studies to rely on what people themselves say as to the languages they use and how often they use them. People are often unable to answer such questions accurately. We are busy living our lives, not observing them, and often simply do not know all that we do or how often we do some part of it. Moreover, any answer to such a question about language is most likely a statement of identity. Self-report will tell about people's values, aspirations, current sociopolitical circumstances; but it cannot be relied on to tell what they do. If one were to take the answers to the census of India at face value, tens of thousands of speakers and even whole language communities would have to be assumed to have disappeared between one census and the next. As the Indian scholar L. Khubchandani has observed, the truth is that the communities are multilingual, circumstances change, and the variety of language which it seems most reasonable or advisable to name first may change.

Information as to the occurrence of a variety can be accurate, of course, only in terms of the set of varieties found in a community. In multilingual situations, as in situations of a series of styles or registers, it is common for one to influence others. The attitude of members of the group may range from ignorance or shocked denial of such influence to cultivation of the relationship as a stylistic resource. Code switching, in the narrow sense of use of a feature of one language in another, may be an *ad hoc* choice of the word that comes first to mind, an allusion to one's status or travels, a gesture to the interlocutor who shares that other language. The range of empirical possibilities is great, and the relation between fact and popular impression loose. A few English words in another language may go unnoticed, may pass as sophistication, may spark a fear that the other language is being corrupted or even in danger of being lost. It is the salient, detachable features of language – words – that most gain popular attention. The many and subtle ways in which languages can influence each other, through adaptation of grammatical categories, shifts in connotations, translation of phrasal patterns, and the like, are less apparent at the surface. And just as a few intrusive words may seem a symbol of loss, so a few remaining words may seem a symbol of maintenance. Just the ability to introduce a certain number of native words on a public occasion may be symbolically meaningful and count as use of the language. (Cf. now Heller, 1988, and Myers-Scotton, 1993).

In short, to describe the language situation of a community, to identify the varieties of language within its repertoire, is to do more than to enumerate a list. On the one hand, it is to discover the relations to each other of the members of a set, a paradigmatic set in linguistic terms. On the other hand, it is to deal with a set of symbols whose significance cannot be inferred from linguistic facts alone, but must be discovered in the life of the community itself. Varieties and features of language, as organizations of linguistic signs, themselves become sociolinguistic signs, unities of form and meaning within a system. Their relations to each other are partly a matter of distribution, of allocation among topics and settings and purposes, and are partly a matter of sheer attribution of meaning in terms of the values and historical experiences of the people in question. The dimensions of contrast underlying these meanings are only discovered through ethnographic inquiry (cf. Scollon and Scollon, 1981).

Occupations, Institutions, Generation, Class, Gender

We are used to thinking of varieties in connection with ethnic identity. There has begun to be sustained work on varieties in connection with occupational and institutional settings. Cazden and Dickinson, 1981; Cicourel, 1981; O'Barr, 1981; introduced education, medicine, and the law in useful articles, and there are many studies of each (on education, cf. also O'Barr, 1982). Age and generation have been less noticed, but now there is work that relates specific circumstances among the elderly to general issues (cf. Coupland, Coupland and Giles, 1991; Coupland, Coupland and Robinson, 1992).

Class has entered sociolinguistic analysis as an indispensable parameter of change and statistical difference, but as a lived reality has hardly begun to appear as a focus of inquiry in its own right. In an attempt to reconcile socioeconomic class (conflct-based) and social network (consensus-based) as sources of variation, Milroy and Milroy (1992) have opened up the use of a notion of life-modes (developed in Denmark by Thomas Højrup). The focus remains on patterns of variation and mechanisms of change in language itself, but the concomitants and consequences of variation and change in lives may more readily come into view. There is evidence to suggest that experiences with school and elsewhere leave many members of the working class (and others) with a sense that their lot in life is deserved, and that language plays a great part in the process. Perhaps the appearance of an equal opportunity to rise through education, joined with a process of selection and rejection mediated in great part by language, is essential to the stability of a society with democratic beliefs, but a persistent hierarchy of wealth and power. Perhaps stigmata of linguistic inferiority are needed, and if already recognized differences did not seem sufficient, others would be seized upon, even invented.

Differences of gender have been the focus of considerable attention. Much remains to be worked out as to the actual relationships among verbal behavior, verbal stereotypes, features of language in the narrow sense, and features of the use of language, such as turn-taking, having the floor, symmetry and complementarity in styles of conversation, dependence of difference on setting and role, and so on. Much of the work has reflected middle-class and academic or professional settings. There is little information on attitudes and practices that may obtain in different ethnic groups, among different classes, regions, and religious traditions. Clearly men's and women's speech is too broad a contrast. There may well be contrasting styles, associated primarily or often with men and women, but some work indicates that status and power may be basic to some features associated with women, such that they may be found also in the speech of men occupying positions of low status or little power.

The study of gender-related differences in speech could be a leading edge of general understanding of language in the country (cf. Coates and Cameron, 1988; Cameron, Frazer, Harvey, Rampton and Richardson, 1992; Corson, 1993b; Kramarae, Schulz and O'Barr, 1984; McConnell-Ginet, Borker and Furman, 1980; Philips, Steele and Tanz, 1987; Tannen, 1993, 1994; Thorne, Kramarae and Henley, 1983). The pursuit of the one focus might illuminate relationships among all the various facets of linguistic diversity: ethnic, regional, occupational and class. In the absence of a clear model of the society as a whole, the pursuit of one dimension as far as it can take us may be the best strategy for gaining a comprehension of the whole. Every ethnic and racial group, region, class, and most occupations have women members; every woman is a member of some ethnic or racial group, a resident of some region, of some class background, with experience of some kind of work, and so also is every man. Such a focus on kinds of person might best integrate in comprehensible fashion the attributes that measurement and models tend to separate.

Classrooms and Values

Let me select just one setting for attention here, that of the classroom. It is important to the life chances of children, and it is representative of the problem of knowledge. A key question in the classroom is what the teacher may make of the attitudes and values toward language use brought by the children.

Sometimes a situation is taken to be a question of knowledge of language when it is in fact a question of knowledge in the sense of appropriate uses of language. Children are assumed perhaps not to know enough English, not to know the right kind of English, or to be shy. Observing a school in central Oregon, Philips (1972) found that the Indian children did indeed talk less than other children in situations controlled by the teacher, but might talk just as much in other situations. A situation in which a single person commands everyone else's right to speak and can demand display of ability in performance goes contrary to the norms of the community from which the children come, where rights to speak are typically equal in public situations and where display of competence is typically self-initiated (and where public groups usually form a circle, rather than having one person in front facing the rest).

Notice that the difficulty is not one of a language other than English. The children come to school as native speakers of a variety of English. *The aspect of language, of membership in a speech community, that is in question is how language is to be used.*.

Of course, schools have long been aware of cultural differences, and there are many programs concerned with understanding them. What is often slighted is the 'invisible' culture (to use Philips's term) of everyday interaction: the expression, through norms of speaking, of community values, of traditional rights and duties between persons, what Goffman has called the ceremonial sphere of deference and demeanor (1956). Teachers may be conscientiously respectful of explicit religious belief and practice yet may profane an unseen order vested in individuals.

An Excursus on Politeness

Perhaps an adequate overall view of these ingredients of everyday interaction can be reached by combining Goffman's distinction with one made in a provocative, important study of politeness in language by Brown and Levinson (1978). Goffman distinguished between *deference*, or what is owed to the other, and *demeanor*, or what one owes to oneself. Both can be taken as involving respect, for the other and for oneself. Brown and Levinson built an extended comparative study on, in part, a distinction between two kinds of 'face', positive and negative. 'Negative face' is like Goffman's deference and is defined in terms of respecting the right of the other not to be intruded upon, impeded, and the like. 'Positive face' has no direct equivalent in Goffman's distinction; it has to do with regard for another's usual wish to have some of his or her likes, preferences, and traits well regarded. We may associate it with Kenneth Burke's term for the heart of modern rhetoric, *identification*.

If we consider the way in which these three spheres contribute to the success or failure of interaction, we can say, roughly, that *identification* has to do with such things as establishing common ground (where one is from, whom one knows, what one does, what one likes, etc.), *deference* has to do with regard for the other's self-respect, and *demeanor* (has to do with expectable regard for one's own. Failure in each respect might sometimes be characterized as 'having nothing in common', 'being rude', 'losing one's cool'. But interaction may fail, or pale, for a fourth reason, the lack of a contribution to the interaction, or of a contribution of interest, from one of the parties. One can find common ground, be polite and self-controlled, and still be too dull to bear.

We glimpse here a logical possibility to be added to the intersection of Goffman with Brown and Levinson. Their categories give two spheres of concern for the other (identification, deference) but only one of concern for the self (demeanor). From another standpoint, their categories give two spheres of concern for respect, for avoiding insult and breach in the other and oneself (deference, demeanor), but only one for concern for what may unite and integrate, rather than maintain boundary (identification). The logic of the relationships points to a fourth category, concerned with what unites, integrates and has to do with the self. Let us call it *expression*, the contribution one may be expected to make to the interest of what goes on. The four spheres can be shown thus:

	Union	Autonomy
Toward other	identification	deference
Toward self	expression	demeanor

Classroom and Values Again

In attending to differences between classroom and community, we must not rely on broad dichotomies. It is not a matter simply of rich versus impoverished verbal environments, or of opposed orientations toward verbal meaning (elaborated and restricted), or of literate versus oral cultures. Such dichotomies are tempting, because we take what is familiar to us as academics, the classroom as one pole, and label what is not familiar 'other'. We have to deal with phenomena that are more various. In particular, the differences are not always aligned in the same way. In one case the salient difference may be ethnic, as between an Anglo and a non-Anglo orientation. In another, the difference may be saliently between two ethnic orientations, neither of which is Anglo (for example, Jewish or Italian). Class orientations may sometimes be those of a middle-class school and working-class parents, but also, sometimes, the other way around, with middle-class parents gradually dropping out of a school and community which is becoming too working-class for them and for the way they want their children to be treated. *The dimensions of difference are various, they contribute to a plurality of types of situation. and dichotomies only obscure the complexity of the reality.*

Clearly one must not rely on a simple assumption of making school and community match. In some communities the parents' expectation of school may be precisely that it is different from home in a specific way. Nor can the sensitivity of teachers be expected to suffice. McDermott 1974; 1977a) has analyzed interactions in a mostly middle-class first grade in the New York area and has concluded that initial assignment to one of two reading groups on the basis of ethnicity-linked command of English leads to a stratification and emergence of differences that has an observable, ineluctable outcome. The advanced group, essentially 'non-ethnic', had initial competence sufficient for confidence, and came to show an autonomous, minimally signaled, orderly sequencing of turns in reading, thus maximizing the teacher's use of time with the group for teaching of reading. In the other group, the teacher did not want to embarrass children by insisting on regular turns for those less proficient. The resulting process of volunteering and competing for turns allows some children tacitly to avoid being called on and directs much of the teacher's attention to interruptions and negotiations about turn-taking itself. The result is likely to maintain, if not increase, the initial stratification that is likely to be lasting. The causes will have been complex and likely not adequately recognized. The initial lack of command of English will be known, but not the contribution of stratification and norms of interaction.

One needs to include teachers among those who contribute to ethnographic knowledge of such situations, but clearly, the problem appears to be one of what happens in the classroom alone only because society, in effect, allows it to appear as such. A different complex of relations between classroom and community could exist. If literacy were a major social goal for all citizens, the society could be mobilized to ensure it. If the literacy of numbers of students is left to depend on turn-taking in reading groups, the invisible failure is that of the society. Other countries have been known to mobilize to ensure literacy. To let literacy depend on the outcome of a crowded classroom is an excellent way to perpetuate the class-linked differences in literacy which children bring to class. Perhaps an essential topic for research is the distribution in the society of the belief that literacy is the business of the schools, as against attitudes or practices that make it a matter of the home before, alongside, or with the school.

Task 2: Recognition of Problem

The preceding section focused on the language situation of the United States as a problem from the standpoint of desire for change in the place of language in the society generally, and desire for knowledge as basis for such change. Questions of language have come to appear as problems in public life in a much more limited way. A fundamental task is to understand the circumstances that lead to recognition or definition of something as a problem for public attention. (On the difficulty of recognizing the existence of something as a part of our society, because of social problems, see Szwed, 1973.)

The linguist Jiri Neustupny has outlined a systematic model of the scope of linguistic problems, ranging from correction in individual behavior to societal planning (in a paper given at the University of Pennsylvania in October 1973; see his book [1979]). Let us consider the latter pole. In Germany, the presence of guest workers (*Gästarbeiter*) is defined as a social problem, and funds are provided to study the linguistic adaptation of the workers and their children in Germany. In the United States the medical system depends in important part on thousands of doctors and interns whose native language is not English, but this has not been defined as a problem. Beyond the circle of top schools of engineering, faculties of engineering in the United States are drawn mostly from other countries. Native-born American engineers command too high a salary in engineering itself to be willing to teach. No problem is publicly identified here. Perhaps incidents will arise of difficulty of communication with hospital staff that will lead to public attention, perhaps not.

The development of what we know about language varieties has obviously not been the result of a systematic scholarly plan. There has been mobilization of ethnic and minority groups around questions of language. The emergence into national attention of the civil rights movement in the 1960s, as well as some riots, coincided with attention to Black English and funds for its investigation. Subsequently the mobilization of Spanish-speaking Americans led to support for bilingual education, defined generally but focused to a great extent on Spanish language situations. The initial legal step, indeed, resulted from mobilization in San Francisco among Chinese citizens. In 1968 the United States Congress passed a Bilingual Education Act, establishing the right of children to be taught in their native language, and as a result of a suit brought on behalf of Chinese-speaking children in San Francisco (Lau v. Nichols), the Supreme Court affirmed the act (see Alcala, Rivera and Thayer, 1974; Paulston, 1981). An effort among Native Americans, stimulated by Deni Leonard and others, to gain recognition for the language rights of Native American communities as a basis for their increased political and cultural autonomy, was in fact sponsored by Senator Daniel Inoye and led to passage of a Native American Language Act in 1990 and 1992. (Funding of course has been a separate matter.)

Such mobilization and national action mostly precedes knowledge rather than drawing upon it. The mobilization around language goes on with little systematic information on which it may draw or in terms of which it may be assessed. Laymen, social scientists and linguists alike proceed largely on the basis of received attitudes and limited information. The elementary, most unifying goal is a place in schooling for a language other than English. That goal is itself hard to win in the United States, and among those who accept it, only some have in mind the further goal of community maintenance of a language other than English. Many who participate in bilingual education see it simply as a way to replace some other language with English (or, say, with French, as may be the case with Cajun and Creole in Louisiana). Few who participate have the opportunity to transcend the class-linked perceptions and prejudices about language that are part of the cultural stratification of the country. Institutionalized forms of English itself are part of the language problems of minority and ethnic groups, but there is little critical analysis of their role in cultural hegemony or of the total language situation (but cf. Edelsky, 1991; Hymes, 1979c; Masemann, 1983; and on minority and ethnic languages generally, Fishman, 1989; 1991; Paulston, 1994; Williams, 1991).

There are three levels of aspiration, then, for efforts at language-related mobilization: a place in schooling for a language not English; community maintenance of a language not English; and critical analysis of the language situation of the country, including the place of standard English itself. Of these three, it is the third that would radically challenge the social order; the second is widely feared as doing so; only the first, minimal goal has been at all strong, and is increasingly under attack and threatened by lack of funding.

The availability of money is not itself a solution, insofar as it brings in its wake other problems. The money enters an institutional order. It may bring about vested interests, either in the existence of a certain class of persons needing to be helped, or in the restriction of employment and funds to persons of a certain background, many of whom may deserve and need employment, but few of whom may have had opportunity for the technical training required by the work to which they are assigned. An example of the first occurred in a school in Colorado, where the availability of funds for bilingual education led to appointment of a special aide, who visited classrooms, seeking children for the new program. The criterion was knowledge of Spanish; that is, knowing Spanish was defined as having a problem. One child selected for assignment to special education was the son of a professor at the University of Colorado. By dint of struggle, the father was able to have his son released from the remedial class. His son, of course, had no problem with language, or anything else in school; both English and Spanish were normally and fluently used in his home. Other children, with fathers less knowledgeable and positioned, might not be so fortunate. At a Georgetown Round Table in 1975 one participant asked, 'Can anything be done to prevent bilingual education becoming a dumping ground?' He reported schools that were closing special classes for various difficulties and disabilities and transferring the children into classes for bilingual education, because money was available for that.

Sometimes funds have been obtained by members of a community on their own initiative, only to find a greater part of the funds going to supervening organizations, educational laboratories, and the like, who may actually exclude the advice of persons with knowledge of the subject. A major problem from one perspective, then, is the need for true community initiative and control. The major problem from the standpoint of sources of funds is likely to be fiscal responsibility and control. And of course the internal political life of any community is such that continuity of leadership may be interrupted, or leadership enlisted in the support of one view as against other strong views within the community. Community practices as to personal transmission of knowledge may not coincide with the institutional structure that comes from participation in larger political and bureaucratic life. What is smoothly running from a central point of view may be appalling closer to the ground. Ethnographic monitoring of the circumstances of bilingual education is needed (cf. Edelsky, 1991, and Hymes, 1979c).

It is recognized as a problem that knowledge of many of the languages of the United States, such as the Indian languages, has been almost entirely in the hands of persons not from the communities in which the languages are spoken or of which they have been a part. No solution to the language problems of such communities, indeed, can come without members of those communities playing a central part. At the same time scholars who are not members of those communities cannot simply turn over the problems to persons who are. There are too few who are, to begin with, and a certain bias of social position frequently accompanies the role of being the first linguistic specialist from one's community, just as a certain bias of social position frequently accompanies the role of being a professor from outside the community. The satisfaction that one older person takes in cooperating in linguistic work may appear to a younger professional an affront, perpetuating an image of a native as only a source, not an analyst. There must be native analysts, but those who have been able to enjoy the status of a respected source of knowledge need not be disdained. Without the partnerships that included them, there would be little knowledge left for descendants of many of the Native American languages.

The worst case is when persons are hired for their ethnic identity and not their professional competence. It is no service to an ethnic group to right the wrong of past exclusion by associating it with shoddy work. The anti-intellectualism of many Hispanics and Native Americans is understandable, given past exploitation. When their principal claim on a newly won position is their access to knowledge that comes from their ethnic identity, they can hardly help but resent continued writing about such materials from others not of their background. Yet a world in which knowledge of a group was the exclusive property of the group and no other would be a compartmentalized, parochial world. Those who share an element of socialist aspiration cannot accept the easy solution of appointing the community, or its nearest representative, as arbiter. The community or its representative may be wrong, from the standpoint of some more general social and political position. It is a double standard if members of ethnic groups are granted a monopoly on knowledge of their own backgrounds, but not excluded from knowledge of other backgrounds. A fair challenge would be: If you do not want others to write about your language, or background, then don't write about anything else yourself. If non-Indians are not to write about Indians or Indian languages, the Indian may not write about whites. To each his own, only. But the tensions of this situation will continue to reproduce themselves as long as there remains so great an inequity in the distribution of access to knowledge and the rewards of professional expertise. Someone like myself, in the middle of many such situations, gets angry in turn at the person who wants to deny any others the right to write and at the Anglo who doesn't understand why a non-Anglo would feel that way.

A widely recognized problem is the lack of local resources and help for communities that undertake some initiative about a problem of language. A less acknowledged problem is the fact that many local communities, and those nearby and willing and able to assist, inherit the generic ignorance and misconception of things linguistic that pervades American society. A minister living on a reservation for 30 years may invent his own way of writing the Indian language, but it may be inadequate. Teachers in an Indian-sponsored school may understand the importance and nature of cultural differences and may do everything they can to make the semester in which they have adult Indians for composition class a success for them, a basis on which they can go onward in education. Yet their background in English may include nothing that enables them to realize that difficulty with the articles in English is not a sign of inattention or lack of precision. They may never have encountered a Pole, Japanese or Armenian, holding a major academic position, who has similar problems with English articles, and so may not realize that what appears simple has proven a subtle puzzle for many foreign-born speakers and linguists alike. Their insight into the native culture may include nothing about the language. They may prove to have taken for granted that the Indian language is simple, when in fact it has a morphological structure more complex by far than that of English. In short, goodwill and effort may abound, elementary knowledge of language differences be nil.

Both locally and nationally, the desire and need to take action outstrips knowledge, not only knowledge not yet in hand that ought to be obtained, but also knowledge that has been shared in the linguistics community for generations and that has penetrated the wider world almost not at all.

The fundamental language problem, I believe, is the twin ignorance just indicated. Needed knowledge follows rather than precedes public action; the knowledge that we already have is little known. It does not seem to me possible that any mobilization around a particular issue of language or any accession of funds can be of much long-term value apart from a thorough-going conception of the needs in terms of knowledge and training of the country as a whole. It is a contribution to extend the sphere of linguistic common sense to include more of those who will act and decide just as it is to extend the sphere of new knowledge. Both are essential to our future.

Greater public understanding may help as well to break the cycle of crisis first, research afterward. Distinctive varieties of English existed among

81

African-American citizens for generations before they came to be defined as a problem during the 1960s. Varieties of Spanish have existed among children in many schools before coming to be defined as an object of national concern; varieties of other languages exist that have not been defined as a public problem. A considered approach to the language situation of the United States as a whole as the fundamental problem may defuse individual issues a bit and gain ground on issues to come. Perhaps the next time that a school system is ordered to assign children bilingual classes, as happened in New York City with regard to Spanish in 1975, there will already exist, as there originally did not, research on the basis of which tests could be designed and administered fairly and accurately. No such research existed in the New York City case; yet the law required four separate tests, for speaking, hearing, writing, and reading, and what the law required was, willy nilly, done.

The need to break the cycle of action first, research afterward, is especially evident in the case of bilingual education. It came under attack before it had much opportunity to discover what it might appropriately be. There is something to be said for the assumption that problems cannot be solved by throwing money at them (national defense seems to be an exception to that rule); but the need for practical programs and careful research grows with increase in the Spanish-speaking population, influxes from Southeast Asia, and the persistence of a multitude of other language needs. One does not solve problems by papering them over either.

Social scientists and linguists who are not members of language minorities need to work to break the cycle of mobilization and action first, research second. Their contributions in research can be more valuable as a background for policy than as a sop and catch-up. There is much for them to understand in analyzing the cycle and changing it that is a contribution to the sociology of knowledge itself (I am indebted to Rolf Kjolseth (1972) for discussion of this issue). One should attempt not only to anticipate public consciousness and research support, but also to influence public consciousness through research. The best ground for such an effort, as suggested above, is a concern with the country as a whole. Such a concern challenges the various sciences of social life to transcend their own parochialism and to recognize the fundamental nature and unity of their subject matter in the sphere of language. The sociology of language tends to come as a congeries of topics – bilingualism, linguistic nationalism standardization, pidginization and creolization, politeness, and so on. For the sake of a foundation to the understanding of language problems, we must deepen our ability to see particular topics as phenomena thrown into salience by particular circumstances; we must see them as sharing fundamental dimensions with others. Particular constellations of phenomena must be seen as aspects of a single subject, the social organization of means of speech (cf. Wertsch, 1983). Choice among languages in one setting may be analytically part of the same semantic field as choice of pronoun in another; both may express degrees of intimacy or social distance. Choice of language in one setting may be analytically part of the same semantic field as choice of accent in another; both may express ethnic identification. And so on. The historical roots of a wide variety of language situations and problems about the world can ultimately be understood as diverse aspects of a single long-term process, the expansion of European mercantilism, colonialism, and capitalism (cf. Parker, 1983). The distribution of languages in Montana today is a reflex of the economic history of the state, region and country.

Such an integration of our field of study unites the so-called micro and macro levels of the sociology of language. Our scholarly forces are so meager that their unity is necessary if they are to have much impact. The unity is not a matter of numbers so much as it is a matter of conceptual strength. If in particular studies we cannot answer questions about general historical processes and social relationships, we can at least raise them. No study of the Quakers' special use of language should go forward without raising the question of the consequences throughout religious life in Europe in the seventeenth century of the assumption that the individual could interpret the voice of God apart from a tradition; without at least asking the significance of the difference between mass and sermon as ritual organizations of language use; without at least wondering whether the experience of silently reading the word of God in the Bible did not encourage the practice of waiting in silence to hear God's voice; without at least a glance at Ranters, Levelers, Anabaptists, and others, and a wondering as to the way each chose to devise a liturgy and ministry, each choice implying some view of the role of language. And so for other topics.

The fundamental vantage point must be what means of speech are available to a group and what meanings they find in them and give them. Insofar as we are able to articulate a general foundation for understanding the place of language in social life, we will have a leverage that transcends particular cases and particular facts. Such a program declares an interest distinct from the interest of any particular group, but one consistent with the interests of most. It is a necessary pole to the pole of practical work, justifying a claim to pursue knowledge as well as of change.

Task 3: Cultural Hegemony through Language

It is probably through education – taken in its broadest sense, as schooling and instruction of all kinds – that the peculiar, latent, tacit American view of language most powerfully exercises cultural hegemony. To see this, to see that there is a characteristic American culture and policy in this regard, comparative analysis and systematic history are both badly needed. One important aspect of the subject has been suggested by Fishman, J., 1972: 195; 1975: 1714; cf. Fishman and Leuders,1972):

A true meeting of education and the sociology of language will enable both to discover why proportionately so many dialect speakers do and did seem to become readers and speakers of the standard language (and even of classical languages) in other parts of the world whereas so few seem to accomplish this in the USA today.

A related observation has been made by Charles Ferguson. In a trip to China in the fall of 1974, as one of a party of linguists, he was unable to discover any evidence of reading problems; it was difficult to convey the notion. The observation suggests that reading problems have to be understood partly as a *product* of American society and its particular history in education, rather than as an inevitable and natural circumstance (just as Margaret Mead's early fieldwork in Samoa indicated that adolescence was not an inevitable and natural problem, but a function of a particular society).

The heart of the matter, I have suggested, is that language has been a central medium of cultural hegemony in the United States. Class stratification and cultural assumptions about language converge in schooling to reproduce the social order. A latent function of the educational system is to instill linguistic insecurity, to discriminate linguistically, to channel children in ways that have an integral linguistic component, while appearing open and fair to all. All have equal opportunity to acquire membership in the privileged linguistic network. If they fail, it is their fault, not that of the society or school (cf. Hymes, 1980b; 1987d; Stein, 1972).

What is usually left out of account is what the child brings to school in linguistic competence and community membership, and what part of instruction in relation to this is necessary for the acquisition of a national *lingua communis*, what part an instrument of class hierarchy.

I cannot demonstrate such an analysis. American scholarship has hardly addressed the facts of the matter. Language has been invisible as a problem for critical social science and educational history. Planning and policy about language have been thought of as something found in Belgium and Quebec, perhaps, where political mobilization around whole language identity has made public controversy. In the United States there has been neither a public agency singled out as responsible for a language policy, nor much consciousness of policy. Amnesia toward the American past and passivity toward the American present, so far as language is concerned seem characteristic of both American scholarship and the American public, except where the mobilization of Spanish speakers newly stirs concern. The widespread sharing of cultural assumptions about language has rendered their particularity almost invisible.

A first attempt at enumerating the assumptions would note the following:

1 Everyone in the United States speaks only English, or should.
2 Bilingualism is inherently unstable, probably injurious, and possibly unnatural.

3 Foreign literary languages can be respectably studied, but not foreign languages in their domestic varieties (it is one thing to study French spoken in Paris, another to study the French spoken in Louisiana).

4 Most everyone else in the world is learning English anyway, and that, together with American military and economic power, makes it unnecessary to worry about knowing the language of .a country in which one has business, bases, or hostages.

5 Differences in a language are essentially of two kinds, right and wrong.

6 Verbal fluency and noticeable style are suspicious, except as entertainment (it's what you mean that counts) (cf. Lanham, 1974).

Notice that some of these assumptions would obtain, even if there were no language other than English in the United States. Class relationships would implicate language as an instrument of hegemony still.

We desperately need a critical social history of such assumptions and the associated practices regarding English and education. Leonard's (1929) early study of eighteenth century doctrines, and Finegan's (1980) recent survey are useful guides. (See now the contributions of Cmiel, 1990, and Kramer, 1992). The literature of the women's movement makes important contributions (for example, Bodine, 1975). Many studies that address the institution of education in the country critically have not seemed to have much to say about language (Carnoy, 1972; 1974; Greer, 1972; Katz, 1968; 1971, 1975; Lasch, 1973; Useem and Michael, 1974), in contrast to studies focused on classrooms (e.g., Cazden, 1992; Cazden, John and Hymes, D. (Eds), 1972; Edelsky, 1991; McDermott, 1977; Heath, 1982; Philips, 1983 [1974]; Stubbs, 1986. Studies made in other countries may be helpful in stimulating research in the United States (e.g., Bisseret, 1979, reviewed in Hogan, 1980; Illich, 1983; Appel, 1983; Snyders, 1965; cf. de Terra, 1983; Williams and Roberts, 1983).

What is amazing is that even the rather self-conscious and explicit implementation of a policy of *linguacide* (as an element of ethnocide) in the treatment of American Indians has not found a historian. Here are some excerpts from an official document (Atkins, 1888: 17, 25, 26):

These languages may be, and no doubt are, interesting to the philologist, but as a medium for conveying education and civilization to savages they are worse than useless; they are a means of keeping them in their savage condition by perpetuating the traditions of carnage and superstition. . .

To teach the rising generation of the Sioux in their own native tongue is simply to teach the perpetuation of something that can be of no benefit whatever to them. . .

> I sincerely hope that all friends of Indian education will unite in the
> good work of teaching the English language only, and discourage in
> every way possible the perpetuation of any Indian vernacular.

These comments were prompted by a dispute about missionaries among the Sioux, who had learned the language, and translated the Bible into it, and intended to use Sioux in the schools they had established. They were forbidden to do so. There are Indian people alive today who remember, indeed, being beaten for speaking their language in school as children. An old man at Umatilla reservation (Oregon) spoke some years ago of when he and a schoolmate had soap put into their mouths and their mouths taped shut for speaking their language. The schoolmate died. At least one grandmother at Warm Springs let grandchildren think she knew no English so that they would have to use the Indian language to her, and so by individual resourcefulness she transmitted a knowledge of the language to another generation. These government and institutional policies, personal experiences and family histories make a rich tapestry that has yet to find systematic voice. The efforts of Indian communities today to develop language programs and to determine language rights have received little systematic attention as well until recently. (Leap, 1981, is an exception. On endangered languages, including Native American, see now Hale, 1992; Robins and Uhlenbeck, 1991).

The public school systems of urban centers are in need of social historians as well. Practice has gone far beyond instruction in a *lingua communis*. In New York City high schools, for example, it was required that one pass a speech test to graduate. The test included details of pronunciation: traces of phonetic habits from Yiddish, Italian, or regional or working-class English were grounds for failure. There flourished private tutors who taught students, not how to speak well, but how to speak to pass the high school graduation test by making the required recording correctly. Until not too long ago Brooklyn teachers themselves had to pass a test of reading a word list without a trace of Yiddish or the like. Without color, one might say, or the interest of an identity.

These instances could be multiplied and should be. We need to know as fully as possible about past tension and struggle in the imposition of linguistic hegemony and escape from it as well. The recent surge of the Official English movement has brought forward valuable accounts of current and past attitudes (Adams and Brink, 1990; Baron, 1990; Crawford, 1992; Daniels, 1990). Ferguson and Heath (1983) are helpful as to the nation as a whole, and an earlier work of value is Laird (1970), complemented by essays in a tribute to him (Boardman, 1987).

A systematic history would show, as has been suggested, efforts to eradicate linguistic diversity and to implant uniformity down to the last colorless detail, bolstered by belief in the inferiority of anything other than a variety of language enshrined in schools and a certain body of texts, often enough motivated by linguistic insecurity on the part of many educators themselves, and by fear of immigrants. But other strands would appear as well: writers of dictionaries and grammars who asserted American as against British norms, for example, and had a word to say for vitality as against mere correctness, and who sought out local speech.

One needs to continue the work of a scholar like Andresen (1990), finding a distinctive American tradition toward the study of language earlier than, and surrounding, what linguists usually count as their history. The new history of women in scholarship has shown that a great deal of past tension and struggle can be discerned, including the recent history of linguistics itself (Falk, 1994). Research that combines the techniques and perspectives of social history with the kinds of perception and question that arise within descriptive sociolinguistics and the ethnography of speaking will be a diachronic counterpart of work needed with regard to the present.

The topic of assumptions that support hegemony leads readily to the critique of disciplines, especially linguistics.

Task 4: Critique of Social Science and Linguistics

The work that is needed with regard to the present consists of thoroughgoing analyses of language situations. A cadre of scholars for such work still is hardly to be found. The number has grown, yet it still is difficult to identify a coherent and concerted engagement in linguistically informed research relevant to American life.

The difficulty is that such work requires skills that are partly linguistic and partly social, whatever the disciplinary origin of the investigator. Sociologists, psychologists, and even anthropologists do not often learn how to notice a feature of speech, how to represent it so that its occurrence can be traced, how to calibrate what is particular or emergent in a text or discourse and what is common. A certain amount of linguistics is needed simply to perceive the relevant features of the data – that a pronunciation has altered, that a word order is reversed, that a grammatical category is surprisingly frequent or absent. Linguists do not often learn how to notice features of social interaction, how to relate behavior to social relationships, activities and institutions.

What one needs at the base of the enterprise is something neither social science nor linguistics separately much provide – a social inquiry that does not abstract from verbal particulars, and a linguistic inquiry that connects verbal particulars, not with a model of grammar or discourse in general, but with social activities and relationships (cf. Dittmar, 1983). The social scientist lacks the observational skills and the linguist lacks the framework for making the connections. Introductory courses in either subject usually lead away from integration, rather than toward it. One is most often taught linguistics as if one were going on to study models of language abstracted from social interaction. One is most often taught social inquiry as if one were going to do research in which relations among features of speech did not matter.

All this is not entirely true. The study of language has evolved in various quarters into the study of 'pragmatics' or 'discourse' or 'communication', to which people from many disciplinary backgrounds contribute. (With regard to pragmatics, see the four volume bibliography by Nuyts and Verscheuren, 1987; with regard to discourse of relevant sorts, see the integrative analysis by Schiffrin, 1994; with regard to cultural communication, see Hymes, 1964; Carbaugh, 1990; Leeds-Hurwitz, 1989;1993; Scollon and Scollon, 1994; with regard to relevant social psychology, see Giles and Coupland, 1991).

Indeed, it must seem odd to say that there is a problem when almost every imaginable level and aspect of language is probably acknowledged somewhere by someone, and the relevance of language, and even of features of language, to social life and thought is nowhere denied, and in many places proclaimed. There is even some reawakening of interest in the issue to which Whorf's name has been given, that of the way in which patterns of language may cohere with patterns of cultural outlook. There is certainly proliferation under the umbrella of discourse. Courtrooms, classrooms, medical interviews, psychiatric interviews, and the intrinsic interest of children as acquirers and users of language, are the loci of diverse work. Sociolinguistic models for research into ongoing linguistic change have established themselves as a significant branch of the general field. Some linguists have broken away from the domination of formal models to investigate grammar in terms of a wide variety of processes and kinds of explanation. Some have launched efforts to use linguistic insight in the critical understanding of everyday life (Fowler, Hodge, Kress and Trew, 1979; Kress and Hodge, 1979; cf. the perspective of Lee, 1992). The work of Michael Halliday has always had these concerns (cf. Halliday, 1977; 1978). It is increasingly accepted that linguistic elements should be analyzed and explained in terms of their *functional relevance*, meaning not only their function within a grammar as such, but their relevance to the needs and interests of users of language in conveying and processing information, making discourse coherent, managing social relationships. Indeed,

> Contemporary discourse analysis tries to avoid isolating specific language forms, focusing on a single structure, selecting a single process, or indeed lifting any feature of a discourse out of its context: to do so risks distorting the meaning of the feature (Corson 1993a: 182).

These are welcome developments against a tendency to look only to generic psychological processes and presumed universal social requirements, or to *ad hoc* occasions, and to have little to say about cultural patterns or institutional constraints. Where educational linguistics has developed, such patterns and their linguistic connections will be in view (cf. Edelsky, 1991;

Stubbs, 1986). But much work is conceived still in terms of experimental models of conventional psychology and sociology or as only an adjunct to study of a particular language or established branch of linguistics (for example, dialectology, historical linguistics), or only in terms of general, not particular accounting, such as linguistic work on conventional metrics as an adjunct to phonological theory. Much work in discourse and pragmatics depends on *a priori* models for its interpretation of examples, even sometimes doubting that cultural differences can matter (for critique of such models, see Hymes, 1986; 1990). The history of recent linguistics is written as the history of formal theories, not as including other kinds of study (Harris, 1993; Huck and Goldsmith, 1995). Most of all, the peculiar combination of social theory, ethnographic perspective, and linguistic skills required by the thesis of this chapter is hard to find institutionalized.

That, I think, is the heart of the matter. Will the many impulses to the study of language in social life eventually envelop and supplant the historical disciplines of sociology, psychology, anthropology and linguistics? In universities and colleges a generation or two from now will the named historical disciplines share small offices in old buildings next to classics . . . near where geography used to be . . . while elevators and full-time secretaries are elsewhere in departments of discourse and the like?

Such things happen, yet it is difficult to see from whence the support would come that would allow it to happen in this case. It is possible to imagine that discourse and communication could triumph as rubrics, but without carrying with them concern for the particular, the local, the scrupulously comparative. In dominating, might they not become dominated by the interests of an economically dominant economic system, and the high culture adopted as its *lingua franca* together with what would seem advantageous to those of the middling classes able to enter their institutions?

It is rash to speculate. Whatever comes to dominate, I think that critical understanding and work will require the twin skills to which this essay keeps returning like Bruckner to a theme. The cultivation and transmission of such skills, ethnographic and linguistic, is likely to depend on those disciplines in which they now reside. It is important to say what one can about their present health, or lack of it, in what we now know as anthropology, sociology, and the like, and linguistics. Let me elaborate on this theme with regard, first, to anthropology, and sociology (as matrices for ethnography), and then linguistics (as matrix for analysis of speech).

Critique of Anthropology

The initial impetus of the ethnography of speaking, seeking to build an empirical base for local and comparative analysis of patterns of speaking, has been carried forward to some degree. There are impressive monographic studies (for example, Briggs, 1988; Hanks, 1991; Kuipers, 1990; Merlan and

Rumsey, 1991; Ochs, 1988; Sherzer, 1983; 1990; Schieffelin, 1990; Urban, 1991), and it has proved possible to shed light on particular topics across a range of cases (such as Duranti and Goodwin, 1992; Gumperz, 1982a; 1982b; Hill and Irvine, 1993; Schieffelin and Ochs, 1986).

Still anthropology in the United States seems almost ready to jettison the tradition of its academic founder, Franz Boas, and its linguistic heritage, through Edward Sapir and others, rather than face the challenge of asking anthropological questions about language, and appointing colleagues whose professional and technical responsibility that is. Perhaps 80 per cent of departments of anthropology in the United States are reported to believe they can get along without linguistic anthropology. One might infer that such departments do not study people who speak, or, if they do, that they are unaware that speaking (let alone language) is a developed field of study. It would be hard to point to more than a very few United States institutions where there are enough faculties in anthropology (let alone sociology, psychology or education) with the requisite combination of skills, linguistic and social, to train a new generation. The reasons for this have something to do with the complexity of formal linguistics, perhaps, but also perhaps with long-standing American attitudes toward other languages and language itself, and with limited standards of scholarship.

In short, there is an active tradition of work, involving folklorists as well, making the kinds of contributions one would expect from anthropologists, but marginalized in its own discipline.

Critique of Sociology

A general sociolinguistics, uniting the phenomena of language in social life in terms of the actual abilities, the actual competencies of speaker hearers in actual communities, as a starting point for study – such a general sociolinguistics, integrating skills of linguistics, ethnography, sociology, and social history, and addressing the United States as a little-known country, could gather the diverse threads and opportunities of the present into a significant force (cf. Hymes, 1972a; 1977).

The prospect of such an impetus coming from sociology is not to be dismissed, but does not seem great. Sociologists mostly study language in ways that do not require linguistics – nationalism, language policy, language choice (societal or individual) – where one need only say that one language is different from another. Those using *language* as a category of critique seem to have in mind an unending circle of critique, not discovery of the social world.

Ethnomethodology

The movement known as ethnomethodology is important in insisting that social science attend to its dependence on the resources of language and commonsense knowledge (cf. Cicourel, 1974; Kjolseth, 1972; Mehan, 1972). Turner (1974b: 197) put it nicely: 'A science of society that fails to treat speech as both topic and resource is doomed to failure'.

Insofar as ethnomethodology confronts concrete features of speech, it is the trend in sociology from which a sociological linguistics can be hoped for. That is not to overlook past limitations. In earlier phase its motivation seemed to be to expose sociology, rather than social life, and to reduce the modern world system (in Wallerstein's phrase) to transcribable encounters. The universalizing of Chomskian linguistics infected assumptions about conversation. The reality of distinct cultural traditions was washed away in definition of problem in terms of exigencies of a communication situation, taken as everywhere the same. Focus on selecting a next speaker, on managing interaction over the telephone without access to another's face, on what would be natural and necessary, seemed too much uncritical reflection of middle-class American experience. It may seem obvious that the one to speak first in a telephone call would be the one who answers the phone, but some European countries distribute responsibility differently. It may seem obvious that face-to-face is the stance for conversation, but the Mescalero Apache align themselves shoulder-by-shoulder for a heart-to-heart talk. And so on. What people do is in part a solution to a functional problem, in part a consequence of cultural meanings and definitions of situation.

Still, much may be hoped for from ethnomethodology's continuing development, and convergence with ethnography (cf. Maynard and Clayman, 1991; Pomerantz, 1989; Sanders, 1990/1991; Watson and Seiler, 1992). It may help others to recognize of what is neither cognitively inherent, nor socially stable, but situationally emergent – to understand what is cultural in the use of language as including the novel as well as what is already known. When elements can be used, what they can mean, can be extended far beyond what can be brought to mind, or ordinarily noticed, if circumstances, preceding and obtaining, support (cf. Hymes, 1974, ch. 9; 1975; 1985a; Goffman, 1978; Jefferson, 1974; Silverstein, 1981; Tedlock, 1983).

The fact remains that ethnomethodology is strong only in certain institutions and areas, and that no sociology department, so far as I know, has hired a linguist to aid in training its students. Knowledgeable integration of linguistics and sociology has been due to valiant individual initiative (e.g. Aaron Cicourel, Joshua Fishman, Erving Goffman, Allen Grimshaw – cf. now Grimshaw, 1989, 1990, 1994). Except for such, the linguistics seems to be used more readily in analogy than analysis. An intrinsic sociological purpose for linguistic skills hardly emerges.

Bernstein and Habermas

A variety of occasional work addressing language does come to sociological journals, but it is mostly imperceptive application of standard methods. Two loci of ideas about language do stand out: the work of the British sociologist Basil Bernstein and the theoretical interest in language and communication of Jurgen Habermas, as a development out of the Frankfurt school of critical Marxism. One must admire the independence and boldness of each, and there is merit and relevance in the work of each for the topic of this chapter, but neither singly nor collectively do they constitute an adequate sociological linguistics. As with much of ethnomethodology, a strict ethnography, comprising discovery of specific organizations of verbal means, is lacking, and with it a purchase on concrete situations. A comparative perspective on social types and cultural configurations is lacking. Each has an ingredient of critique, but imperfectly developed for our purpose (cf. Chapter 3 above, and, for Bernstein: Atkinson, Davies and Delamont, 1995).

Bernstein is known for his distinction between *elaborated* and *restricted* codes. His critical contribution is to insist that there is an organization of verbal means, socially constituted and cutting across the presumed homogeneity of a single language; to insist that theories of social order are incomplete in that they do not encompass such organizations of verbal means as essential to the processes by which society is maintained and changed; and to be prepared to assess socially organized codes as different in adequacy or orientation. Two things limit the contribution of Bernstein's work. Externally, his dichotomy has been variously reinterpreted outside Great Britain in ways that often quite mistake its original intent. Dichotomies are easily transplanted to categories of *us* and *them, white* and *black, native* and *immigrant,* and so on. Internally, his many insights have remained penned within a maintenance of his original dichotomy. There has been a retreat from overt linguistic marking of the contrast to an imputed difference in underlying orientation toward meaning, despite overt similarity. Thus, there is a restricted variant in everyone's speech.

The ideal types posited by Bernstein no doubt correspond to aspects of reality, but not to enough of it. Linguistic ethnography is needed to discover the range of code-orientations in relation to family, class, institution and setting. The sociological methods of Bernstein's funded research have belied his insights – questionnaire, interview, self-report, formal experiment. The ingredients subsumed under the original dichotomy have comparative, cross-cultural relevance, but only if freed from the dichotomy. (In general, dichotomies are to be suspected in this field (cf. Hymes, 1974; 39–41, 115). If he is right in suggesting that the orientation of the elaborated code is necessary for reflective analysis of social conditions and social change, still his research has not traced the ingredients of this orientation among the various classes of England. More recent work has suggested that middle-class orientations also have limitations and implicit channeling effects as preparation for certain kinds of occupations, and recent theoretical formulations have suggested a considerably more dynamic conception of linguistic varieties. But the substantive work that would allow us to relate the linguistic ideas to ongoing social life is missing.[2]

Critical theory, as developed by Habermas, seeks to discover in the sphere of symbolic interaction (cultural or communicative competence) a source of critical response to inequality and domination in modern society. The hoped-for transformation of the social order by a concentrated and aroused proletariat has been abandoned (cf. Clecak, 1974; Singer, 1974). The situation was described well by Habermas himself (1973, Chapter 6, especially pp. 195–8, 241), who pointed out that the new focus of attention for Marxist theory is only a following in the footsteps of repressive forces themselves. Justification of the social order in terms of the idea of the free market has been succeeded by justification in terms of the purportedly neutral demands and benefits of science and technology. Yet belief in progress through these means is an illusion that serves to perpetuate actual irrationality and exploitation (cf. Anderson, 1973; Habermas, 1970a, Chapters 4–6; 1973, Chapter 7; Schroyer, 1973).

The revitalization of interest in ethnic and local identity throughout the world is perhaps a sign that many people have drawn some such inference. But it is not enough to consider the integration of the cultural dimension as the crucial problem of modern social theory, especially Marxian theory, and to recognize it as basic to any social transformation. How is one to get hold of the cultural (communicative) nuts and bolts of exploitation and alienation? The postulation of a universal form of communicative competence, inherent in every attempt at discourse, if useful as a regulative ideal by which to criticize repressive speech situations, is of little help in comprehending specific structures of speech which are what their participants want them to be. There must, presumably, be some state of the world that the perspective would accept as worth working toward. Any such state of the world would be characterized by some form of social order, and any form of social order would entail a limitation of the ideal of unrestricted turns at talk in the pursuit of consensus. The universal ideal provides no criterion for preferring or understanding the various specific organizations of speech events which any society will have (Cf. Chapter 3). Which is not to say that there is not liberating power in the Habermas critique and ideal in many situations (cf. Corson, 1993a; 1993b).[3]

No one would be so rash as to claim more than a crude inkling of the dimensions and dynamics of the life of language in the United States. What (to pick one town) is the state of language in Florence, Oregon? What has it been, what is it becoming, what should it become? The questions may seem foolish. One takes states of language for granted as transparent, until and unless someone makes them a problem not to be ignored. Only then one may realize that some do not use language as others do, and that the others think they should 'learn standard English' or 'tell the truth'.

If someone should want to know about the forces that produce migration, marriage, mobility, or any of a number of aspects of the distribution of people and kinds of people, someone in a sociology department would likely be able to be helpful. So also for almost any aspect of American life. Hardly so for language. Most social theory, even critical theory, reasons about language with a prior reason: language is essential; its potentialities are great. One may compare language to money, as Parsons and Rossi-Landi did, or other things to language. But hardly a sociologist is able to articulate social theory with linguistic facts, so as to be able to characterize the state of language, say, in Florence, let alone able to go and find out whether the characterization holds. Nor is there indication that sociology programs, even those emphasizing a perspective to which language is important, plan to require linguistic training of their students or to offer the kind of linguistic training they want themselves. Such knowledgeable integration of sociology and linguistics as occurs is due, as said, to valiant efforts of a few individuals.

This is not to make a plea for any school of linguistics, and, indeed, one theme of this paper is that sociologists should not admire and emulate linguistics so much as criticize and help to correct it. Social scientists should make use of linguistic tools for purposes of their own. The point here is that social scientists need elementary command of linguistics in order to recognize some of the essential characteristics of linguistic problems. The proper analogy is not to linguistics for the sake of writing a grammar or contribution to formal linguistics, but rather to linguistics for the sake of learning a language when, as an adult, one is past the point at which such a thing can be done unconsciously, or for the sake of interpreting a text whose meaning one needs to know. The proper expectation is not of some kind of structural magic, but of preparation to see, as one would need to learn the elements of music in order to understand someone else's accomplishment and one's own response. The catch in all this is that the elements of linguistics may have to be reconstituted by social scientists themselves or sought out in anthropological niches. A linguist may so subordinate the elements of language to a current understanding of purely linguistic theory as to obscure and omit what a student of uses of language needs. Others must come to see linguistics itself as sometimes a linguistic problem.

Critique of Linguistics

Perhaps it is silly to believe that analysis of discourse ultimately requires a foundation in command both of situated practice and specific form (to use a happy expression from Hanks, 1995). So many proceed without it. Still, if the world is as indicated at various points above, and in Note 3 (quoting William Sloan Coffin), it would seem that a purchase on it, in terms of what is said and implied is essential for understanding and change. Yet it would be hard to point to more than a few programs or departments in which the concerns of this chapter have a central place, and in which training for attending to specific form, meaning linguistic form, including linguistic relations, goes together with training for attending to situated practice. Programs in linguistics usually are dominated by domains of formal theory. As mentioned, the very term 'theoretical linguistics' has been reserved for concern with the form of language in general. The greatest activity and support beyond this formalism appears in regard to discourse as an area of 'cognitive' science, where cognitive is restrictive in the sense of denoting general mental processes and certain kinds of meaning.

It would be helpful if social scientists were to abandon an attitude of *laissez-faire* toward linguistics, and were to criticize it from the standpoint of sociology of knowledge and latent social function. Although a great variety of new activity goes on in a more tolerant general atmosphere in linguistics, nothing has arisen to replace or even challenge the pride of place of so-called theoretical linguistics. It is an irony that ought to be widely recognized that a linguist famous for his contributions to political life has shaped a linguistic climate in which the political has no place. Chomsky's conception of linguistics is the bringing to perfection of the trend to focus on formal models, while investing formal models with the ultimate significance of being avenues to human mind and nature, the only general goal worthy of a linguist (cf. the analyses in Hymes, 1974, and Hymes and Fought, 1981; cf. also Prucha, 1983; Slama-Cazacu, 1983; Titone, 1983).

The unintended consequence of the success of this brilliant work was to disable linguists from study of the social and to reinforce assumptions in American life prejudicial to understanding the place of language in it. (For different perspectives, see Newmeyer, 1986; Salkie, 1990).

Recall the assumptions noted in the preceding section (pp. 84–85).

1 *Only English.* Chomsky assumed that the goal of insight into the general bases of human language could be achieved by intuitions as to one's own first language and could perhaps best be achieved by monolinguals. Most linguistic theory and analysis under his aegis focused on English.

2 *Bilingualism is suspect.* Focus on one's intuitions into one's own language again sets bilingualism aside as secondary. A necessary simplifying assumption of the theory is the ideally fluent speaker/hearer in a homogeneous speech community.

3 *Learn literary standard.* The variety of English in which Chomskian linguistics was conducted and to which it was addressed was essentially formal written English. Dialects and vernaculars are assumed to be superficial variations.

4 *English is enough.* See 1 and 3.

5 *Right or wrong.* Most Americans assume that there is a single standard, that grammars, dictionaries, or 'best users' should be appealed to in case of doubt, that the problem of language today is change that makes it less precise, proper, cogent. Chomskian linguists were quick to apply a sign of exclusion, the asterisk, to sentences they judged impossible in English. The goal was initially taken to be to determine all and only the grammatical sentences of the language,

on the analogy of logical decidability. The inability of linguists to agree on what was in and what was out, together with some evidence that education and training influenced their intuitions, became an Achilles' heel of the movement.

6   *Fluency and style are suspect.* Fluency is assumed, and style is not disparaged, so there may be no convergence here. On the other hand, a good many of the utterances set aside as ungrammatical prove acceptable in sufficient context, such as a poetic one; intonation, which is inseparable from the effect and acceptability of utterances, is ignored. There probably is thus a reinforcement of the tendency to assume that the written form of the language is 'real' and normative. An account of the sound pattern of English that preserves the inherited orthography contributed to this effect.

All in all, there has been a considerable reinforcement of the written standard as standard and exclusive concern.

A further reinforcement of traditional American culture is worth noting. The preceding generation of linguists in the United States, focusing on formal analysis of language structure, profoundly distrusted the teachings of schools about language and lay assumptions about things linguistic. One of the purposes of the movement which founded linguistics as an organized discipline in the United States was to challenge such views. Part of the impetus came from the critique of ethnocentrism by the anthropological wing, shaped by Boas and Sapir, and part from the lifelong convictions of Bloomfield, reinforced by his later adherence to a behaviorist psychology and positivist conception of science.

The generation of linguists associated with Chomsky attacked their predecessors as all of a piece, *structuralists*. In discrediting the approach, which came to be known as *neo-Bloomfieldian*, they discredited its critical attitude as well. One particular tenet, the equality of all languages, was not questioned, but the insistence on the autonomy of the goal of linguistic theory and its independence of social considerations eliminated any basis for critique. The image of the maturing child acquiring creative fluency with minimal external influence might have made the circumstances of many actual children poignant, but left no ground for analysis, except to deplore social institutions. The possibility of a constitutive role for social institutions was not granted.

The Chomskian total rejection of the immediately preceding school of thought included an attack on its concern with phonology as starting point for analysis of language. (The misconceptions in this regard are analyzed in Hymes and Fought, 1981). A part of this attack was a depreciation of training in the skills of hearing speech sounds accurately and recording them reliably. It is doubtful that more than a handful of leading grammarians today could transcribe anything actually spoken.

The Bloomfieldian school had accepted, through anthropology in part, an empirical, inductive approach to generalizations about languages stimulated by the experience of rash, false generalizations in earlier general linguistics, and it accepted some possibility of differences among languages being associated with insight into differences among ways of life, as well as being of value in their own right. (In this respect it represented a continuation of the outlook of Wilhelm von Humboldt and J. G. von Herder, which I have labeled Herderian (Hymes, 1974, Chapter 4.) The Chomskian frame of mind interpreted this approach as hostility to theory. Generalizations about language were thought to be near at hand; the differences among languages were thought to be superficial; ways of life were not considered. The link of the Bloomfieldians to ethnographic modes of work was dismissed either as due to a charitable desire to record dying languages or as the legacy of a crippling behaviorism. That an ethnographic mode of work might be necessary for certain kinds of knowledge about language was not considered.

Generic distrust of behavior and observation; reliance on intuitive insight and methodological authority; the view that the reality behind language that matters is universal mind and brain, not social life; that what is to be explained is sameness concealed behind difference (for an insightful alternative, see Bolinger, 1977, and cf. Hymes, 1978b); the view that what matters is what is true of every language, not what has been made of linguistic means by particular people in history – all these ingredients of a Chomskian outlook discourage acquisition of the skills needed for the problems discussed in this book, discourage even contemplating such a program and often enough make the social order appear invisible. Social life appears unordered, and societal differences appear, not as points of leverage for penetration of social reality, but as indications that anything is possible.

Reinforcement of cultural assumptions and prejudices, together with the disarming of linguistics with regard to weapons with which to address serious problems of social life, cannot be said to have been intentional. It might be thought that the outcome would have been different had the Marxist intellectual tradition in the United States not suffered such dissolution after the Second World War. Not because of any specific Marxist propositions about language, but simply because of the postulate of social being as determinant of consciousness, and the example of Marx's critical method, his disclosure of taken-for-granted categories of political economy as not natural but products of a specific historical formation. Such a background might have vaccinated many attracted to linguistics in the 1960s against the underpinnings and consequences of Chomsky's approach. Subsequent renewals of Marxist scholarship have mostly left linguistics alone, or relied on citation of British and continental thought.

That Gramsci studied philology has been noticed, but not turned to account. The beginnings of a left critique of existing disciplines in the 1960s did not reach linguistics. Perhaps, indeed, it would not have reached that far. Linguists were prominent in the opposition to the Vietnam War, on the one hand, and the views of American Marxists about language and social life may not extend beyond those of their liberal colleagues. In any case, the challenge of thinking about language as problematic from a thoroughgoing sociohistorical standpoint has hardly been taken up.

The point to be reiterated is that use of linguistics must include a critique of linguistics. *Unexamined acceptance of existing forms of linguistics is mistaken and misleading.* The diversity of opinion and interest that exists in linguistic circles should not obscure the limitations with regard to kinds of training and legitimate problem that dominate the subject. The dominance of the Chomskian school has been greatly loosened, but the ambience of the discipline continues to be shaped by it.

The logic of linguistics' own development does lead it to the study of discourse and, in discourse, to the study of the relationships among linguistic elements in styles – styles associated with persons, roles, activities and social life. But how far that frontier is crossed is uncertain. The pull of psychology and abstract mind is strong, because there one can hope to find explanations of a familiar kind, explanations in general human terms. What it would be like to find intellectual satisfaction in explanations that connect with social life and historically conditioned conjunctures is almost beyond imagination. The lack of academic employment increases the number of linguists working in practical circumstances, where social life comes into play, but so far does not provide much intellectual framework or coherence for the experience.

The state of affairs in linguistics makes it unlikely that linguists are about to criticize sociology or anthropology for not offering help. If there is to be substantial integration, it will have to come from sociologists and anthropologists determining that there are problems in language and about language that need to be addressed as sociology and anthropology.

Task 5: Reshaping the Study of Language

Language is a unity of diversity *par excellence*, a configuration of common understandings and individual voices. As universal resource, it presumably shares in each community's reproduction of its organization, tensions, satisfactions, way of life. Insofar as communities differ, they presumably differ somewhat in their usage of speech and in the kinds of personal competency they encourage and discourage, require and neglect. What things are said and can be said, how things are said and can be said, presumably is an integral part of the fabric of the community. If one wanted to maintain that fabric, one presumably would want to maintain certain whats and hows of saying. If one wanted to change that fabric, rend it or open it to a different orientation, one presumably would have to change certain whats and hows of saying. Saying, indeed, might be the aspect of life most within the power of persons in a community to change.

If one considers, then, that the sphere of symbolic interaction is crucial to social theory and that within that sphere lie means essential to social change, both from the standpoint of possible levers of change and from the standpoint of desirable levers of change (thinking of desirable change as personal as well as institutional, 'that the educator must himself be educated,' as Marx put it in one thesis on Feuerbach) (Engels, 1941, p. 83), then the absence of a general sociological/anthropological/educational linguistics, able to address the place of speech, is perhaps the greatest linguistic problem of all, for social science and for society.

There is reason to think that some reshaping of the study of language will occur in the next decade or so, simply through the logic of the long-term history of the subject. Linguistics as a distinct academic field is only some 50 years of age in the United States. It grew out of a study of language distributed among a variety of fields, distinct departments of language, anthropology, philosophy; it crystallized around a distinct methodology of its own for the study of structure, and created a new general science of several levels of linguistic structure. The levels wholly internal to language have now been developed to the point at which the organization of language in discourse is the frontier. Now that members of a number of other disciplines have learned enough of linguistic method to contribute, the half-century monopoly has been effectively broken. Linguistics will be the home of study of structure internal to language and of particular languages perhaps, but the larger field of linguistics will embrace contributions from many disciplines.

Such reshaping could occur without any contribution to the problems discussed in this chapter. Two sources of an alternative seem possible. One of those is social scientists and linguists for whom local communities and problems of society motivate their work. If many of them discover the problems of this chapter as problems, much will be accomplished. The other source of an alternative is the recurrent mobilization of members of groups affected by language situations. Perhaps Native American languages, for example, will never have the sustained attention they need and the academic recognition they deserve until they become a problem about language. There is a great deal to be done generally, simply in terms of the motives that lead people to wish to preserve components of the diversity of language in the country and to understand and deal with the processes that affect their languages and them. As argued earlier, however, this source is an intermittent and often premature one.

Moreover, ethnic lines of demarcation are not themselves a sufficient mapping of the country. Some of the uses of language associated with black English, for example, may be shared across class lines with whites who have similar relationships to employment, authority, and power and who have similar verbal needs. We are largely ignorant of what is black and what is working-class about such phenomena.

Institutional studies will contribute much, but they tend to be focused on what is seen as a problem by one party to the situation, either the profession concerned, doctor, lawyer, teacher, or other, or by concern for the problem of client or patient. Research that encompasses all perspectives may not be as common. Still, there is probably most need for work that answers Nader's (1973) call for 'studying up' as well as 'down'.

All of these lines of interest may contribute to the solution of the problem posed, but only, I think, if the problem is posed in its general terms and has a disciplinary and extradisciplinary base united. The scholar must take the conceptual lead, not merely follow after crisis and funds. Members of communities affected by situations must be participants in the development as well. A study of discourse that excluded them might be an intellectual solace, but in the practical world it would probably prove mainly a resource for administration of things as they are. The task of general scope is that of intellectual understanding and disciplinary skills, on the one hand, and of cooperation across institutional boundaries, on the other. (For reflections on this task in regard to education, see Chapters 1 and 2 of this book, and my introduction to Cazden, John and Hymes, 1972).

Such work would broach a truly general study of the language situations of the United States. It would begin to constitute a true sociolinguistics, a general sociology of language. The central assumption would be that every social group, activity, or relationship may give rise to characteristic verbal means. Of any facet of the society, one would be prepared to ask:

- What is involved in talking like an X?
- What is involved in talking to do Y?

That is, what is the verbal concomitant of being, or being seen to be, a certain kind of person or position? What is the verbal concomitant of doing, or being considered to do, a certain kind of activity, work, or purpose? What is the distribution of such verbal styles in the society? Who has access to which style and who lacks it? Who has commitment to which? What are the consequences for institutional outcomes, genuine culture, personal identity and integrity? What would be a rough assessment of the linguistic health of the society? What costs and benefits result from the present distribution of linguistic abilities, the present institutionalization of values, beliefs, and attitudes, regarding features and uses of language?

(For many Americans, particularly perhaps in certain occupations, much of their daily speech is probably not a satisfaction or genuine expression of identity, but a kind of verbal passing. Where, for whom, and about what is there verbal expressivity that is satisfying or rewarding – uses of language felt to be integral to the self or the occasion?)

Such an approach must overcome the separation between questions of language and questions of value that has characterized the development of modern linguistics in the United States (perhaps in a way similar to the situation of modern economics). Values have been taken as obvious, taken for granted, or else excluded on principle, so far as linguists themselves are concerned. Uses of language have been postulated as everywhere essentially equivalent, rather than investigated. Indeed, one of the central tenets of the liberalism of modern linguistics has been the essential equivalence in use of all languages studied by linguists, despite abundant evidence to the contrary. Some even think it the mark of a radical to denounce attention to differences of this sort. Inequality in speaking is to be overcome, it seems, by denying that it exists.

I cannot explain this deep-seated hostility on the part of even cultural materialists toward facts that one would think a Marxist would be the first to see, except as a projection of a professional bias (all languages are equal in the sight of linguistics) and a reaction against the prejudices of the society at large, prejudices which do equate difference with inferiority. But I cannot see any way for a science of language to contribute to the transformation of linguistic inequality that it does not recognize as existing. I see no possibility for a truly social science of language on the basis of this attitude, an attitude that I would call militant, not radical. It is essential to this attitude that social shaping of verbal means and abilities is denied. Amidst all the costs of inequality and exploitation, language is privileged, on this view, and remains unscathed.

There is a grain of truth in this view. The potentialities of language are great. It is capable of transcending situations to a degree; it is a resource more within the control of people than many others. These possibilities of language should be developed politically. But the militant view of equality does not see a need for development; it sees a need only for an end to prejudice. Reality is different. Language, verbal means, like other resources of human life, become shaped to specific ends. Their adaptation to some purposes lessens or precludes their ready adaptation to others. They carry something of their history with them. The great poetry of one variety cannot be the great poetry of another.

It is utopian (in the negative sense) to imagine as an ideal for communicative competence and language a state of society in which anyone can say anything to anyone in any way, a state in which there are no constraints on communication and language. Social life, social order, would be impossible. What one can do, thinking in terms of aspirations, is to envision the costs and benefits of different forms of social order, including the costs and benefits of different forms of communicative, linguistic order. I apologize for the obviousness of what I have just said. My excuse is that it is a point of view which has little support within the dominant practice or theory of linguistics today.

These issues of background and domain assumptions, then, pose great obstacles to the development of the sociolinguistics that is needed. We have far to go to gain acceptance of the fundamental assumptions of a socially constituted linguistics:

- that verbal means and the social matrices in which they exist are interdependent;
- that the organization of verbal means must be viewed from the vantage point of social matrices;
- that one must discover ways in which verbal means are organized by virtue of social matrices (using 'social matrices' here as a general term for activities, institutions, groups, etc.)

It is here that the linguistic competence we need may be dependent on the contribution of social scientists. The term *linguistic competence*, indeed, is used in two ways in my title. It refers to the object of study of a true sociolinguistics: the actual abilities of definite persons in a definite social life. It refers also to the abilities that scholars must have, if they are to be able to study such competence. 'Toward linguistic competence', in this sense, refers to efforts toward a cadre of scholars competent to undertake such work.

The nature of the needed competence can be seen by drawing out in a somewhat different way the implications of what has been said in relation to language and linguistics.

The elements and relationships analyzed in linguistics are but a part of the verbal means (indeed, communicative means) employed in the conduct of social life. The organization of these means as a whole cannot be grasped within ordinary grammar. The paradigmatic and syntagmatic dimensions of language find their full scope in what Ervin-Tripp has called 'rules of co-occurrence' and 'rules of alternation' (see discussion in Hymes, 1974; 59, 201). These two types of rule govern the organization of verbal means in the speech styles and in discourse and the organization of the use of such styles in situations. The true scope of a socially constituted study of language is thus the study of speech styles within culturally constituted ways of speaking.

Grammar in the usual sense contributes analysis of many of the resources of speech styles, but not all. The grammar of discourse has additional properties. Two crucial properties are these: 1) a speech style involves selection and grouping of features across the usual levels of linguistic analysis, coordinating them in a novel way independent of such levels; 2) a socially significant speech style often involves only a portion of the occurring features.

Now, a grammarian is used to seeking total accountability at each level of analysis – all of the message form is referable to phonological elements and relationships, to morphological elements and relationships, to syntactic and semantic elements and relationships. This kind of accountability can be pursued to a fair degree in abstraction from social context.

It is not possible to pursue accountability of speech styles in abstraction from social context, and much of the interest, both in formal properties and in meaning, of speech styles may lie in the relations among social contexts, not in the relations of the linguistic features themselves. It is possible that linguists, given their usual training and outlook, will find the study of speech styles, of discourse grammar, neither feasible nor interesting. They may pursue it to a point, but when its social foundation becomes unavoidable and a major part of what there is to study, they may draw the line. One sees some evidence of such a line now.

This restriction might be overcome, and the linguistic skills needed for a true sociolinguistics become adequately available in response to the social and political mobilization of groups within the country – yet such groups have little basis on which to consider what kind of linguistics, if any, they might profitably have.

The restriction might be overcome if social scientists work to develop the subject. Here the most promising prospect, I think, is a confluence of sociology, social psychology, education and anthropology,[4] as disciplines in which the empirical study of American social life is much developed and in which critical perspectives are considerably developed, as well, with the kind of work done in the ethnography of speaking, which so far has been mostly addressed to other societies.

Let me conclude with a few comments on this last field. The ethnography of speaking has gone through two stages. The first was the development of the perspective itself, drawing on ideas of Sapir, Burke and Jakobson, so as to make the case for study of the patterning of verbal means beyond grammar and for cross-cultural relativity of the role and meaning of language. The first concern, then, was to justify a discipline based on the social constitution of language in both structure and function.

The second stage has been the undertaking of field studies explicitly devoted to questions of the structure and function of means of speech. It is striking that until the last decade cross-cultural differences in this regard had been virtually ignored. It was a rare ethnography from which one could learn much about such matters. The usual comparative guides and collections were virtually useless.

A third stage has several tasks:

1   to go beyond case studies to comparison and the greater precision and depth of analysis which comparison and contrast of types of case makes possible. It was indeed a goal from the start that comparison and contrast would lead to sharpening of terminology and dimensions of description within a generalized framework;
2   to use the generalized framework in our own society, as part of the development of social theory;
3   to apply a critical, reflexive perspective to its own work.

Postscript

Throughout this chapter the concern has been to recognize adequately the ways in which use of language in our society is culturally particular and diverse, not to be taken for granted, not to be explained away. At the same time such use of language is of course open, creative, emergent. That was Sapir's later view of the cultural as personal (cf. Hymes, 1964: 29, n. 8; 1974: 20, n. 6). The next part of this book is concerned with recognizing the personal and emergent in narrative, through the interplay of recently recognized linguistic and cultural means.

Notes

1   This chapter is based on a lecture with the title 'Toward Linguistic Competence,' given at the Festival of the Social Sciences in Amsterdam in April 1975. The festival was organized by Alvin Gouldner, and I should like to dedicate the chapter to his memory. The text of the lecture, somewhat edited, was published in *Sociologische Gids* (1976), **76**, 4: 217–39, and I thank the editors of the journal for their interest in it. The original address was somewhat changed in organization, material added and omitted, and some points rephrased for inclusion in Bruce Bain (ed.) *The Sociogenesis of Language and Human Conduct*, New York, Plenum, 1983: 189–224. This chapter has been further edited, and the last part considerably reorganized as well as amplified with additional references.

2   I write without having seen the promised fifth volume of his series, *Class, Codes and Controls*. The fourth volume (Bernstein, 1990) is a penetrating dissection of the ways in which educational institutions manage the organization and sequential presentation of knowledge (classification and framing), giving it their own stamp, whatever the curriculum may be taken to be. Such institutional analysis is perhaps Bernstein's greatest strength. (cf. Chapter 9 of this book.)

3   On the dialectic between the particular, for which linguistic ethnography is crucial, and the universal, let me quote William Sloane Coffin (1993: 7). Having said that the notion of national sovereignty has become obsolete, he remarks,

> the three most powerful movements in the world are nationalism, ethnicity, and racism . . . once again, we are putting asunder what God has joined together.
>
> But it would be a mistake to leave it at that and not recognize the many legitimate differences that exist within our common humanity. Nationalism, ethnicity, race, gender, our different sexual orientations – all have their rightful place, and the universalism that is their opposite tends to blur, deny, and too often repress what is particular about them. It is totally understandable that people want to preserve and deepen their

roots in their own land, language and culture, and that they also want to champion a gender or races that for so long have been so cruelly maligned. It should come as no surprise that everywhere people are asserting the particular over and against the general. It is not even surprising that nations themselves are breaking up, for while the nation-state is clearly too small for the big problems of life, nation-states often appear too big for the small problems of life.

The challenge today is to seek a unity that celebrates diversity, to unite the particular with the universal, to recognize the need for roots while insisting that the point of roots is to put forth branches. What is intolerable is for differences to become idolatrous. When absolutized, nationalism and ethnicity, race, and gender are reactionary impulses. They become pseudo-religions . . . No human being's identity is exhausted by his or her gender, race, ethnic origin, or national loyalty.

4   When this paper was written, it was addressed first of all to sociologists, and *sociology-* and *sociologist* were common terms. In point of fact, of course, several disciplines are relevant and have made significant contributions, and in the latter part of the revised paper, several names are noted.

Part III
Narrative and Inequality

Chapter 5

Narrative Thinking and Storytelling Rights: A Folklorist's Clue to a Critique of Education

Introduction: Dell Hymes

This chapter has its origin in instances of its own subject – use of narratives to explore and convey knowledge. In the course of a conversation with Courtney Cazden, I mentioned material recorded by Joanne Bromberg-Ross. She had recorded consciousness-raising sessions of a women's group, and presented a portion to my seminar. One session in particular contained a marvelous demonstration of interdependence between two different modes of clarifying meaning. The topic was what was meant by strength in men and women. Discussion began with discussion of terms. An unresolved back and forth about terms was followed by a series of personal narratives. Suddenly definitional discussion returned, stated in a way that made it clear that there had been no break in metalinguistic focus. Narrative had solved the problem of differentiating two kinds of strength (one good, one bad), when direct definition had floundered. The second mode of language used continued the purpose of the first, coming successfully to its rescue.

These two foci, terms and stories, often appear to contrast, rather than to complement each other, as here. My telling of the example from Bromberg-Ross reminded Cazden of instances of contrast from her experience at Harvard, which she recounted. I urged her to write them up, for they highlighted the possibility that one form of inequality of opportunity in our society has to do with rights to use narrative, with whose narratives are admitted to have a cognitive function. Cazden's written account follows next. After it, I will cite other observations and suggest some general implications. The most pertinent and obvious implication can be stated right off. If differential treatment of narrative experience plays an important role in present educational practice, then folklore can claim a special place in the study and change of education in this regard.

Ways of Speaking in a University: Courtney Cazden

We who work in universities may find contrasts in ways of speaking in our own classrooms. Two personal reports from graduate students and one case study of changes in language use over an undergraduate's four college years point to a particular contrast between narrative and non-narrative ways of clarifying meaning (exemplified, I realize, in the following account).

One fall I gave my class in Child Language to two different student groups: two mornings a week to a class of graduate students (master's and doctoral level) at Harvard Graduate School of Education, and one evening later in the week as a double lecture to a class in Harvard University Extension. The latter is a low-tuition, adult education program whose older than college-age students are either working for a college degree through part-time evening study or taking single courses for personal or professional interest. My Extension class had a mixture of the two groups – degree candidates like the tuna fisherman from San Diego who works as a bartender while progressing slowly toward a BA and then law school, and teachers in local day care centers, bilingual programs, and Perkins Institute of Helen Keller fame. Each class knows of the other's existence, and students have been encouraged to switch when convenient – as an evening make-up for the morning class, or the chance to experience real Harvard atmosphere for the Extension students. One evening, I noted two black students from the Graduate School in the Extension class. Instead of sitting in a far corner, they were near the front. Instead of remaining silent, they participated frequently in the evening's discussion. Finally, the man spoke publicly about his perceptions of the difference in the two classes. I paraphrase his unrecorded comments:

> In the morning class, people who raise their hand talk about some article that the rest of us haven't read. That shuts us out. Here people talk from their personal experience. It's a more human environment[1]

I remember a similar contrast described to me two years ago by a Tlingit woman graduate student from a small village in Alaska. She spoke about discussion in another course during her first semester at Harvard. Here the contrast was not only between ways of speaking, but how these ways were differentially acknowledged by the professor. Again I paraphrase:

When someone, even an undergraduate, raises a question that is based on what some authority says, Prof X says 'That's a great question!', expands on it, and incorporates it into her following comments. But when people like me talk from our personal experience, our ideas are not acknowledged. The professor may say, 'Hm-hm', and then proceed as if we hadn't been heard.

In Philips' (1983) sense, contributions to class discussion based on narratives of personal experience did not 'get the floor'.

Michael Koff (not his own name) came to Harvard College from a working-class community in Boston. Yearly interviews with him had been conducted at the Bureau of Study Council as part of a study of the impact of college experience. Some years later, for a Graduate School term paper, Bissex (1968) analyzed the transcripts for linguistic indicators of what she called 'the Harvardization of Michael'. She found a cluster of co-occurring shifts between Michael's sophomore and junior years, including one from *for instance* to *I mean*.

In Michael's sophomore interview, there are twenty-five occurences of *for instance* and other words used to introduce examples, compared with ten, three, and four in his freshman, junior, and senior years. His language as a sophomore is, as he says, 'concrete': every page of the transcript includes at least one illustrative incident, and the last half of the interview is almost entirely anecdotal. These incidents always function to clarify points. Michael does not trust the 'big, vague general words that do not mean anything'; he trusts the meaning that resides in concrete experience (Bissex (1968): 11–12).

> One of the things that I developed an interest in over this past year is some young high school people who live in a housing project ... Somehow if I wanted to talk about life in the project, I either said, 'Life is terrible!' or 'Life is not too bad.' It didn't mean anything. It's easier to, I mean, for instance, just talking here, it would be easier if I could think of something – some specific instance. [pause] For example, this family in Larchwood Heights. . .
>
> Michael Koff, sophomore

Michael's junior interview is marked, in contrast, by 24 occurrences of *I mean* compared with nine, seven, and four in his freshman, sophomore, and senior years. *I mean* has replaced *for instance* in its function of introducing an intended clarification of a previous statement. The interesting difference is in the nature of the clarification during his sophomore and junior years; the shift from concrete illustration to restatement, generally on the same level of abstraction as the original statement (Bissex (1968): 16).

> I mean, you just look at things differently. I – ah – it's hard to say what. It's hard, I mean, because you can only put your finger on some

of them. You feel you're growing up. I mean, certain things become less important, certain things become more important . . . I mean, the things that you think are important drop out and new things take their place.

Michael Koff, junior

Although narratives have an honorable history as 'the temporizing of essence', Burke, 1945: 430, they are often denigrated, particularly by social scientists, as 'mere anecdotes'. Evidently there is a press in at least some speech situations in this university to substitute other modes of explanation and justification.

A Narrative View of the World: Dell Hymes

Let me try to generalize, or at least extend, Cazden's observations. We tend to depreciate narrative as a form of knowledge, and personal narrative particularly, in contrast to other forms of discourse considered scholarly, scientific, technical, or the like. This seems to me part of a general predisposition in our culture to dichotomize forms and functions of language use, and to treat one side of the dichotomy as superior, the other side as something to be disdained, discouraged, diagnosed as evidence or cause of subordinate status. Different dichotomies tend to be conflated, so that standard : non-standard, written : spoken, abstract : concrete, context-independent : context-free, technical/formal : narrative tend to be equated.

When we think of differences in verbal ability, for example, many of us think in terms of command of standard varieties of English, command of the vocabulary, syntax, and written genres associated with standard varieties. We tend to group standard norms and verbal acuity together. William Labov's widely reprinted essay, 'The Logic of Non-standard English' (1972b) has done something to change that situation, by contrasting two examples of discourse, the cogent flow of one with the stumbling of the other – the cogent discourse being in a non-standard variety, the stumbling in a standard. Still, it is probably hard for narrative to get a hearing or approval in our schools, however apt its inner form of idea, if its outer form of pronunciation, or spelling, word-form and sentence-form, is not approved.

There is a connection here with Bernstein's well known contrast between *elaborated* and *restricted* codes. (More recently Bernstein speaks of contrasting coding orientations, each with its *elaborated* and *restricted* variants.) The orientation that Bernstein calls *elaborated* is associated with such things as independence of context, objectivication of experience, analysis of experience, a kind of metalinguistic potentiality. The orientation called *restricted* is associated, among other things, with dependence on context and a taking of pre-established meanings and values for granted. One suspects that the contrast is in some respects a version of the older contrast between '*abstract*' 'elaborated' and '*concrete*' 'restricted' modes of thought. Certainly it is Bernstein's view that an 'elaborated' orientation is necessary in order to go beyond the socially given. This is part of his defense against charges of favoring the middle-class and putting down the working-class: an 'elaborated' orientation is necessary for the kind of analysis that could lead to a transformation of the condition of the working class. Other sociologists have taken up the notion of a link between an 'elaborated' code or orientation, and a radical social perspective, taking the one to be a condition of the other (Mueller, 1973, and Gouldner, 1975–6).

Now, if one applies Bernstein's contrast to everyday genres, then one is likely to take written communication as 'elaborated', as against spoken. (Various writers have done so.) A main basis is the assumption that written communication is *ipso facto* context-independent. That assumption, of course, is false. Our traditional stereotypes about the functions of writing perpetuate it, but an empirical examination of the uses and interpretation of writing would falsify it. A written document may be dependent on knowledge of non-linguistic context for its interpretation just as speech may be. One may need to be present, or privy to a description of the scene, in order to know the referents of pronouns in spoken narratives (this kind of example is typical of work in the Bernstein vein). One may equally well need to be privy to an implicit scene to know the true referents of norms in a written narrative or document.[2] Personal letters afford many instances. Even written documents in the most formal style may be deceptively explicit. A diplomat, a bureaucrat, a college administrator has to learn to interpret written communications as if present to a drama in which they are context-dependent utterances. In other words, it would work against adequate understanding of the cognitive uses of language to treat difference of channel as a fundamental difference. Actual uses of writing may not have the properties conventionally attributed to them. To think of spoken narrative as cognitively inferior to written statement, because less independent of context, is to rely unreflectingly on a stereotype.

Again, if one applies Bernstein's contrast to everyday genres, then one is likely to take discourse employing abstract terms, definitions, numbers, and statistics as self-evident examples of a cognitively superior 'elaborated', orientation. But the form is not a necessary evidence of the function. Abstract terms, definitions, numbers, and statistics may be present as a consequence of rote learning, rather than complex creative thought. One may find abstract, analytic forms that are bound to their immediate context, unable to transcend it, and one may find concrete narrative uses of language that leap toward alternative futures.

In sum, our cultural stereotypes predispose us to dichotomize forms and functions of language use. Bernstein's contrast of codes, distinctions between spoken and written, between narrative and non-narrative, tend to be absorbed by this predisposition. And one side of the dichotomy tends to be identified with cognitive superiority. In point of fact, however, none of the usual elements of conventional dichotomies are certain guides to level of cognitive activity. In particular, narrative may be a complementary, or alternative mode of thinking.

Even if dichotomous prejudices were overcome, so that narrative, even oral narrative in non-standard speech, were given its cognitive due, the greater equality that resulted would be an equality of modes and genres, not of persons. The stratification of our society, including its institutions, such as schools, would favor the telling of some stories over others, because of the position of the teller. The structures of relationships and settings would discourage some displays of narrative skill, inasmuch as true performance of narrative depends on conditions of shared background, similarity of identity, and the like (cf. Wolfson, 1978). Some evidence and thinking in narrative form would not be admitted, or not be counted. If reasons were to be asked, or given, very likely they would draw on the dichotomizing stereotypes just sketched. Narrative forms of evidence would be dismissed as anecdotal, even where narrative might be the only form in which the evidence, or voice, was available. But the dismissal would be an application to others of a principle the user would not consistently apply to himself or herself – a principle, indeed, that no one could consistently apply, if I am right in thinking that narrative forms of thinking are inescapably fundamental in human life. The truth of the matter would be that only the anecdotes of some would count.

Even if overt performance of anecdote (narrative) were to be excluded, there would still be covert appeal to narrative forms of understanding. Terms, formulae, data, statistics, would be interpreted silently in terms of representative cases, and representative cases inevitably embody representative stories, what Kenneth Burke ((1945): 59, 324) has called 'representative anecdotes'. From Burke's point of view, every pattern of thought and terms must appeal to such anecdotes. One's choice is not to exclude them, but to choose ones that are appropriate and adequate. To exclude the anecdotes of others by a rule against anecdotes in general is in effect to privilege one's own anecdotes without seeming to do so.

In sum, if one considers that narrative may be a mode of thought, and indeed, that narrative may be an inescapable mode of thought, then its differential distribution in a society may be a clue to the distribution of other things as well – rights and privileges having to do with power and money, to be sure, but also rights and privileges having to do with fundamental functions of language itself, its cognitive and expressive uses in narrative form.

Cazden's account, and the uses to which Bernstein's categories have been put, suggest that we do indeed tend to think of our society, and our educational institutions, as stratified in ways that define certain kinds of narrative as inferior, and people to whom such kinds of narrative are natural as inferior as well. Certainly the students at Harvard that Cazden discusses are being encouraged to repress or abandon personal narrative in certain settings and roles. Very likely something similar happens in many schools at many levels of education. The student or child is told in effect that his or her own experiences do not have weight (except perhaps as diversion). Not that there is not an essential purpose to going beyond individual experiences. But if, as the Bromberg-Ross recordings indicate, narrative of individual experience is a complementary mode of solution of cognitive questions, then a pattern of discouraging it is a pattern of systematically discouraging what is at least a valid starting point, and may be an essential means of thought.

The irony, or better, contradiction, is of course that academics are not themselves like that. Consider graduate work or teacher training. When a student is considered a candidate or initiate for a profession, he or she becomes the recipient of gossip and lore of the field, of insight and orientation passed down in narrative form, of personal experiences that were meaningful to those who tell them, that have shaped understanding of the field. What many of us know about our subject comes in part from conversations with colleagues, from the stories they have told us, not from reading and evaluating published works. And from those accepted as co-members of the profession we do not discount verbal interest and effect. Indeed, we may relish it, if the result is a good story that makes a point with which we agree. We pay it the compliment of introducing it into our lectures.

The implication of such observations is that the narrative use of language is not a property of subordinate cultures, whether folk, or working-class, or the like, but a universal function. The great restriction on its use in a society such as ours has to do with when it is considered appropriate and legitimate. Generally speaking, it is considered legitimate, a valid use of language in the service of knowledge, when it is used *among co-members of a group.*

If the narrative function is excluded in an institutional setting, such as a college or school, the implication is that the students are defined as *not* co-members of a group with those who teach them.

Perhaps some of the decline in education in the country is connected with this suppression of the narrative function. Certainly it is more and more the case that teachers come from districts outside the district in which they teach, even from outside the city. Possibly schools worked better in the past when staff and students shared more of the same world of experience, and narrative use of language was more acceptable between them. This factor could only be a partial one, but it may nevertheless be significant.

Students may come from homes in which narrative is an important way of communicating knowledge. They may take part in peer groups in which experience and insight is shared through exchange of narrative. A classroom that excludes narratives may be attempting to teach them both new subject matter and a new mode of learning, perhaps without fully realizing it. Again, difference between the culture of the teacher and the classroom, on the one hand, and the culture of the children outside the classroom, on the other, may be a problem. If so, a teacher may not be able to be an ethnographer in the community, but she or he can be an ethnographer of what is present in the classroom itself. Giving children turns at narrative may allow them to bring the outside culture inside. Finally, a teacher who permits herself or himself personal narrative, but not the children, may not bring children closer but underscore a barrier (as well as be perceived perhaps as wasting time).

Consider graduate studies again. Success on the part of a graduate student, in the eyes of the faculty, is in part a matter of socialization into the profession. That socialization is a matter in part of acquiring the lore and outlook of the profession, an informal education. A student who had mastered facts and theories and methods and who had no stories and no interest in stories would trouble a faculty. On the one hand, the already initiated want to be considered entertaining or at least useful sources of lore that is of interest. On the other hand, the initiates at appropriate steps should show themselves to be entertaining, or at least useful, sources of lore in turn (as when having returned from field work). There is a desire on both sides perhaps for the link between generations to be more than names of documents and in bibliographies.

(Fame can be defined simply as the case in which a larger, non-professional circle knows some of the names and is interested in some of the stories; others not themselves the object of interest find audiences for whatever narratives they themselves can tell that involve the name. Stories could be studied in terms of their range of distribution: department-wide, campus-wide, profession-wide, general intellectual circles.)

This argument goes somewhat against the grain of a major thrust of our society for generations. That thrust has been to transcend the parochial, the local, the rural, in the interest of the opportunities and accomplishments of a general public sphere – the often told journey to the city, or the larger city. (Though even in the city one finds the successful able to indulge their sentiment for their starting point and the events along the way, others wanting or required to listen.) But perhaps this argument also helps to point up a major dilemma of our society: success in technical, professional fields is defined in such a way that someone cannot both stay at home or return there, to serve, and feel successful. This is a major problem for persons with strong ties to their communities of origin, such as Native Americans. One needs advanced training in order to be competent, to be able to cope with problems faced by the community of origin, but the advanced training embodies a message of on, upward and away. Perhaps the fundamental failing of higher education in the United States is to educate for status and not for service, or to define service without regard to considerations of locality, so that local is inevitably seen as lesser. Perhaps the treatment of personal narrative in educational settings plays a part in all this.

Warm Springs Interlude

Much of my sense of this problem comes from experience over the years (over the summers, mostly) at Warm Springs, Oregon. Let me try to convey something of this experience. In doing so, I draw on a letter written (24 August 1976) to Dennis Tedlock, responding to questions about the directions of the journal he then edited, *Alcheringa*, and leading into general questions about the role of language in poetry, ethnography, and social life. Just before writing, my wife, Virginia, and I had been reflecting on a quality of the use of language in the life of Indian people we know. It is a quality one comes to have a sense of through being around them over a period of time.

In one way it is a sense of a weighted quality to incident in personal lives: as when one friend, Hazel Suppah, told us that her son had been out to look at a root cellar her family had built many years ago. He came back to say, 'You know, it's still good. I think we could use it.' All this in the context of a visit off the road to where an old man had lived years ago, the house now fallen in, and the barn, nothing disturbed but only gradually reassimilated to the land. Hazel had lived nearby when young; the old man had come over to their place when lonesome. One bike lay prone against a slight rise, now a magnificent red bronze, green growing around and through the lines of its structure, the lowest and nearest point, a pedal, already partly within the soil. Hazel was looking for an old-style wooden trough (resembling a canoe) that Walker had had out for watering horses. It was gone, and she realized it must be the very one that the Tribe had installed in the resort at the other end of the reservation, with flowers planted in it. If she'd known the land had been sold to the Tribe, she would have come to get it herself.

We rummaged all around the land, nothing to be heard but insects, the white peak of Mt. Hood just visible from certain points behind the high hills across the highway from which we had come. All those old places are vacant now and most everything in them taken, years ago, by men who built power lines across. The Indians themselves didn't take an interest then; Hazel said they all had the same things themselves then. Now these old places, the isolated homesteads allotted to families in the founding of the reservation more than a century ago, to make Christian farmers of them, are another world and time to Indians themselves, who cluster mostly around the end of the reservation where the Agency, the Tribal administration, the mill, the restaurant and the housing projects are. Places that one can go out to in order to find and pick up things, memories, like berry patches. We brought back an intact old kerosene can for Hazel; she was sure her daughter would want to go out and get the two others there. A weather-polished twinpronged grey piece of wood, having nothing to do with the farm, was found by my wife and now shows between two trees just outside the window of our cabin back across the mountain. Two matching bronze sections of a broken harness, metal, a few links of chain on each, I carried about in each hand as we walked all round the rises on which the buildings half-stood, up to the fences, down to the run-off creek, and finally put in the back of the car. Well, I got carried away with trying to convey something, and forgot to put in the sunlight, along with the stillness. Back to functions of language.[3]

Virginia pointed out that in going around with a friend from Warm Springs one often saw a bit of experience becoming an event to be told, being told and being retold until it took shape as a narrative, one that might become a narrative told by others. Hazel had such stories about the old man who'd had that place, Dan Walker, stories I had heard from others. Her son's remarks had the weight of a theme, a kernel of a story, the first act perhaps. Perhaps we'll hear the rest after it has come about. My oldest Wasco friend, Hiram Smith, once did this to me. We had looked about some twenty minutes in a store in The Dalles, drifting out at last. Later, to his daughter, Hiram reported, 'Oh, that young guy in there, he didn't know nothin' about fishing equipment, Dell and I just turned around and walked right out.' No-nonsense partners, us.

Many must have had experiences of this kind. Such experiences seem to point to something a bit beyond our current concerns. There is a current movement to go beyond collection and analysis of texts to observation and analysis of performance. That is essential, but perhaps only the second moment of three. The third is what Hazel Suppah often did, what Hiram Smith did, what members of cultures world-wide often do, I suspect. Continuous with the others, this third is the process in which performance and text live, the inner substance to which performance is the cambium, as it were, and crystallized text the bark. It is the grounding of performance and text in a narrative view of life – that is to say, a view of life as a source of narrative. Incidents, even apparently slight incidents, have pervasively the potentiality of an interest that is worth retelling. The quality of this is different from gossip, or the flow of talk from people who have nothing but themselves to talk about – their illnesses, their marriages, their children, their jobs, etc. Not that the difference is in the topics. The difference is in the silences. There is a certain focusing, a certain weighting. A certain potentiality, of shared narrative form, on the one hand, of consequentiality, on the other.

If such a view and practice is the grounding of an essential texture of certain ways of life, then it needs to be experienced and conveyed if others are to understand and appreciate the way of life. Indians do not themselves think of such a thing as their 'culture'. They use 'culture' as we do popularly, for *high* culture, dances, fabricated material objects, things that can go in a museum and on a stage. Norms for speaking and performance go further into general norms of etiquette and interaction that are at the heart of certain qualities and problems, yet not explicitly acknowledged .

Ethnography is the way in which one can find out and know this aspect of a way of life. Of course one could ask in an interview, or on a questionnaire: 'Do you ever make up little stories about things you see or do?'

('Oh, I guess so.') 'Could you tell me one?' ('Well, let me see, once. . .') Even if successful in getting little texts – texts almost certain not to be truly performed (see Wolfson, 1978) – such an approach would not discover the texture of the text, the way in which it is embodied in the rhythm of continuing life and observation and reflection of life. One has to go around and be around to come to see how the world is a world closely observed.

Conclusion

All this offers folklore, and other disciplines with a special interest and knowledge of narrative, including theology (Hauerwas and Jones, 1989), an opportunity for both many empirical studies and a principled critique of present society. The narrative use of language seems universal, potentially available to everyone and to some degree inescapable. Humanity was born telling stories, so to speak, but when we look about us, we find much of humanity mute or awkward much of the time. The right to think and express thought in narrative comes to be taken as a privilege, as a resource that is restricted, as a scarce good, so that the right to unite position and personal experience in public is a badge of status and rank. My account is to be listened to because I am an x; yours is of no interest because you are only y; all this independent of narrative ability. The one who is y may be an excellent raconteur, x a bore.

To be sure, the excellent raconteur may be enjoyed if he or she chooses time and topic with discretion. But very likely we hear narrative as much these days, and enjoy it less. The decline in narrative performance among ethnic groups assimilating to the mainstream of life in the United States has been deplored often enough. On the thesis of this paper, the result is not a decline in quantity, but perhaps in quality. If the Michael of Cazden's account enters the security of an established profession, and gains standing in it, probably he will find that his narrative accounts of his professionally relevant personal experiences are considered appropriate, count for something, whether or not he tells them well. Successful people, interviewed on TV shows, are recurrently asked to tell 'how they got their start. No doubt many develop a moderately interesting narrative, if only because it is needed and they have opportunity to practise it. But sheer narrative ability, apart from success, seldom finds a place. Orson Bean is a superb narrator, and sometimes Johnny Carson gave him his head, but on other shows, he has gotten short shrift from MCs looking only for short repartee and embarrassed by the presence of small works of art.

Study of the interaction between ability and opportunity with respect to narrative experience is very much needed. The findings have a special bearing on education. Folklore has a special role to play in providing such findings.

Notes

1 More than the students are different in the two classes. During the double three-hour Extension lecture, we take a break for coffee and informal talk. The evening hour, and the second presentation of the same content, probably made me more relaxed as well. Participants and situation are thus confounded in their influence.

2 Thus, from White's essay on metahistory (1973a):

> . . .it can be argued that interpretation in history consists of the provisions of a plot-structure for a sequence of events so that their nature as a comprehensible process is revealed by their figuration as a *story of a particular kind.* What one history may emplot as a tragedy, another may emplot as a comedy or romance. As thus envisaged, the 'story' which the historian purports to 'find' in the historical record is proleptic to the 'plot' by which the events are finally revealed to figure a recognizable structure of relationships of a specifically mythic sort.
>
> In other words, the historian must draw upon a fund of culturally provided 'mythoi' in order to constitute the facts as figuring a story of a particular kind, just as he must appeal to that same fund of 'mythoi' in the minds of his readers to endow his account of the past with the odor of meaning or significance (p. 294).

One can argue, in fact, that just as there can be no explanation in history without a story, so too there can be no story without a plot by which to make of it a story of a particular kind. (p. 297).

This perspective is developed in detailed analyses by White (1973b), but these elements of the perspective are stated in clearer, more quotable form in the article (1973a).

3 Some readers may be embarrassed by this bit of personal narrative. If so, the embarrassment helps make my point.

Chapter 6

Narrative Form as a Grammar of Experience: Native Americans and a Glimpse of English[1]

There is some distance between analyzing texts addressed to children for their patterning and the work of researchers in child language development observing children acquiring and using language. And yet, I believe that some things which are beginning to be found out about Native American myths and tales have implications for the study of child acquisition of language.

Narratives are undoubtedly part of a child's experience of language. These Native American texts turn out to be subtle organizations of lines. The lines are organized in ways that make them formally poetry, and also a rhetoric of action; they embody an implicit schema for the organization of experience. The patterns may be more finely worked out sometimes in myths, but are also found in personal narratives. In the serious and scheduled occasions when children were (sometimes still are) the specific audience for myths, and those when children are simply present when myths or other narratives are told, it is not only that samples of language are being presented. Over and over again, at every level, an implicit organization of experience into satisfying patterns is conveyed and may be internalized.

Such texts have usually been presented as blocks of prose. In lines, of course, but lines dictated by typesetting and page margins. It is not possible to understand what these stories do, and what they are, when you see them that way. I would not rule out the possibility that there are people with minds so subtle and fine that they can actually do it. However, even with languages that I've worked with for decades, I can't discern what the stories do and are when they are presented in prose form, and so I think it unlikely others can. One cannot see the proportions and weighting of the material. One cannot see the relationships among the story elements that show there to be an implicit logic of experience and of literary form.

Andrew Peynetsa's 'Coyote and Junco' (1)

Let me give two examples, beginning with a rather straightforward example from Zuni, where the telling of myths and personal narratives still goes on today. This is a short story about Coyote, a trickster hero, and Old Lady Junco, who puts him in his place.[2] This version was recorded by Dennis Tedlock and published in his important book, *Finding the Center* (1972). If one wants a sense of the life of this kind of literature, it is a wonderful book to look at because the presentation on the page in lines does something crucial, something that is only beginning to be done. It slows down and guides the eye. One reads for form as well as for information (Burke, 1941).

SON'AHCHI

      LO————NG A

     SONTI   GO

AT STANDING ARROWS

OLD LADY JUNCO HAD HER HOME

and COYOTE

Coyote was there at Sitting Rock with his children.

He was with his children

and Old Lady Junco

was winnowing

Pigweed

and tumbleweed, she was winnowing these

with her basket.

She winnowed these by tossing them in the air

She was tossing them in the air

     while Coyte

Coyte

was going around hunting, going around hunting for his

     children there

when he came to where Junco was winnowing.

'What are you DOING?' that's what he asked her. 'Well,

     I'm winnowing,' she said.

'What are you winnowing?' he said. 'Well,

pigweed and tumbleweed,'

     that's what she told him.

     'Indeed.

What's that you're saying?' 'Well, this is

     my winnowing song,' she said.

'NOW SING IT FOR ME

so that I

may sing it for my children,' he said.

Old Lady Junco
sang for Coyote:

           HINA   HINA
     YUUWA   YUUWA
           HINA   HINA
     YUUWA   YUUWA
           HINA   HINA
       YU   YU
  (blowing) PFFF   PFFF
           HINA   HINA
       YU   YU
  (blowing) PFFF   PFFF

That's what she said.
'YES, NOW I
can go, I'll sing it for my children.'
Coyote went on to Oak Arroyo, and when he got there
       MOURNING DOVES FLEW UP
and he lost his song.
He went back
(muttering) 'Quick! Sing for me, some mourning doves made
    me
lose my song,' he said.
Again she sang for him.
He learned the song and went on.
He went through a field there
and broke through a gopher hole.
Again he lost his song.
Again, he came for the third time
to ask for it.
Again she sang for him.
He went for the third time, and when he came to Oak
    Arroyo
BLACKBIRDS FLEW UP and again he lost his song.
He was coming for the fourth time
when Old Lady Junco said to herself (*tight*) 'Oh here you come
but I won't sing,' that's what she said.
She looked for a rock.
When she found a round rock, she
dressed it with her Junco shirt, she put her basket of seeds
    with the Junco rock.
(*tight*) 'As for you, go right ahead and ask.'
    Junco went inside her house.
Coyote was coming for the fourth time.
When he came:

'Quick! sing it for me, I lost the song again, come on.'
  that's what he told her.
Junco said nothing.
'Quick!' that's what he told her, but she didn't speak.
'ONE,' he said.
'The fourth time I
speak, if you haven't sung, I'll bite you,' that's what
  he told her.
'Second time, TWO,' he said.
'Quick sing for me,' he said.
She didn't sing. 'THREE. I'll count ONCE MORE,' he said.

Coyote said, 'QUICK SING,' that's what he told her.
She didn't sing.
Junco had left her shirt for Coyote.
He bit the Junco. CRUNCH, he bit the round rock.
Right here (*points to molars*) he knocked out the teeth, the
  rows of teeth in back.
(*tight*) 'So now I've really done it to you.' 'AY! AY!'
  that's what he said.
THE PRAIRIE WOLF WENT BACK TO HIS CHILDREN,
  and by the time he got there, his children were dead.
Because this was lived long ago, Coyote has no teeth here
  (*points to molars*). LEE——SEMKONIKYA. (*laughs*)

Tedlock and I don't entirely agree on how to analyze narrative texts. In studying narrative among the Zuni in New Mexico and the Mayan Quiché in Middle America, he emphasizes the oral origin of the texts and the dependence of their organization on the voice. We both agree that whatever poetry is, in any culture, it is an organization or grouping of lines according to some patterning. But for Tedlock, the discovery of what these lines might be depends upon listening for pauses, The organization of a narrative into lines is determined by the presence of pauses. A new pause indicates the end of one line and the beginning of another.

From a linguistic, theoretical point of view, there is a problem with determining the organization of lines by pauses. If you only have one recording, how do you know that the person would pause in the same place if she told the story again? Also, pauses have to be present, whether motivated by literary concern or not, simply because no one can tell a sustained story in one breath. Pauses can be an artifact of how long you can hold your breath. Some pauses are likeiy, then, to be accidental or simply inevitabie, and not necessarily a stylistic device. You would have to have repeated tellings of a story to discriminate the ways in which occurrences of pause were common to any telling in a community, characteristic of a particular narrator, characteristic of a particular story, specific to the one telling in a motivated way, possibly incidental.[3]

Relations of Two and Four

There is another way of organizing the patterning of this story. Every American Indian group has some number which is the number around which a lot of things revolve. If a rite is going to be done a number of times, it will be the sacred number of times, or some multiple of it. Zuni has a pattern number, a sacred number, four. If there are going to be several people in a Zuni story who are brothers or sisters and who follow a course of action, there will be four. If the same thing is going to happen several times until it comes to a climax, it will happen four times, and so on. (Among Chinookans, as you'll see later on, it's five.) Now it seems to be the case in Zuni that the number four goes with the number two. You'll see that in this story, there's a repeated rhythm of 'then this, then that.'

The story has four parts. In the first part, the two actors are introduced, Coyote and Old Lady Junco. The story says first that she lives here and then that he lives there. The story says that then she was doing this, then he was doing that. He's come to her at the end of Part 1.

In Part 2 she's winnowing the seeds. He asks her about the winnowing, and he asks her again about the winnowing. Then he asks her about the song, and she sings the song for him. End of Part 2.

In Part 3, he goes off, loses the song and comes back. He goes, loses the song, comes back and gets it again. He goes, loses the song, and comes back, and then, naturally, she should give him the song again, but no. This is where the numerical pattern is not just a mechanical device. You can't just start counting twos and fours and get anywhere. Indeed, what happens here is what happens in some other Zuni stories. The expectation has been built up that this fourth time will be like the preceding times when she sings it for him again. You're ready for that and it doesn't happen. You're out on hold, dramatically, as she prepares for what will now be the fourth section of the story. This fourth section will be an elaborated double four, an eight-part telling of what does in fact happen the last time. You move up to it, you're ready. And then there's a big surprise. In the fourth part, he demands the song, and she doesn't sing. Then he carries out a threat and gets his comeuppance. This takes eight stanzas using the four-part pattern, first by just doing the this/then that, this/then that pattern, and then saying, 'I'll count four times'. He gets you through the sixth stanza by the time he's counted the four times, and the last two stanzas are to wrap it up. At the end of the story there is also a reversing of the order of action. Now her action is referred to first, his second; then she speaks first for the first time. The reversal of the turntaking order signals a reversal of who is in control of the situation.

This is a short story. According to Tedlock, it took four minutes to tell, the four of which I'm sure is accidental. One could just read it and think it was cute, funny, and amusing. It's the kind of story with a moral point that is often told. By wasting his time trying to learn a song and being no good at it (a shameful failure) both Coyote and his children pay a price in the end. Obviously, to forget a song is no way to behave, but a Zuni would find it amusing to hear of someone who has done so.

There's a rhythm to the story, a subtle patterning of this/then that. The patterning is not talked about anywhere; there are no names for it in Zuni so far as I know. Nevertheless, it's there, just as syntactic relations may be subtly and powerfully present and nobody has a way of referring to them in the native speech community. The child who heard Zuni stories from a person like Andrew Peynetsa, the narrator of this story, was following a kind of logical patterning that organized the experience into symmetrical, regular relationships. The storyteller also exploited the pattern for effect at the end of the story by putting the audience on hold and then carrying over and doubling the pattern. There's an artistry here that you can't even notice unless you realize this sort of thing is going on in the story.

Often the pattern is marked by initial grammatical particles. At certain points the word for 'meanwhile' in Zuni (taachi) recurs and marks off units. Then the repetition of the word for 'again' (taas) marks off units. But much of it is not overtly marked. Turns of speech also count as units, but most of the words are just part of the actual unfolding of the logic of the event, of a sequence of actions. This is a linguistic point, of course. Many people find that new things are understood about linguistic forms once we look at them beyond the sentence in discourse. This story is an example of that. Given that there does seem to be this internal patterning, the lines of the story can be arranged differently from the version based on pauses. You will see what a difference that makes to the analysis of the text, to the seeing of something that is really there.

Andrew Peynetsa's 'Coyote and Junco' (2)

[i] [Coyote meets Junco]

Son'ahchi.   (A)
    Sonti Lo:::::ng ago:
At Standing Arrows,
    Old Lady Junco had her home.

Meanwhile Coyote,   (B)   5
    Coyote was there at Sitting Rock with his children,
        he was there with his children.

Meanwhile, Old Lady Junco was winnowing,   (C)
    pigweed and tumbleweed she was winnowing;
      with her basket she winnowed these by tossing them in the air 10
        she was tossing them in the air.

Meanwhile Coyote,   (D)
    Coyote was going around hunting,
      going around hunting for his children there,
        when he came to see where Junco was winnowing.   15

                       [ii] [Coyote asks Junco]
'What are you doing?'   (A)
    that's what he asked her.
'Well, I'm winnowing,'
    she said.

'What are you winnowing?'   (B)   20
    he said.
'Well, pigweed and tumbleweed,'
    that's what she told him.

'Indeed. What's that you're saying?'   (C)
'Well, this is my winnowing song,'   25
    she said.

'Now sing it for me   (D)
    so that I may sing it for my children,'
    he said.
Old Lady Junco sang for Coyote: 30
    'Yuuwa hina, yuuwa hina,
    'Yuuwa hina, yuuwa hina;

    'Yuhina, yuhina,
        pfff, pfff (blowing);

    'Yuhina, yuhina,   35
        pfff, pfff (blowing)'
        that's what she said.

              [iii] [Coyote keeps losing the song]
'Yes, now I can go,   (A) (a)
    I'll sing it for my children.'
Coyote went on to Oak Arroyo,   (b)   40
    as he got there,
      mourning doves flew up,
        and he lost his song.
He went back.   (c)
    'Quick! sing for me,   45

some mourning doves made me lose my song,'
    he said.

Again she sang for him.   (d)
    He learned the song.

Again he went on;   (B) (a)   50
    he went through a field there.
Again, he broke through a gopher hole,   (b)
    again, he lost his song.
Again, he came for the third time   (c)
    to ask for it.   55
Again, she sang it for him.   (d)

He went on for the third time,   (C) (a)
    again he came to Oak Arroyo;
Blackbirds flew up,   (b)
    again he lost his song.   60
He was coming for the fourth time.   (c)
Old Lady Junco said to herself,   (d)
    'Oh here you come,
        'but I won't sing,'
           that's what she said.   65

She looked for a round rock,   (D) (a)
    she found a round rock,
        she dressed it with her Junco shirt,
           she put the basket of seeds with the Junco rock.
'As for you, go right ahead and ask.'   (b)   70
    Junco went inside her house.

                       [iv] [Coyote threatens Junco to his cost]
Coyote was coming for the fourth time. (A) (a)
When he came,   (b)
    'Quick! sing it for me,
     'I lost the song again,   75
        'Come on,'
        that's what he told her.
Junco said nothing.   (c)

'Quick!'   (B) (a)
    that's what he told her.   80
She didn't speak.   (b)
'One,'   (C) (a)
    he said.
'The fourth time I speak,   (b)
    'if you haven't sung,   85
        'I'll bite you,'
           that's what he told her.

'Second time. Two,' he said.	(D) (a)	
'Quick sing for me,' he said.	(b)	90
She didn't sing.	(c)	

'Three.
  'I'll count once more,'
    he said.
	(E) (a)	95

Coyote said,
  'Quick sing,'
    that's what he told her.
	(F) (a)	

She didn't sing.	(b)	
Junco had left her shirt for Coyote.	(G) (a)	100
He bit the Junco,	(b)	
CRUNCH, he bit the round rock		
right here he knocked out the teeth,		
the rows of teeth in back.		
'So now I've really done it to you.'	(c)	105
'AY! AY!'	(d)	
that's what he said.		
The Prairie Wolf went back to his children;	(H) (a)	
By the time he got back there,	(b)	
his children were dead.		110
Because this was lived long ago,	(c)	
Coyote has no teeth here.		
LEE:::::::::SEMKONIKYA	(d)	

Recognition of the overall principle of patterning allows us to observe some further niceties of pattern that bear on the relationships between the actors and are part of its aesthetic effect. With regard to reversal of turntaking precedence, mentioned earlier, notice that there is a symmetry in the story as a whole. Scene [i] begins with Old Lady Junco, and the alternating sequence of actors is J-C-J-C. Scene [ii] begins with Coyote, and the sequence is C-J, C-J, C-J, C-J. Scene [iii] is similar almost throughout, the sequence being C-J, C-J, C-J, J. Old Lady Junco holds the last stanza alone. This anticipates the reversal in the corresponding fourth segment of the next and last part, where Coyote initiates the action three-fourths of the way through the section (6 stanzas), but Junco is first in the next stanza, the last in which both appear. The sequence of actors in these seven stanzas of the last scene is C-J, C-J, C(J), C-J, C(J), C-J, J-C-J-C. Thus the relationship of the two begins and ends with Old Lady Junco having primacy in form as well as content.

    The niceties include variation as well as symmetry. Old Lady Junco is not explicitly present in two of the stanzas; Coyote is multiply present in three of them, if explicit turns at talk are counted; something is perhaps present in the opening and final untranslatable expressions, characteristic of myths, *Son'ahchi Sonti* . . . and *Lee semkonikya.*

Taking these expressions first, there would seem to be three levels of enclosure to the narrative: the world of myth itself, and what it represents as to the ordaining of how things should be, recognized but beyond ordinary words; Old Lady Junco, beginning and ending this narrative, and, so far as it goes, remaining; Coyote.

As to turns at talk, the logic of the scene and the regularity of the turn-taking imply that Old Lady Junco does not respond in stanzas (C) and (E), even though that is not stated. Four stanzas (A, B, D, F), describe her as not responding. Two stanzas (C) and (E) do not describe, but *enact* her silence. Now, it is in the four stanzas (A, B, D, F) that Coyote demands she sing. (In (B) 'Quick' seems an abbreviated repetition of the 'Quick, sing it for me' of (A); cf. (D) and (F)). The two stanzas in which her response goes undescribed (C, E) are the two stanzas in which Coyote threatens by saying how many more times he will count. Somehow the enacted silence is appropriate to threat. Perhaps it is appropriate to a threat of counting because she knows what the count will bring about. Perhaps there is a gradual intensification: say nothing, not speak; silence, not sing; silence, not sing.

There seems to be a gradual intensification on Coyote's part. After two attempts (A, B), he twice speaks twice (C, D). After a second threat (E), he speaks only once (F), but enclosed within two expressions of saying. In the final stanzas of denouement (G) and outcome (H), Coyote has a multiplicity of actions, or steps of action. In (G) a three-step action (bite Junco, bite the rock, knock out the teeth in back (b)) are followed by a response of crying out, the last thing heard from him (d). In (H) there are perhaps three consequences: in going back to his children, he gives up the song and Old Lady Junco; he finds his children dead; he forever has no back teeth (abc)).

Perhaps this elaboration of turns and actions is deliberately ironic, dashing Coyote up against the insuperable wall of the formal close. In any case, the management of omission and explicit mention of response on Old Junco's part has her not respond in pairs: twice not speaking (A, B), twice not singing (D, F), twice unreported (C, E), followed by a summation (Gc). It is difficult not to believe that the narrator was keeping track of twos and fours in several overlapping respects.

Victoria Howard's 'Seal and her Younger Brother Lived There'

Now let me turn to a different kind of case. In terms of what we know about cultural patterns in narratives right now, there are only a few areas that have been looked at from this point of view. I've been working mostly in a corner of the Northwest (in Oregon and Washington) with a language known as Chinookan, whose speakers are almost gone. What we have in the way of texts now is all we will ever have, and yet, as one looks at these stories one begins to see the effectiveness of this kind of analysis. Looking around that region in the last year or two, I've been able to find this same kind of patterning in a number of languages adjacent to each other. The stories are full of fives and threes. If somebody acts a series of times, it will be five times, If there is a series of brothers, it will be five. Five seems to be the overall pattern and three, the one that goes with it. And the two numbers are integrated in a subtle way, a kind of dialectical way. You can get a sequence of five in which the third is the end of the first sequence and the beginning of the next. Thus, five gives you two threes.

Now, when I tell you what this means, of course, it's going to sound simple. Doesn't everything have a beginning, a middle, and an end? And yet the stories contain patterns at the level of three sets of lines in a group, at the level of three larger groupings, stanzas, or whole sections, and at the level of the whole story. So there's a pyramid in this level of organization. There are twos and fours in the Zuni case, threes and fives in the Chinookan case. The patterns are there at every level, yet are not talked about, and have been discovered only recently.

This patterning is also present where something is simply being described. When Coyote is travelling (and he's always travelling) you may say in Chinookan, *gayuya, gayuyaa, gayuyam,* 'he went, he kept going, he got there.' Or the pattern occurs when a boy who is deserted discovers that his grandparents left him fire so he won't freeze and will survive. 'He turned, he looked, he saw the fire.' At that level and at every level, the same kind of patterning occurs.

In the following example, I think you will see also how this patterning works. A little bit about the context and background of the story will be helpful in understanding it. It's a fragment of a story, a fragment which must have been simply a moment of dramatic suspense in a full original version. Throughout Oregon, Washington and British Columbia, there are recorded stories of revenge in which a man or two men seek to revenge either a father or a sister. Brothers revenge a sister, sons revenge a father. In doing so, in order to get into the household of the enemy, they disguise themselves as women, becoming transvestites temporarily. In that disguise they are almost always found out, four times if it's a four-part culture, five times if it's a five-part culture. They are almost found out by some little mistake, by not proceeding exactly the way the women they are imitating habitually did. In a few of these stories, the last 'almost discovered moment' is when they are going upstairs to bed where they're going to cut off the head of the man they're after, and a little child underneath looks up and sees in one case a knife hanging down, in another case a penis hanging down, and calls out, 'This is not a woman.' But, an older person in the house shushes the child and says not to talk like that. This almost discovery is frustrated, then, and the heroes (they are clearly the heroes) successfully carry out the revenge.

Now in the following Clackamas Chinook text the perspective of the whole story is transformed. All that's left is the episode of suspense just described, and it is told from the point of view of those who are revenged upon, not from the point of view of the heroes carrying out the revenge. It's told even more subtly from the point of view of the girl who experiences what is wrong and is not attended to. The fragment is worked into a new whole, so that it too has three parts, all told from a single point of view. These things can be seen easily enough if the text is presented in prose form on the page, without recourse to its organization in lines. Here is how it was presented by Jacobs, who collected it (1959: 340–1).

Seal and her Younger Brother Lived There (1)

1   They lived there, Seal, her daughter, (and) her (Seal's) younger brother. I do not know when it was, but now a woman got to Seal's younger brother (and remained as his wife). They lived there.

2   They (all the people) would go outside at night (in order to urinate). The girl would speak, she would tell her mother, 'Mother. There is something different (and dangerous) about my uncle's wife. She is just like a man when she goes out (and urinates).' 'Do not speak like that! She is your uncle's wife!'

3   They lived there like that for a long time. They went outside in the night-time (in order to urinate). And then she would say to her, 'MOther! There is something different about my uncle's wife. When she goes outside it (her urinating) is just like a man.' 'Do not talk like that!'

4   Her uncle and his wife would lie together in bed. Some time afterwards the two of them lay close to the fire, they lay close beside it. I do not know what time of night it was, something dripped on her face (on Seal's observant daughter). She shook her mother. She said to her, 'MOther! Something dripped on my face.'

5   'Hm. Do not say that. Your uncle (and his wife) are copulating.)' Presently then she again heard something dripping down. She said to her, 'Mother! I hear something dripping.' 'Oh don't now. Your uncle (and his wife) are copulating.

6   The girl got up, she fixed the fire, she lit pitch, she looked where they (two) were lying in bed. Oh dear oh dear! Blood! She raised her light to it. In his bed her uncle's neck was severed. He was dead. She screamed.

7   She said to her mother, 'I told you something was dripping. You said to me, Oh don't say that. They are copulating. I told you there was something different about my uncle's wife. When she went outside she urinated exactly like a man.'

8 You said to me, 'Don't say that!' She wept. Seal said, 'Younger brother! My younger brother! They (the house posts in younger brother's house) are valuable standing there. My younger brother!' She kept saying that.

9 But the girl herself wept. She said, 'I tried to tell you but in vain, my uncle's wife urinated not like a woman but just like a man. You said to me, Don't say that! Oh oh my uncle! Oh my uncle!' The girl wept.

10 Now I remember only that far.

This story demonstrates a mode of acting of a mother who insists upon the decorum of speech at the expense of actual evidence of experience. That's what the official moral of the story must be according to the grammar of these things in Chinookan. In another way, the story is telling something about the daughter through her experience of wetness. She first hears it, then feels it on her body, and then produces it by crying. In crying the child is assuming maturity. If you look at the verbal elements like metapragmatic speech (Bruner, 1981) (or metanarrative, as some people call it), you will notice that the mother's speech is a perfect example of Bernstein's 'restricted code' (1971). It's positional speech in terms of her status as a mother with a certain social position. The girl's speech is not very extensive at the beginning but the whole last part of the story is turned over to her. She retells the story metapragmatically in an elaborated code and in a burst of elaborated speech so that the story is, in effect, an account of her assumption of a new level of experience and understanding. This is all done in a few lines of the text.

Upon closer examination, however, there are important relationship patterns that do not emerge from the text when presented in blocks of prose. By presenting the more subtle patterning of lines on the page, we can get a much better idea of the kinds of organization of experience being captured in the story. Compare the block version with the one below.

Seal and her Younger Brother Lived There (2)

[i] [The wife comes]

They lived there, Seal, her daughter, her younger brother.
I don't know just when, now a woman got to Seal's younger brother.

They lived there.
  They would 'go out' outside in the evening.
The girl would say,   5
    she would tell her mother:
    'Mother! Something is different about my uncle's wife.'
    'It sounds just like a man when she 'goes out'.'
'Shush! Your uncle's wife!'

A lo. . .ng time they lived there like that.   10
    In the evening they would each 'go out'.
Now she would tell her:
    'Mother! Something is different about my uncle's wife.
    When she goes out, it sounds just like a man.'
'Shush! '   15

[ii] [The uncle dies]

Her uncle, his wife, would lie down up above on the bed.
Pretty soon, the other two would lie down close to the fire,
    they would lie down beside each other.

I don't know when in the night, something comes on to her face.
She shook her mother,   20
    she told her:
        'Mother! Something comes on to my face.'
'Mmm. Shush. Your uncle, they are 'going'.'

Pretty soon now again, she heard something escaping.
She told her: 25
    'Mother! Something is going t'uq t'uq.'
    'I hear something.'
'Shush. Your uncle, they are 'going'.'

[iii] [The women lament]

The girl got up,
  she fixed the fire,   30
    she lit pitch,
      she looked where the two were:
      Ah! Ah! Blood!
She raised her light to it, thus:
  her uncle is on his bed,   35
    his neck cut,
      he is dead.
      She screamed.
She told her mother:
    'I told you,   40
      'Something is dripping.'
    'You told me,
      'Shush, they are 'going'.'
    'I had told you,
      'Something is different about my uncle's wife.   45
      'She would 'go out',
        with a sound just like a man she would urinate.'
    'You would tell me,
      'Shush!'
She wept.   50

Seal said:
>'Brother! My younger brother!'
>'They are valuable standing there.'
>'My younger brother!'

She kept saying that.   55

As for that girl, she wept.
She said:
>'In vain I tried to tell you,
>>'Not like a woman,'
>>>'With a sound just like a man she would urinate,   60
>>>>my uncle's wife.'

>'You told me,
>>'Shush!'
>'Oh oh my uncle!'
>>'Oh my uncle!'

She wept, that girl.   65

Now I remember only that far.

Throughout the text, relations of threes and fives are organizing what is going on, making it a satisfying experience, an aesthetic experience, for the narrator and for a native audience. You can see it in the case of the first scene having three parts, each of which begins by saying 'they lived there,' culminating the third time with 'a *long* time they lived there like that.' The second scene begins by repeating three times the words 'lie down'. In the second scene three things also happen. In both the first and second scenes, after an introductory mention of where people are, there follow two exchanges between the mother and daughter, each ending with hushing by the mother. Then there is a final scene, which, like the preceding two, begins by specifying where someone is. The girl acts in two verses, each of five lines. In the first, she acts (four times), followed by an expression of what she perceives (a common pattern in such myths). In the second verse, what she perceives is elaborated in three lines, framed by her action and response. These two verses lead to the longest verse of the myth, one central to its interpretation (the girl's long speech of reproach to her mother, accusing her of being responsible for what has happened). This verse has in fact ten lines and five explicit pairings of daughter and mother as addressor and addressee. The frame encloses four reported, enacted speech acts, followed by an end of speech in weeping.

The story takes only a few minutes to tell or read, but its apparent bareness, if skimmed as prose, belies an underlying process of arousal and satisfying of formal expectations of some complexity.

Conclusion

Let me speculate a little about the significance of such findings for language acquisition, first of all with regard to what it may mean in the American Indian case. Such patterns appear again and again and ultimately we may find them in some form in all American Indian narratives. This would mean that the patterns would have been adhered to in formal settings of the telling of myths in winter and in informal story telling settings as well. Children would have been obliged to listen to these recurring patterns over and over again, in a variety of settings. There's no explicit way of talking about these patterns in Chinookan, or in the other Indian languages, just as there are no words for transformations or parameters or the other syntactic relationships of their languages. Yet over and over again, people were being inducted into an understanding of a form of action as a way of organizing experience. In cultures where the telling of stories was a major way of understanding, explaining and dealing with experience, experience was put into the form of personal or culturally shared narrative. Again and again, instead of a chaos of events, experience was organized into sometimes subtle patterns.

Such organization is very antithetical to major currents in literary criticism in our own society. There, deconstruction and a sort of widespread revolt against stories that have endings and expectable patterns have replaced acceptance of the kind of literary form which took shape for most peoples of the world for most of human history. Traditionally, it has been 'the arousal and satisfying of expectations', to use Kenneth Burke's characterization of literary or poetic form in relation to the audience, that was accomplished through devices such as the ones seen in these Native American texts (Burke, 1925). Such devices give experience a shape, a satisfying shape which is convincing. As things come out this way, accounts are convincing not only because they may be believed in terms of the actors and actions, but also in terms of form. This form may be hidden in a sense, since no one talks about it, but it is responsible for making the story seem to come out right, to be warranted in the sense of fitting a deep-seated cultural norm for the form of reported experience.

Why would people go to all the trouble? Why not just tell the story of Seal or any other story as a sequence of events: this happened, this happened, then this happened? Why, along with remembering the sequence of incidents and who did what to whom, why also be constantly mapping incidents into an organization of lines, verses, and stanzas which follow hidden, implicit, proportioned relationships? My own speculation, one that may never be provable, is that a North American Indian conception of children made this organization of language very reasonable all together. Among the Chinookans and some other peoples, children, when they first gave voice, were believed not to be babbling but to be speaking a special language they shared with spirits. There were shamans appointed who had the power to interpret this language. The concern was that if the children didn't like it here, they might go back where they were before. The keeping of children was of tremendous importance. There was tremendous value placed on the individual child, and so, in a sense, children were being wooed into adult life. Rather than imagine these communities as living in a simple state of nature where everything is going along as it has to or must, I think one wants to think, at least in part, of people organizing a great literature addressed officially to children. They are the audience. All sorts of terrible things may happen in the stories, but they are addressed to children nonetheless. The children, in a sense, are being inducted into a world which is ordered, in which experience again and again in the form of a story, at least, has a recurrent, regular, often multileveled form. Stories always come out in terms of the discourse pattern, regardless of how they come out in terms of the action. There is this invisible, heard-but-not-seen web of order to all experience, or a potential web available for any experience that could become a story. There's 'a cool web of language winds us in', as Robert Graves said (1958: 48). Anything that happens can become a story, and if it becomes a story and it gets shaped into the story form, it will have a structure just by the carrying out of these principles of patterning, of arousal and satisfying expectation.

This patterning runs so deep that I've begun to find it in unexpected places. When Edward Sapir worked in the west in Oregon in 1905, he was working on a language called Takelma. Sapir was staying with a man who spoke an Athabaskan language called Chasta Costa. When he was there at night, not having anything else to do, he worked on Chasta Costa, too, and published what little we know of it. He wanted texts, as all good linguists of that generation did, but this man didn't know any stories in Chasta Costa. There was a popular magazine in the house that had some jokes in it, so Sapir got the man to tell him one of the jokes in Chasta Costa. And lo and behold, what did the man do but turn it into a four part pattern, with turns of talk and everything. It's all there.

Thus it seems that this patterning gets carried over into conversational English a lot of times. Older people who were raised with these patterns often carry them over when they tell stories of their own experiences in English. We have here not simply a linguistic fact of interest (that sometimes particles and recurrent linguistic items are not boring or monotonous) but examples of particles that actually show structure in narrative discourse. We also have the providing by a culture of an envelope or web of form for all experience, which, at least potentially, is available for inducting children into a kind of cultural security, both cognitive and aesthetic simultaneously (cf. Chapter 5).

Is this implicit patterning of discourse peculiar to American Indians and not found anywhere else? Well, it's hard to say, for there's so little work as yet in this area. I have looked at some other materials, a few in English. For example, I looked at a couple of the stories that William Labov collected in

New York and which Courtney Cazden reprinted in an article (Cazden, 1970); sure enough, there's some of this patterning there. At first I did not see it as consistent, but as more *ad hoc*, perhaps simply fixing on something like 'so' to begin a series of segments of a story or fixing on 'like then', or 'so then', or 'and'. Still, these markers are not randomly distributed throughout the story, but come in sets. They cluster. It might seem that 'and' is doing the work for a few lines, after which so then takes over. Further familiarity with the texts shows that there is more to it than that, a logic or an aesthetic, that conveys and reinforces intended meaning (see now Chapter 8).

Again, in some material collected in Gloucestershire, England, by Simon Lichman, 1980, (ms.) of old people telling stories about the revival of mumming tradition, there are recurrences that look a lot like American Indian material. There were two things in particular. First, there was the bringing around of each section of the story to an ending on the same reference point, in this case the Vicar who suddenly overheard the man doing a little step in the garden and found out that mumming was still alive. Second, there was the use of the first word of a line as a point of reference, so that when the man gets to the climax of the story, he has a set of three lines, the first beginning with 'that's' and the two that follow beginning with 'it's'. Now it may be accidental that he chose these three words to be first in each line. But because of the fact that they are so similar grammatically and that they come first, I don't think the choice is accidental. It seems to me that there's a tendency to take advantage of things that come first, especially particles, conjunctions, adverbs, things of that sort. Even in English today, to do a little more with them is not unusual. They show up in threes, fours and twos, or in sets for one section of a story, then moving on to another section.

In terms of storytelling ability we may be in much poorer shape than the traditional American Indian. We may not have as many good storytellers. Good storytelling gets washed out by all the media and events that influence people's experience with the language. When we do find people lapsing into the performance of a story in which they're really trying to tell it effectively to somebody they know, we do find some of these devices turning up. You find people lapsing into quotatives, which are sometimes thought to be a particularly American Indian device. People use, 'He says. . .' 'He says. . .' to mark off the different sections of a story. Or groups are marked by initial 'ands' and 'buts'. Wolfson (1982) has found stories of this sort, although she collected them for a different purpose, namely to study the occurrence of the historical present in conversational narrative. Looking at stories from the point of view I have been suggesting here, you begin to see they have sections which tend to be marked off by initial elements which recur in that role. It may be *ad hoc* to the particular teller or the particular story, but it makes me think that this is something which is a general human tendency. It may be a universal tendency to use words that come first as markers of relationships in stories and to use these relationships to segment stories into sets with lines, or sets with parts. In working this fall with folklore students on their collections of personal history narratives (in English), Virginia Hymes, has found a considerable variety of devices, (tense shifts, among others) marking similar relationships.[5]

In sum, perhaps something that was honed into a truly literary form in traditional American Indian cultures over generations is actually more pervasive than that. For American Indians, the use of words as markers of relationships is also reflected in their English, or it may come out when they are making up a story from a magazine lying on a table. The patterning may not be so pervasive in Boston or Philadelphia, yet it may be something that's partly there, that comes to the foreground in some cases and that ought to be looked for in more than purely formal features. Patterning may very well bear some of the life of literary aesthetic impulse in the shaping of experience in narrative, even in today's English and in children's experience of narrative discourse.

The work discussed here is based on the following ideas. First, all oral narrative discourse may be organized in terms of lines. Second, each change of predicate is likely to coincide with a change of line, the distribution of pauses may coincide with the relevant line units, but the fundamental criterion is syntactic, not phonetic.[6] Third, lines are grouped into what can best be called verses. Fourth, the relationships between verses (and often but not always between lines) are grouped in an implicit cultural patterning of the form of action, a logic or rhetoric of experience, if you will, such that the form of language and the form of culture are one and the same at this point. Fifth, such patterning frequently, but not necessarily, is marked by devices at the beginning of lines.

These patterns may be universally present but made use of in different degrees and ways. Among American Indian peoples these principles appear to be elaborated into a subtle fabric as principles of literary art, such that performances of myths and even personal experiences may have a subtle fabric. In modern society such principles appear to be present in narrative as well; the degree to which they are present is yet to be discovered.

What are the implications of these patterns for language acquisition and the teaching of language? Clearly, these findings suggest that the richness of syntax which linguistics finds in every normal child may be accompanied by a richness of narrative organization. The degree to which this is so cannot be assumed in advance. One has to know something of the state of the art of narrative in the community in question, and many communities have been buffeted in ways that erode traditional narrative art. Such kinds of competence have disappeared from many American Indian communities, as far as the Indian language itself is concerned. Yet patterning may be potentially present in any community's use of language and part of what the child brings to school at least to some degree.

It is likely that children who have experienced the satisfactions of such patterns in their homes and neighborhoods will find much of what is offered in reading books lacking in interest. There may be conflict between what is assumed by teachers as the *narrative* style and the *homebased* styles (Heath, 1983; Michaels, 1981).

It is difficult to say much that is practically pertinent until analyses are made of a range of materials in a variety of communities. Still, it seems safe to say that it is erroneous to think of schooling and writing as the sole sources of experience of literary form. If, as I believe, the principles that underlie traditional American Indian artistry are potential in every language, every speech community, democratically ready at hand for everyone, then it would be a sad mistake if these ubiquitous tools were never taken up and used. Modern society does debase local tradition and creativity but does not succeed in eradicating it. Inasmuch as the generative principles of language and narrative are universal, and the need to 'traditionalize' experience intrinsic to meaningful human life, we can expect some degree of preschool, and out-of-school, oral narrative experience to be as lasting as humanity itself. Its richness will wax and wane with forces over which schools have no control, but schools will be more effective if they realize its presence and take it into account. Insofar as schools see themselves as outposts of great tradition, missionaries to their districts, the indigenous oral patterns and potentialities may be factors to be taken into account in transmitting another message. Insofar as schools can see their mission as the etymologically appropriate one of educating in the sense of drawing out, discovery of this kind of patterning can be a source of encouragement and stimulation.

Notes

1   This chapter began as a transcript of an address delivered at the Sixth Annual Boston University Conference on Language Development, Boston, October 1981 (see Hymes, 1982). I have revised the original somewhat for clarity and consistency, but have kept its informal tone. I had forgotten how different this piece sounded in that regard, and began to edit the orality out (you not became 'one', contractions were expanded ('can't' became 'can not', etc.). When I mentioned what I was doing to my wife, she remarked that things in which I had such a tone were often better. Some points of the the two texts have been revised or discussed further.

2   This text is reproduced with permission of the author, Dennis Tedlock. Differences in the size of letters represent differences in loudness of voice. Differences in the place of words within a line indicate differences in the height of the voice. In the alternative presentation the format of the original article has been revised in keeping with my more recent practice.

3   It is likely that intonation contours, or tone groups, are the controlling factor in the use of the voice in organizing narratives. Pauses partly covary with intonation, partly do not. In at least one telling of a Hopi narrative, related to this one (a winnowing song is the same) there is considerable variation in the length and

content of lines, such as shown by Tedlock for Zuni (Hymes, 1992b). Within that variability, however, there is a quite systematic organization of the story through the patterning of particles for now and for quoted speech (see Hymes, 1994), patterning of the sort discussed next. For further discussion by Tedlock, see Tedlock (1983), and cf. Hymes (1992a). Tedlock shows ways in which the voice contributes expressive emphases and implications, distinct from the recurrent pattern relations. In effect, the underlying relations are like the expectations an audience has for iambic pentameter, or Germanic alliterative verse, or Greek dactylic hexameter. A singer or reciter may ring changes upon that base, and a good one certainly will do so.

4   The presentation of this narrative, like that of the Zuni, has been revised in keeping with my later practice. The story is discussed in detail in Chapters 8 and 9 of Hymes (1981). Note that the point of division between scenes ii and iii is different from that in those chapters and the first publication of this article.

When first analyzing the story, I had been impressed by finding another Chinookan text (Louis Simpson's 'The Deserted Boy', Ch. 4 of the same book) to have an elaborated climax in its middle section and thought that the same held here. Certainly there is continuity of action from the mother's 'shush' to the girl's getting up, fixing the fire, etc., and the last three verses of the story, alternating reproach and lament, are a unit. But, as mentioned, the first of these last three verses can be seen as a pivot, ending one sequence of three as it begins another, within a scene of five verses in all. And if one thinks of the story as unfolding in time, it is almost impossible not to imagine that the integrity of the first three verses would carry over for an audience to the next verses, repeating 'They lived there' three times (clearly distinct from the next scene of being in bed) and ending as they do on the mother's 'Shush'. If an introduction and two sets of 'Shush' give momentary closure in the first scene, an audience could hardly fail to have a sense of momentary closure the second time the same thing happened, that is, at the end of the sixth verse.

The psychologically realistic pattern actually makes more formal sense as well. Each of the first two verses begins with an account of location, as does the third. (Specification or change of location is a common principle of marking initial boundaries within these myths). Also, the first scene ends with the alternating speech of mother and daughter, as does the third and final scene; so now does the second, middle scene.

The girl's major speech is thus not the abrupt beginning of a scene, but the pivotal center of two interlocking sequences of verses. It was reasonable to look for elaboration at the center of a unit, but in this story elaboration comes at the center, not of the story, but of its final scene. For remarks on this myth, see also Hymes (1995c).

5   For further work in English, see now Chapters 7, 8 and 9, and Virginia Hymes (1995).

6   The work of Virginia Hymes has since made clear that intonation contours are fundamental indications of verses. Such contours are both phonological and syntactic. When it is not possible to know such contours, other features of narration usually make it possible to infer the relations which organize verses. In particular, turns at talk, indicators of time, of change of participant and place, and traditional patterns of step-by-step action do so.

Chapter 7

Oral Patterns as a Resource in Children's Writing: Ethnopoetic Notes

This chapter is essentially a set of notes to two books which document and discuss children's writing (Himley, 1991; Shuman, 1986). I want to show that the writing uses patterns of oral narrative. That in itself is not surprising (cf. Dickinson, Wolf, and Stotsky, 1993). One basic kind of pattern, however, has seldom been taken into account, that of the organization of lines in verses, stanzas and scenes.

Line and Stanza in the Work of Gee

Gee (1989; 1991; 1992) takes account of lines and stanzas in a certain way. Stimulated by work in what can be called *ethnopoetics*, Gee recognizes that oral narrative is built up of intonational units and lines, and of groups of these. He indeed refers to 'lines and stanzas, units which I believe are the basis of speech' (1989: 14) and to 'the line and stanza structure of human thought' (1989: 61). The difficulty is that Gee heads straight for meaning, not pausing to consider details of form.

In spoken narrative the elementary unit is an intonational unit. Gee's correct understanding of this is well grounded in work of Wallace Chafe and Michael Halliday (cf. Gee, 1991: 21–2). Others working in ethnopoetics call such a unit a line. Gee (1991: 22) calls it an 'idea unit'. A line may consist of more than one, and is 'something that would show up as a sentence in writing'. Gee's lines, in other words, are not necessarily spoken lines. He knows that narrators have alternatives when they organize a sequence of words into intonational units, but puts narrative on the page in a way which displays only those equivalent to sentences.

143

In the work of Virginia Hymes and myself, intonational units are not all equivalent syntactically.[1] Some have sentence-like contours, some do not. Tone groups may be equivalent to a phrase, which may or may not be equivalent to a sentence. It is sentence-like contours that have proven to be the central building blocks of narrative form. This has been found to be so in several varieties of English and for several Native American languages. These units are distinguished as verses. A verse may involve more than one line.[2]

It is verses that enter into relations governed by culturally significant groupings, and thus the larger organization of a narrative. If narratives are normally marked by repetition and parallelism, they also involve succession (cf. Hymes 1991a; 1991b; 1992; 1993a; 1993b; 1994).

In American English, and a variety of Native American languages, patterns of succession usually involve three or five units. The relation does not hold among lines as such, but among lines, or groups of lines, which are verses, and among stanzas and scenes. This finding has been made repeatedly, so much so as to indicate that Gee's finding that stanzas are often four lines long (1991: 25) must be an artifact of a decision as to what counts as a line. There are indeed language communities in which relations of four (and two) prevail, but so far as is known, American English is not one of them.

Alternative Analyses of 'The Sea'

Let me give a brief example of the difference. Gee (1991: 17ff) presents a narrative from a woman suffering from schizophrenia. She was told to talk freely for a certain amount of time. The doctor gave no response during the time she spoke. Her text was judged 'disturbed' and not fully coherent. Gee argues that the text is a typical example of making sense in narrative.

One can agree with Gee and admire what he has done, and at the same time think that there is even more to be said about the text as a typical example of narrative sense. Part 1 of the narrative is about the sea. Gee analyzes it as having five stanzas. Each stanza has four Gee lines, except the coda, which has two. Gee shows 'idea units' (phonological lines) with a slash within his longer, sentence-equivalent lines. Here is how they are related.

Strophe	Stanza	Gee lines	Idea unit (phonological lines)
1	1	1	1/2
		2	3
		3	4
		4	5, 6, 7
	2	5	8, 9
		6	10
		7	11, 12

Strophe	Stanza	Gee lines	Idea unit (phonological lines)
	8	13	
2	3	9	14
		10	15,16
		11	17
		12	18,19
	4	13	20,21,22,23
		14	24,25
		15	26
		16	27,28,29,30
Coda	5	17	31,32
		18	33

Gee is right that these lines are a distinct part of the longer narrative which
they begin, and are part of five groups, and that the first and second pairs of
groups ('strophes' in his terms) go together. But five or three part relations
at one level lead one to expect them at other levels as well. They do appear,
if one attends further to succession of phonological lines in terms of verbal
parallelism and repetition, and the tendency of narrators to bring units
around to the same or a related ending point. Gee's sense of the organization
of the whole part, somewhat revised, is confirmed at other levels as well. Let
me show the text in that way. (Verses are flush left. Capitalized words have
prominent pitch, as in Gee. Closing braces mark the end of pairs of units).

[I] [The sea]

Well, when I was LITTLE,   (A)
   the MOST EXCITING thing that we used to do is
   there used to be THUNDERSTORMS on the beach that we lived on
And we walked down to MEET the thunderstorms
And we'd turn around and RUN HOME,   5
   running AWAY from the
     running away from the THUNDERSTORMS.
That was the MOST EXCITING   (B)
   one of the MOST EXCITING times we ever had was doing things like
                         [that
   besides having like when there was HURRICANES OR STORMS out
              [on the ocean.   10
The WAVES
   they would get really BIG
And we'd go down and PLAY in the waves when they got big.

And one summer the waves were ENORMOUS   (C)
   they were just about   15
     they went STRAIGHT UP AND DOWN

So the SURFERS WOULDN'T ENJOY them or anything like that
They'd just go STRAIGHT up and down
     the HUGEST HUGEST things in the world.
Then they would   (D)   20
     they would
     they went ALL THE WAY OVER the top of the edge of the road
and went down the road TO OUR STREET
So that's HOW BIG the waves were
     they were HUGE   25

It was SO MUCH FUN just watching them   (E)
They made BIG POOLS on the edges of the beach
     that lasted for maybe ABOUT A MONTH   }
The waves were SO SO STRONG
and you'd get SO MUCH OF A CHANGE in the beach that year}   30
That was when I was REALLY YOUNG
     maybe about 7-YEARS-OLD or something
That was uh that was really EXCITING   }

The first three stanzas, as shown above, have the same scope as in Gee, but read differently. Parallelism in details finds a place. Here in the first stanza each of three verses has one of three occurrences of 'thunderstorm'. Each has an initial marker ('Well', 'and', 'and').

Gee points out the resumptive parallel ('Most exciting') that begins the second stanza links it to the first. Here the first verse of the second stanza also seems extended like the first of the first stanza. The second verse is linked in turn with the third by its ending point ('big'); the third begins with 'And we . . .', as do the second and third verses of the first stanza.

Gee (1991: 25) notes that his second pair of stanzas go together as being about waves, and takes the second stanza of the pair (fourth stanza in all) as lines 20–30. I perceive line 25 as having an ending point ('big') parallel to that of the third stanza (huge).

Moreover, the lines that follow participate in a different pattern, one of three pairs, with different verbal repetition. The first two pairs (26, 27–8, 29, 30) both make emphatic use of *so*. Both end with the beach and a period of time (month, year). The third pair continues that reference to time ('that was when'). Its own paired beginning ('That was. . .') is broken off in its second verse, then repeated to bring the whole round to its beginning ('exciting'). In sum, there are not just two pairs of stanzas, and a coda, but a fifth stanza itself composed of pairs (of verses).

This analysis of the text gives the following profile, which can be compared to that above for Gee's analysis. Such a profile helps to display the consistencies at each level.

Act	'Scene'	Stanza	Verses	Lines
I	i	A	abc	1–3, 4, 5–7
		B	abc	8–10, 11–12, 13
	ii	C	abc	14–16, 17, 18–19
		D	abc	20–22, 23, 24–5
	iii	E	ab	26, 27–28
			cd	29, 30
			ef	31–32, 33

I will return to Gee's work for an example of a young person's writing at the end. Let me start with an example of a child's very first writing.

Matthew's First Writing

Let me turn now to Himley's exploration of 'the particular ways [her son] Matthew has been drawn across time to the semiotic resources of written language' (1991: 140).

The texts come from her Chapter 6, after discussion of perspectives on such work. Himley's careful discussion of the texts should be read for an appreciation of all that is going on in them. If these observations lead others to her book, I shall be pleased, especially because the tradition in which she locates it, that of Patricia Carini, was important to my colleagues in Reading and Language Arts at the University of Pennsylvania.

Himley herself (p. 155) points out the likely presence of oral patterning in regard to the dialogue in connection with Matthew's third text (the first of the series of four about the disappearance of the TV):

> After the narrative crisis is set up in the opening three lines, the flow of information – that is, the way the text is developed locally – reads like the transcription of a spoken language dialogue. The unit of text, more phonological than graphological, as well as the absence of periods, supports the interpretive possibility that the writer relies on spoken language for resources for the text generation.

My purpose is to show that the spoken language resources involve ethnopoetic relations.[3]

Text 1 (1st grade, fall 1980, about age 5 years, 10 months)

Once upon a time there were two little boys.
Their names were Matt and Matt.
Their Moms and Daddys were lost.
They had to spend their own money to buy food
so they could eat breakfast and lunch and dinner.   5

One day their Moms and Dads came home.
    They asked how they got food.
[—] 'How do you think?'
    'With money.'   }
[—] 'Did you have enough money?'   10
[—] 'Yes, we were almost out.'   }
[—] 'I'm glad you did not die.'
[—] 'We almost did,' said Matt Himley. }

In the original text (pp. 141–2) there is no separation between lines. Lines seem conditioned partly by the space available, and sometimes run over. Punctuation is not used; capitalization occurs, but not always or only in the first word of a sentence. I follow Himley's normalization.

    Two temporal expressions 'Once upon a time' and 'One day' begin parts of the story. Probably the story should be taken as having just those two parts. If so, the first has five elements. The third element is one point of focus (their moms and daddies were lost), the fifth spells out another (they could eat). The second part has three pairs of turns at talk. The initial turn is indirect, the remaining five direct. (Perhaps 'One day their Moms and Dads came home' is a separate unit with a single line. It seems more likely that it and the following line of indirect discourse together are the first of six paired units). Ms. Himley notes the effective edge in the repeated 'almost', and the naming and rhythm of the final line.

Text II (5th grade, May 1985, age 10 years, 5 months).

Matt Himley gave the text (pp. 146–7) its title and perhaps its paragraphs:

1999
'They finally did it,' I whispered to myself
    as I woke up to see the city in crumbles.
The bomb must have landed about 80–90 miles away
    since I was only knocked down and bruised up.
I was looking at a huge black cloud to the west   5
    when my heart stopped. Where was my mom?

Since the house wasn't damaged very much
    I went inside to see what I could
Then I just remembered
    that my mom said
    that she was going to the grocery store.   10
I went into the garage to get my bicycle.
The wall of the garage must have sheltered it
    because it was almost exactly like I left it.
And then I set out to find my mom.

When I got to the grocery store   15
    everyone was up and around.
When I saw my mom
    I was very relieved.
She was sitting against the magazine rack,
    with one eye open and one eye closed.   20
We hugged and kissed for a while.
And the(n) with our hands around each other
    we went home.

In some oral traditions words equivalent to 'And then' mark verses and larger segments. Matthew here uses the pair to close the second and third parts. Indeed, he shows a fine sense of marking the endings of sections throughout. The first ends with the poignant question, 'Where was my mom?'

In the printed story three parts are indicated by space. Their status as units is shown by consistent internal patterning. The first has three verses, the second five, the third five. Subordinate clauses, introduced by conjunctions, are prominent, and the rhythm appears to make frequent uses of pairs of clauses in a unit.

The first stanza marks the second line of pairs of lines, using 'as', 'since', and 'when'. (The final line, 'Where was my mom?', seems in apposition to the preceding phrase, as if preceded by a colon).

The second stanza marks its first, second, and fifth verses with an initial word: 'Since. . .', 'Then. . .', 'And then. . .'. The third has no marker, but is a pivot, culmination and onset in one. The fourth marks its second clause ('because. . .').

The third stanza is like the second. The first, second, and fifth verses are initally marked: 'When. . .', 'when. . .', 'and then. . .'. Again the third sentence is straightforward without a marker. So is the fourth. Altogether, a kind of patterning expectable in a tradition that makes use of three and five-part relations: three stanzas, with three, five, and five verses, respectively.

A major contribution of Himley's book is to trace four stages in writing the same story. The writing took place over a three- to four-week period. The first version (p. 153) was written in school.

Text III (2nd grade, fall 1981, age about 6 years, 11 months)

[i] *The Day the TV Disappeared*[4]

Once upon a time I was playing Atari
    and my TV disappeared.
I didn't know what to do.
I ran to my mom.

I said, 'The TV disappeared.   5
    'What should I do?'
My mom said,

'Calm down.
'Should I call the police?'
I said, 'Yes!'   10

The second version (pp. 155–6) is not dated, but seems to have followed closely: 'Apparently attracted to the imaginative possibilities suggested in the first version, Matthew begins again' (p. 146).

[2]

Once upon a time I was playing Atari,
    and my TV disappeared
I didn't know what to do.
I went upstairs to tell my mom.

She said to calm down.   5
[—] 'But what should I do?'   }
[—] 'Do you want to call the police?'
[—] 'Yes!'   }
[—] 'Do you know where the phone is?'
[—] 'Of course.'   }   10
[—] 'Then go.' [—]
[—] 'OK.'   }
911 I dialed.
'Hello, please.
'My TV disappeared,' I said.   15
'My address is 8201.
'Please come over.'
[—] 'We'll be over in a second.' }

Ding dong.
'Where is the TV?' said the police.   20
[—] 'It was there.'   }
[—] 'So what happened?'
[—] 'I don't know.'   }
[—] 'Then I don't.'
[—] 'Well, we can't find it.'   }   25

The end.

Ms. Himley supplied the quotation marks that distinguish the last two lines as separate turns. That status fits the pervasiveness in these stories of pairs of turns at talk, whether three pairs, as seems the case here, or five.

To be sure, the nature of a pattern of three pairs in this case is not certain. One would expect the parties to the exchange to have the same position in each pair. If the 'we' of the last line is spoken by the police, as one might think, that implies that the preceding line ('Then I don't') goes with it as a concluding turn. If so, then the police indeed have three second-position turns (lines 20, 22, and 24–25), but the boy has only two initiating turns (lines 21, and 23). The first initating turn in the stanza, the line and signal that start the stanza, 'Ding dong', is external to the police. To be sure, Schegloff (1968) discovered that the first thing that happens in a sequence with phones is not the first thing said, but the ringing, which counts as a summons, and the ringing of doorbells likewise counts as a summons.

Putting the voice of the police in the second position of each of three adjacency pairs does maintain a dialogic form. Perhaps the 'ding dong' is taken as implying its correlate, admission to the house, and the police are responding to that step. Admitted, they ask. Told, they ask. Told again, they give up. This would seem to fit Himley's observation (p. 156):

> Matthew has invented a kind of paragraph: he indicates an external action (e.g., dialing the phone, the doorbell ringing) and follows that action with the dialogue, or speech act, relevant to that action. These bits of clues about the action and setting seem like nascent exposition, or perhaps even stage directions, as the text does now resemble a script.

But it is hard to make cogent sense out of this. If the ringing of the doorbell is to be taken as external to the police, it is even more external to the boy. No consistent pattern of relations seems possible that way.

Perhaps there is no consistent pattern. Yet the story itself has already indicated a way of taking the ringing of the doorbell that fits. In the preceding stanza there appear to be five pairs insofar as a signal and utterance by the same person count as a single turn. The boy both causes the phone to ring ('911 I dialed'), and then speaks (lines 13 and 14–17). The lines 'Ding dong' and 'Where is the TV?' said the police, are parallel to that. Together, the two cases appear to indicate an incipient convention on Matthew's part: signal and words by the source of the signal, counting as one turn.

This interpretation is equally consistent with the remark by Himley. The stanza has three pairs, then, with the police in first position, and the boy in second. The boy has the last word, summing up with 'Well' and an inclusive 'we'. If you don't know, then we (both of us) don't know. Which makes sense, and a lot more sense than having the police say both 'I' and 'we', with 'Well' continuing a turn, rather than, as one would expect, introducing it.

Having noticed this textualizing strategy, connecting an action with ensuing dialogue, in this text, Himley spaced the next, third version of the story in order to emphasize it.

The third version (pp. 157–60) is of such length as to benefit from indications of units and relations at the right margin. In Part I, scene [v], I have taken Himley's colon after 'Hide, Tom' as indicating it is spoken by the protagonist with the next two lines. Thus, the officer is hidden as of line 93, then steps forward to save the day at 100.

[3]

Once upon a time I was playing Atari [Part I]   [i] (A)
and my TV disappeared.
I didn't know,
because I went to get something to drink.
I went upstairs to tell my mom.   5

My mom said,   (B)
      'Calm down.'
'But I can't,' I said.   }
'Then sit down.'
'OK, but what should I do?'   }   10
'Do you want to call the police?'
Yes!'   }
'OK. Do you know where the phone is?'
'Yes, in your room, right?'   }
'Right. Go!'   15
'OK.'   }

911 I called.   (C)
      'Hello. My TV disappeared
      My address is 8201.
      Please come over.'   20
'We will be over in a second.'
'OK'

                                               [ii] (D)
Ding dong.
      'Where's your TV?'
'It was right there,' I said.   25
'So what happened?'
'I don't know,
      I will get my mom.'
'OK' said the policeman.

'Mom, the policemen are here.'   (E)   30
'I will be down in a second.'
'OK'
'Now where's the table?'
'That's what we're trying to find out,' said the policeman.

'I went to get something to drink.   (F)   35
      I got a cup and some Pepsi.'
'Is anything gone now?'   }
I said, 'No, but I might know where everything is going.'
'Where?'   }
'There is a robber that has a machine near Ridgeland
                              Park.   40

Should I call a friend that lives near Ridgeland?'
'OK,' said the policeman.   } .

383–8377 I dialed.   (G)
          'Hi, Matt.
          Can I come over?'   45
'I will call my mom.'
'OK'

771–7044.   (H)
          'Hi, Matt.'   50
'Ya?'
'Yes, you can.'
'I will be over in a second.'
'OK,' said Matt.

Dingdong.   [iii] (I)   55
'Hi, Matt.'   }
'What do you want to do?'
'Well, first I should introduce these people.
This is Captain Tom from the police station.
Now this is why he came here.   60
My TV disappeared
          and Captain Tom might know where it is going.' }
'Where?' said Matt.
'To Ridgeland Park.   } ?

Want to go there?'   (J)?   65
'OK'   }
'Let's go.
          But one thing, I can't play.'
'OK'   }
'Well, let's go.'   70
'OK.'   }

'Captain Tom?'   (K)
'Yes?'
'Can we ride in the cop car?'
'I guess so.'
'OK'   75

After they got there,   [iv] (L)
          Matt Himley said, 'Where does he live?'
'Right over there.'
'OK'   80

Don't run.'
'OK'

'I will go first.
        Get down.'
'Yes, sir.'   85

'Don't call me sir,
        call me Tom.'
'OK, Tom.'

'Get down.'   90
'OK'

Ding dong.   [v] (M)
'Yes?'

'(Hide, Tom).
'My name is Matt.
    His is, too.'   95

'So what?'
'We've been walking for days.
        Do you mind if we have a bite to eat?'

No! Get out!'

'Hold it,' said Tom.   100
        You're coming with me.
        'Thanks, Matts and Margaret.'
'You're the one who should get thanks.'

'Then thanks.
    You can go home now.   105
'OK.'

'Matt, can you come over now for real?' [Part II]   [i]
'I will ask. . .
        Yes, I can.'

'Then come on!'   110
'OK! What do you want to do?'

'Let's play Space Invaders and kill 'em.'
'OK, let's go.'

7777 Big score.
Time to go.   115

'Bye, Matt.'
'Bye.'

Boy, am I sacked.   [ii]
'Matt! Matt!'

'What?'   120
'Time to get up.'

'Tough luck.
    'Bye.
    I'm going to school.'
'Fine.'   125

Lunchtime.   [iii]
'What are we having?'
'Soup.'
'Be down in a second.
    Did anything disappear?'   130
'The pot!
The table and the stove,
    the sink, the floor –
    everything (the machine is going crazy).}
Let's get out of here, let's go.   135
Help! Help!   }
Everything is disappearing.
Let's go to the police office and report it.'   }

        the end.

Notice the recurrent grouping of signals and turns at talk in groups of three
pairs (23–29, 35–42, 118–125) and five (77–90, 91–106, 107–117). The final
sequence of five turns (126–138) is an extravagant three pairs within its last
turn.

Scene [iii] of Act I is puzzling. The last five lines are a clear stanza,
introduced by a change of topic and explicit address (72–76). The three,
pairs of turns at talk just before (64–71) have coherence, three questions
answered with OK, but do follow directly on what precedes. Perhaps what
precedes is a five element stanza (55–63), but it seems more likely that 64–65
is a Janus-faced turn, counting doubly, implicitly at least, so that line 64
completes three pairs with 55–63.

Sometimes the initial group is more complex than others (17–20, 43–47,
48–50 (this might alternatively be three pairs), 77–81).

There is one more written story:

[4]

Once upon a time I was playing Atari
    and my TV disappeared
so I told my mom
    and my mom called the police
The policeman said   5
    he'd be over in a second

So he rang the bell
  and he came in
    and said he might know
  where everything is going   10
  so he caught the robber
    and put him in jail
  the end

Himley points out that this is summary, not narrative, and more typical of
written language in having exposition, not dialogue (164). Even so, it is
shaped as if it were oral. It has five parts. An introduction (1–2) and close
(13) enclose three units, each marked with initial *so* (3–6, 7–10, 11–12).[5]

Gee again: Wilma's Text

Gee concludes his book, *The Social Mind* (1992), with a statement of its major
theme (p. 143):

> . . .in our everyday lives and in much traditional psychology, what we
> think of as 'mental' is in fact, 'social'. Meaning and memory,
> believing and knowing, are social practices that vary as they are
> embedded with different Discourses within a society. Each Discourse
> apprentices its members and 'disciplines' them so that their mental
> networks of associations and their folk theories converge towards a
> 'norm' reflected in the social practices of the Discourse. These
> 'ideal' norms, which are rarely directly statable, but only discoverable
> by close ethnographic study, are what constitute meaning, memory,
> believing, knowing, and so forth, from the perspective of each
> Discourse.

It follows that practices within and across Discourses are always and
everywhere *political* and *ideological* (pp. 141–2).

His concluding discussion draws on a narrative written by a ninth-grade
Puerto Rican girl, written, unsolicited, in connection with research conducted by Amy Shuman. Shuman (1986: 9ff) presents it exactly as written,
quotation marks and all, on lined notebook paper, except that pseudonyms
replace the names of people and the school.[6]

Gee (1992: 143–5) reproduces the first part, 'Seventh Grade', as
published by Shuman, then summarizes the two remaining parts, 'Eighth
Grade' and 'Ninth Grade'. He presents the first part in lines and stanzas. He
finds it to have ten stanzas, grouped in three main sections. In brief: [7]

	Stanza	Lines
I: School		
IA: Going to school		1–4
	2	5–8
IB: Moving from place to place	3	9–12
	4	13–17
IC: Ending the day and going home	5	18–20
	6	21–24
II. The Class Generally	7	25–28
	8	29–31
III. Friends	9	32–35
	10	36–39

Punctuation and Capitalization as Evidence of Lines and Stanzas

As inferences from a written text, Gee's identification of the separate lines seems right. His identification of stanzas, however, does not.

Gee expects stanzas to be groups of four lines, and often finds them to be so. Still, there are inconsistencies. His stanza 4 has 5 lines, and his stanzas 5 and 8 have 3. Gee is in fact right about these stanzas, I believe, and they indicate what is right about the others. The evidence lies in punctuation and capitalization.

The author, Wilma, in fact implies stanzas of three and five lines throughout. Contrasts in her use of capitalization and punctuation imply as much, and indicate an awareness of ethnopoetic relations. (The full text follows this discussion, which presents the reasons for its organization).

Notice line 17, the last line in the fourth stanza in 'Seventh Grade'. 'Which' is capitalized, following a period. Clearly it marks a unit (a verse) of its own. So does the capitalized 'Which' following a period in line 24. But the uncapitalized 'which', following no mark of punctuation, of line 26 does not. The stanza containing it (G, as indicated in the presentation of the text below) thus has three verses.

The uncapitalized 'and' of lines 22 and 38 is subordinate and not the marker of a verse. The stanzas containing the lines (F, J) thus have three verses. Contrast the capitalized 'And' in line 31, indicating a distinct verse.

Again, the uncapitalized 'until' of line 33 in stanza I is subordinate, and the stanza thus has three verses. Notice the contrast with the capitalized initial Until' of the third verse in stanza (G).

On these assumptions, lines 10 and 11 of stanza C, uncapitalized, are to be indented as part of a single verse with line 9. The third verse of the stanza is line 12, which begins with an uncapitalized 'which,' but a 'which' preceded by the punctuation of a double dash.

157

My account of the third stanza differs from Gee in taking 'A couple of us caught the bus together' as its first line. In keeping with an expectation of groups of four, Gee put it as the fourth line of a preceding stanza, but such a line, initiating a change of location, is characteristically the beginning of a new group. In consequence, the second stanza has left three lines and verses (5, 6, 7).

The first stanza has four lines, but the second ('I was scared') is subordinate to the first, in being unmarked by preceding punctuation. Line 10 in the third stanza is parallel. Both follow clauses beginning with 'When'. The first stanza, then, has three verses, the two lines beginning with 'When', and two strongly parallel lines beginning with 'but'.

A Logic of Relations among Stanzas

Organization of stanzas as groups of three and five verses is congruent with finding the series as a whole to consist of ten stanzas, and indeed, of five pairs of stanzas. Gee does not discuss his reasoning in this regard, but very likely it has to with internal relations of content, to which he later draws attention (p. 149). The case is not unique. Organization of a scene in terms of five pairs is, in fact, an important part of the narrative analyzed in Chapter 10.

Gee gives the pairs of stanzas each a heading, as seen above. Division into three superior parts seems superfluous. It has been found in many languages, including English, that in a series of five there is often a connection between the third and fifth elements, a connection which integrates the series as a whole. Such a connection involves the third unit as a pivot, serving as an intermediate outcome for the first three elements and as an onset for the last three.

Gee himself perceives the third pair of stanzas as an outcome for the first three pairs of his Part I, having to do with a temporal sequence of going to school and how it works out. One can see the third pair also as the beginning of a sequence with the remaining pairs. This second three-part sequence is linked, not by steps in time, but by a theme, that of favorable outcomes: 'Which I learned very quickly' (24), 'And were treated fairly by both teachers' (31), 'As you know we still are very closed and trust each other' (39).[8]

The third and fifth pairs are also linked as outcomes by the concern with friends in both. The first mention of friends in the story is in line 21 in the sixth stanza, and the last pair of stanzas focus on friends.

The Rest of the Story

As mentioned, Gee summarizes the rest of the text. Analysis of the original text shows it also to reflect ethnopoetic patterns. The profile below displays them. Runs of three and five lines are common, and each part has a balanced pattern of five lines as well (II 21–25, III 1–5). In one case an uncapitalized 'and' begins a verse. That seems warranted by the preceding period. In the second scene of '8th Grade' and the first scene of third part pairing relations among verses, like those found in the first part among stanzas, occur.

The third part does have just two scenes, unlike the three of the second part and the five of the first. Together the two parts could have five scenes, matching the first part, but it would be a mistake to put them together. Clearly they are distinct. The author gives each its own title, and begins each in the same formulaic way: 'This is how it all started', 'It all started. . .'.

In sum, ethnopoetic relations of a sort expected in American English obtain throughout (including the number of major parts, three, although that alone could be due to the popularity of that number in its own right). The ethnopoetic relations are reflected in details of capitalization and punctuation. These devices are not simply grammatical, but also rhetorical, as they were for Shakespeare and others in the Renaissance.

Here are profiles of the three parts, followed by the text.

I. *Seventh Grade*

Scenes	Stanzas	Verses	Lines
i	A	abc	1–2, 3, 4
	B	abc	5, 6, 7
ii	C	abc	8, 9–11,12
	D	abcde	13, 14, 15, 16, 17
iii	E	abc	18,19, 20
	F	abc	21–22, 23, 24
iv	G	abc	25–26, 27, 28
	H	abc	29, 30, 31
v	I	abc	32–33, 34, 35
	J	abc	36, 37–38, 39

II. *8th Grade*

Scenes	Stanzas	Verses	Lines
i	A	abc	1, 2, 3
	B	abc	4, 5–6, 7
	C	abc	8, 9, 10
ii	D	abc	11–13, 14–15, 16–18
	E	ab(cde)	19, 20 (21, 22–23, 24–25)
	F	ab cd ef	26, 27–29, 30–31, 32–33, 34, 35–36
iii [coda]	G	a	35–37

III. *9th Grade PATH* [9]

Scenes	Stanzas	Verses	Lines
i	A	ab	1–5, 6–8
	B	ab	9–11, 12–15
	C	ab	16–18, 19–23
ii	D	abcde	24–25, 26, 27–29, 30, 31–33
	E	abc	34–36, 37–38, 39–41
	F	abc	42–44, 45, 46–50

Ethnography, Linguistics, Narrative Inequality

[I] *7th Grade*

When I first came to Paul Revere (A)
    I was kind of scared
but it was going to be my first year there
but I was supposed too get used too going there.

I started early in the Morning (B) 5
I was happy.
Everybody talking about it sounded scarry, and nice.

A couple of us caught the bus together. (C)
When we got there,
      since I was a seventh grader 10
        I was supposed to go to the audotorium
– –which I did.

From there I appeared in the boy's gym. (D)
I didn't know until they announced where we were at.
From there I appeared somewhere else. 5
That was my home room.
Which they called advisory.

I copy something from the board called a Roster. (E)
After that a Bell rang.
We waited for another Bell and left. 20

I met with my friends (F)
    and cought the bus back home.
They explained how to use the rosters.
Which I learned very quickly.

The Classroom I was in like a regular elementary school (G) 25
    which was only from one room to the other.

I didn't understand that. (I)
Until our teacher explained that was called Mini School.

Well we did a lot of things. (H)
Went on a lot of trips. 30
And were treated fairly by both teachers.
I didn't hardly had any friends
    until I started meeting a lot of them.
I had a friend by the name of Luisa and Alicia.
Those were the only two friends I had at the beginning of the year. 35

Almost at the middle I met one girl by the name of Barbara. (J)
We were starting to get real closed to each other
    and were starting to trust each other.
As you know we still are very closed and trust each other.

160

II. *8th Grade*

This is how it all started.   [i] (A)
On the first day of school we went to our 7th grade classroom first.
Our teacher will tell us where we will go.

Barbara and I were hoping to be together.   (B)
Mr A. called both of our names together.   5
And said 'Yoos are in mini school again
      and have Mr K. for your advisory. [']

When we were on our way up there   (C)
      we decide not show up until the second day.
We walked the halls.   10

The second day we show up together   [ii] (D)
      we noticed
           w[h]ere we were at.
We only knew a couple of people from our elementary school
           like Jimmy, Emma, Nancy, Courtney and Jeanine.   15
We continue going everyday
       until we started meeting more and more
           it seem like it was going to be a super year.

Everybody was getting along with one another.   (E)
Which I liked that.   20
There were no argument between races or color
      if you was white
          you were suppose to hate Puerto Rican
      it didn't worked like that
          everybody got along.   25

We almost did the same thing in the 7th grade.   (F)
But in the 8th we cutted a lot
      and we know the school by heart
         and did not obey the teacher.   ]
Since that was our sencond year   30
      we didn't bother.
We were really bad
      made almost all the teachers had a hard time with us.}
Did everything we could of done to get in trouble.
We had pink slip   35
      like we never seen before.}

I enjoy this year very much.   [iii] [coda] (G)
      had a nice time
         and enjoy every bit of it.

III. *9th Grade P.A.T.H.*

It all started	[i] (A)	
when the first day of school came		
and we were happy		
especially Barbara and I		
though we were going to 9–2.		5

It all started   [i] (A)
    when the first day of school came
        and we were happy
    especially Barbara and I
        though we were going to 9–2.   5

So we went to K
    he called everybodys name
        and told them where they belong.   }

Barbara and I were waiting   (B)
    he called Barbara's name first   10
        and said P.A.T.H. 9–7 Ms S.

We thought
    that was going to split us up
        since they kept saying
            they were going to split us up into one. }   15

He waited   (C)
    and called everybody's
        safed mines for last.
When he called my name
    and said P.A.T.H. 9–7 Ms. S.   20
        I jump with such of joy
            that I thought
                that was going to be the end of us. }

Well over P.A.T.H. is good   [ii] (D)
    if you could hang onto somebody strict.   25
We stayed in one classroom all day.
and only have two brakes at 9:30 and 1:15
    and 50 mins. for lunch
        thats all.
We have to be in before 8:00.   30
or have our mother call
    before we come in
        thats if we are going to be late or absent.

As soon the clock hits 8:00   (E)
    you are not allow to sharpen pencil   35
        or nothing.
We start writing until brake
    after brake we start writing again until lunch.
The only think I like about PATH
    you learn a lot   40
        because she reviews what you had in the 7th and 8th grade.

Like I say   (E)
     if you could hang until something that's very strict
         you do alright.
But don't let her take over you at all.   45
     Stay quite
         when she talks to you in front of the class
            but when it by your self
               and her let everything out
                 and you'll get everything your way.   50

Notes

1 What I can say about oral narrative in English depends on work over the years of Virginia Hymes, who joins me in this tribute to Susan Ervin-Tripp. When we were at Berkeley, Virginia for a time assisted Sue (and Wick Miller) in their research on children's acquisition of language.

2 At the end of the next chapter, Leona's story shows the difference between lines (as tone groups), and verses. In texts known only from transcriptions without specific indication of intonation contours, a variety of lexical and syntactic events and kinds of repetition and parallelism usually identify verses. Cf. Tannen, 1989: 96–7, on the pervasiveness of repetition as a ground of conversation itself.

3 Himley footnotes the work of Michael Halliday at this point, and aptly so.

4 In the paragraph quoted above (cf. n. 3) Himley writes (p.155) as if dialogue begins in the fourth line. It actually begins, not in the fourth, but in the fifth and sixth written lines, with 'I/said, "The TV disappeared./. . ."' line 5 as analyzed here).

5 An interplay of written poetic form and young children's conversational narratives is shown in Minami and McCabe (1991). They find a convergence between the characteristics of *haiku*, a literacy game called *karuta*, and the narratives of seventeen Japanese children. Their narratives were exceptionally succinct, usually freestanding collections of three experiences, with stanzas almost always consisting of three lines. Their analysis was influenced by the work of myself and Gee.

6 Shuman's book is an important contribution to general issues of the interplay of orality and literacy, taking up fight stories ('what counts is the recounting'), storyability and tellability, collaborative uses of literacy, retellings and recontextualization, and familiarity and distance, on the basis of a number of years of field work.

7 The full text (as analysed) is given at the end of the chapter.

8 Cf. the integration of a series of ending points by a common theme in Hymes, 1981: 206–6, and in the text in Chapter 10.

9 P. A.T. H. (or PATH) is a pseudonym for the acronym of a special program for girls who needed special attention (Shuman, 1986, p. 201, n. 6).

Ethnopoetics and Sociolinguistics: Three Stories by African-American Children

Introduction

When sociolinguistics emerged on the American scene in the 1960s, the service of society was an important part of its context. To be sure, issues of theory and method in relation to formal linguistics loomed large, but these issues were engaged in partly because it was believed that the kind of formal linguistics advocated by Chomsky could not serve society. The need was particularly felt by some concerned with language in education. The Chomskian image of a fluent, creative, ideal speaker, of a child as the site of the ineluctable unfolding of an innate ability, stood in poignant contrast to the realities and diversities of the actual life of language in urban neighbourhoods and schools. The Chomskian withdrawal from observation and inference of use in daily life stood in conflict with two linked concerns that are particularly strong for those concerned with children in urban education settings: to start where the child (actually) is, and to recognize abilities that may be unseen at school, or misconstrued when seen (cf. the essay translated in Hymes, 1984).

In this regard the work with narratives of William Labov in New York City has been especially salient. More recent work of Sarah Michaels with children's narratives, begun at Berkeley while working with John Gumperz, has been valuable as well. In this chapter I should like to show that a dimension can be added to such work, one in keeping with its general purpose of disclosing actual ability and accomplishment.[1]

Ethnopoetics

The additional dimension comes from the field of ethnopoetics, which began to emerge as a field in the 1970s, somewhat after sociolinguistics. To be sure, ethnopoetics is associated primarily with the verbal art of other societies, notably societies traditionally studied by anthropologists. The development and range of such work can be seen in personal collections such as Bright, 1984; Hymes, 1981, and Tedlock, 1972, 1983; and and group collections such as Sherzer and Urban, 1986; Sherzer and Woodbury, 1987; Swann, 1983; Swann and Krupat, 1987. Ethnopoetic analysis has been used by E. Basso, 1985; Briggs, 1988, and Metcalf, 1989 to illuminate events and activities central to a community; it can also disclose personal voice, for example, in my own work (Hymes, 1981, Chs. 6, 9, 10; 1983c; 1985a; 1987a; 1987b). Work has also been done with narratives in American English, as in the work of Virginia Hymes with the Appalachian stories of Charlotte Ross, and related work of students from the Department of Folklore and Folklife at the University of Pennsylvania, although much of it is unpublished.

The principles and patterning found in this work have not yet played a part in the work of sociolinguists, concerned with the interplay of literacy and oracy in our society. Yet it appears that ethnopoetics has discovered a universal aspect of language use, one that may be essential to the analysis of discourse.

A good many scholars present texts in terms of lines. What is rare is recognition that stories may consist not only of lines, but also of groups of lines, indeed, that such groups may bespeak a throughgoing rhetorical art that organizes the story and shapes its meaning. Put otherwise, it is rare to find a model of the mind of the narrator that understands it as proceeding along not one track, but two – not only a track of what, but also a track of how, organizing performance through the synchronization of incident with measure.

The elementary principles of ethnopoetic analysis may be taken to be:

1   Performed oral narratives are organized in terms of lines, and groups of lines (not in terms of sentences and paragraphs).

2   The relations between lines and groups of lines are based on the general principle of poetic organization called equivalence (Jakobson, 1960). Equivalence may involve any feature of language. Features that count to constitute lines are well known: stress, tonal accent, syllable, initial consonant (alliteration), and such forms of equivalence are commonly called metrical. Lines of whatever length may also be treated as equivalent in terms of the various forms of rhyme, tone group or intonation contour, initial particles, recurrent syntactic pattern, consistency of contrast of grammatical feature, such as tense or aspect. The latter kinds of equivalence are particularly found in Native American traditions.

3   Sequences of equivalent units commonly constitute sets and do so in terms of a few pattern numbers. Sets of two and four are commonly found together in many traditions, as are sets of three and five in others. Where one of these sets is the unmarked pattern, the other

   pattern may serve to mark emphasis and intensification (cf. Hymes, 1985b; 1987a). In both the unmarked and marked cases the formative principle is that of arousal and satisfaction of expectation (Burke, 1925).

4   Texts are not ordinarily constituted according to a fixed length or fixed sequence of units. Rather, each performance of a narrative may differ from each other, responsive to context and varying intention. The patterning of a text as a whole is an emergent configuration (cf. Hymes, 1985a).

5   Variations and transformations in narratives appear to involve a small number of dimensions, which may prove universal as elements in a model of the mind of the narrator. The active dimensions can be related to the first six components of a heuristic for the ethnographic study of speaking (Hymes, 1974, Ch. 2; see also Malcolm, 1991).

We are only at the beginning of what can be learned, but enough has come to be known to indicate that these principles of narrative performance are not limited to any language, cultural tradition or area, but rather appear to be universally human. We can imagine children as being born with the capacity to acquire mastery of such form. Local circumstances determine the particular principles of grouping acquired – two and four, three and five, or some other.

Local circumstances condition also the degree of mastery acquired. As with grammar, so with discourse; not every one has access to all that has come to be done with it, or is given encouragement to extend its range. The systemic potential of English, say, far exceeds any lowest common denominator of competence among those who speak it.

When texts come come from a culture grounded in oral tradition and a narrative view of life (cf. Chapter 5 of this book), it is not surprising to find text after text that shows thorough architecture and rewarding artistry. In a society such as our own, where personal narrative commonly competes with mass media amidst a perpetual circulation of paper, and personal experience is discounted as anecdote, it would not be surprising to find that architecture and artistry are often less. When texts come from experiences that lack personal identification or circumstances that discourage acquired modes of telling, effective shaping seems even less likely.

It appears, however, that effective shaping of stories is far more pervasive than one might expect, that the impulse to narrative form is far from paved over or drowned out, even in unfavorable circumstances. The principles and approach discussed here make possible a new dimension and new degree of precision. Let me here reanalyze three short narratives told in English by urban African-American children, two in the context of a research project, one in a classroom. All show competence of form in even brief compass, and the last a complexity not hitherto observed.

The analyses are given in detail in order to both demonstrate the presence of the patterning, and to indicate the nature of what might be found by others in other materials. It is likely that the domestic ethnography of the United States in which so many anthropologists now engage encounters a multitude of narratives, analysis of whose form in this way would be illuminating both for the work in question and for the general nature of verbal competence. Linguistic ethnography ought not to begin at the water's edge, but own a responsibility to inherent form wherever it appears, classroom, corner, doctor's office, suburban train.

A Text from Labov's Work in New York City

The research conducted in the 1960s in New York City by William Labov (see Labov, 1972c; 1972d) has become a sociolinguistic landmark. Variations in pronunciation which had been set aside as free were shown to be predictably governed; the irreducible heterogeneity of an urban metropolis was shown to contain a speech community in terms of agreement on the social meaning of certain changing sounds; an initial cornerstone of linguistics as a science, regularity in the outcome of sound change, was shown to be observable not only after the fact but in progress, contrary to the expectation of many. Out of this work came also an influential framework for the analysis of narrative (see Labov and Waletzky, 1967; Labov, 1972a). That framework is known for a definition of narrative in terms of a minimum of two temporally ordered sentences, and for considering narrative in terms of the question said to be faced by any narrator, 'So what?' A well formed narrative includes an answer to that question, a dimension Labov calls evaluation. An example frequently used in talks was one in which the narrative line concludes with a statement not part of the temporal order, to the effect that 'And that man was my own brother.'

Labov's interest in the transformation of experience into narrative (1972a) led him to compare young people's stories of their own experience with their accounts of television programs they had watched. One of the latter is shown below as published by Labov (1972c: 367)[2]:

a   This kid – Napoleon got shot
b   and he had to go on a mission.
c   And so this kid, he went with Solo.
d   So they went
e   and this guy – they went through this window,
f   and they caught him.
g   And then he beat up them other people.
h   And they went

i	and then he said
	that this old lady was his mother
j	and then he – and at the end he say –
	that he was the guy's friend.

The story is one of a series of accounts of a television program popular at the time, *The Man from UNCLE*. Labov reports (1972a: 367) that it is typical of many such narratives of vicarious experience that his group collected:

> We begin in the middle of things without any orientation section; pronominal reference is many ways ambiguous and obscure throughout. But the meaningless and disoriented effect of 17 [the number of the story in the article] has deeper roots. None of the remarkable events that occur is *evaluated*.

Labov contrasts the story with a second, one of true personal experience (which is considered below).

An ethnopoetic perspective shows the story to have a considerable degree of structure. Recognition of such structure helps one recognize that evaluation is actually present.

Syntactic and lexical parallelism show the story to have two parts. Each part is built on a distinct framework. In the first part the framework is 'this kid', 'this kid', 'this guy'. In the second part the framework is 'And then he'. The two parts are distinct. The second part has no variant of 'this kid', etc. 'And then he' does not occur in the first part.

Several features of the story indicate that it rings changes on these frameworks in pairs of lines. Notice repetition of 'so' in the third and fourth lines (the only occurrences of 'so' in the story). Notice the parallelism of 'they', 'they' in the next two lines. Notice the parallelism of 'he said/that' and 'he say/that' in the last lines. I take each case to consist of two lines. (Labov shows them on the page as each two lines, but assigns each a single unit symbol (i, j)). Until this point each line after the first has begun with a particle or particle pair (–, and; and so, so; and, and; and then, and). Initial 'that' fits this sequence, especially given the expectation of pairing that has been established. (Thus the series given at the end of the preceding sentence concludes: and then, that; and then, that.)

Recognition of two parts and of parallelisms within them indicates that the story should be displayed as follows:

This kid – Napoleon got shot	1
and he had to go on a mission.	2
And so this kid, he went with Solo.	3
So they went.	4
And this guy – they went through this window,	5
and they caught him.	6

And then he beat up them other people		7
and they went		8
and then he said		9
that this old lady was his mother		10
and then he – and at the end he say		11
that he was the guy's friend.		12

Notice the occurrence of pause and recasting in lines 1, 5 and 11 (marked in the transcription by a pair of dashes). This feature occurs at the outset of the story, and at the outset of the concluding segment of each part. One may suspect it is an expressive marker that goes with units at boundaries.

There is clearly a formal competence, an ability to organize narrative lines in terms of initial particles, and to group them in terms of recurrent parallels. The short text is indeed a model of symmetry. Its profile is as follows:

A	a	1, 2
	b	3, 4
	c	5, 6
B	a	7, 8
	b	9, 10
	c	11, 12

The particular narrative task, talk about a television program, may have elicited little more than the ingredients of formal competence. Nonetheless, recognition of the shape of the story makes it clear that the culminating segments (B bc) provide evaluation and point, the answer to Labov's basic question 'So what?'. Contrary to Labov's italicized comment (quoted above), evaluation is present: 'that he was the guy's friend' is analogous to 'and that guy was my own brother'. What is missing is not evaluation, but sufficient information ('orientation') to understand what is being evaluated, the point of the evaluation.

A Fight Story

To the account of the television program just analyzed, Labov contrasts a narrative of personal experience. Here it is as presented in Labov (1972a) (and Cazden, 1970)

a	When I was in fourth grade –
	no, it was in third grade –
[b][3]	This boy he stole my glove.
c	He took my glove

d	and said that his father found it downtown on the ground.
	(And you fight him?)
e	I told him that it was impossible for him to find downtown
	'cause all those people were walking by
	and just his father was the only one that found it?
f	So he got all (mad).
g	So[4] then I fought him.
h	I knocked him all out in the street.
i	So he say he give.
j	and I kept on hitting him.
k	then he started crying
i	and ran home to his father.
m	And the father told him
n	that he ain't find no glove.

The story is parallel in structure and evaluative features, Labov writes (1972a: 368), to another fight story. The point is said to be self-aggrandizement, and almost every element is said to contribute to that evaluation, being designed to make the teller look good and the other boy bad. The story

> follows the characteristic two-part structure of fight narratives in the B[lack] E[nglish] vernacular; each part shows a different side of his ideal character. In the account of the verbal exchange that led up to the fight, Norris is cool, logical, good with his mouth, and strong in insisting on his own right. In the second part, dealing with the action, he appears as the most dangerous kind of fighter, who 'just goes crazy' and 'doesn't know what he did'. . . his opponent is shown as dishonest, clumsy in argument, unable to control his temper a punk, a lame, and a coward.

Labov points out earlier that when he ran home, 'his very own father told him that his story wasn't true'. And adds here (1972a, p. 368), ' No one listening to Norris's story within the framework of the vernacular value system will say "So what?" The narrative makes its point and effectively bars this question.' The story makes its point not only in terms of values but also in terms of form.

The rationale of Labov's grouping of the story into fourteen units (1–14 in Labov, Cohen, Robins and Lewis, 1968, a–n in 1972a) is not explained nor is it entirely evident. We do not know if the lines or units correspond in some way to intonational contours or tone groups. The emphasis in the analysis on narratives as temporally ordered clauses suggests that syntax is the basis of the units. There is, however, a syntactic inconsistency. In units d, e and i, a verb of saying and what is said are given as a single line. In m, n what is said is distinguished as a separate line. Perhaps m, n show emphasis and a sense of pairing analogous to that at the end of the preceding story. I suspect that the separation of m, n is correct, but then the exact parallel in e ('x told y/that. . .'), where both object and 'that' are present, should be regarded in the same way. (d lacks object, i lacks both object and 'that').

It can be guessed that a sense of pairing of segments is present in Labov's groupings: ab, cd, ef (in the first part); g, ij, kl, mn (in the second part). Yet features of content or participant role do not coincide consistently with the designated segments. New segments are indicated within a single actor's turn and talk at two places (c, d; m, n), but not within an extended other (e). (c–d, g–h, k–i, m–n) are pairs of segments with a constant single actor, while (e–f, ij) have change of actor. Possibly no consistent rationale is intended.

Ethnopoetics makes it necessary always to raise the question of the criteria underlying segmentation into lines, and to seek to discover what groupings the lines may have, together with the meanings signalled by such patterning. Such a questioning of the present story discovers an organization that supports Labov's sense of it, and so adds a dimension to what the narrator knows and does.

In earlier analysis (Hymes, 1987c, 1991a) I took the story to use three and five part relations in such a way as to yield the following profile (Labov's letters are at the right):

A	a	1–5	(a, b, c, d)
	b	7–11	(e)
	c	12	(f)
B	a	13–14	(g, h)
	b	15	(i)
	c	16	(j)
	d	17–18	(k, l)
	e	19–20	(m, n)

The story can be displayed as follows:

A (a) When I was in fourth grade –	1
no, it was in third grade –	2
this boy he stole my glove.	3
He took my glove	4
and said that his father found it downtown on the ground.	5
[And you fight him?]	6
(b) I told him	7
that it was impossible for him to find downtown	8
cause all those people were walking by	9
and just his father was the only one	10
that found it?	11
(c) So he got all (mad).	12

B (a) So then I fought him.   13
            I knocked him all out in the street.   14
   (b) So he say he give.   15
   (c) And I kept on hitting him.   16
   (d) Then he started crying   17
            and ran home to his father.   18
   (e) And the father told him   19
            that he ain't find no glove.   20

The first five lines (a), and the five lines of (b), are taken as units. (a) shows intersecting three-part relationships, an integration found in many American Indian languages, the Finnish Kalevala, narratives from Appalachia and Philadelphia. The third element is outcome of one triad and onset of a second. (In effect, 3 + 3 = 5).

Overall the analysis shows Labov's findings as to two-part structure in fifth narratives, and presentation of self, to be present not only in content, but also in shaping of poetic form.

An analysis suggested by Virginia Hymes shows integration of triads, pairing, and presentation of self, but in relations among stanzas.

If all capitalized lines that begin a sentence are significant of how the story was told, lines 1, 7, 12, 13, 14, 15, 16, 17, 19 count. (Line 3 has initial 'This' in Labov, but completes 1–2). The result is a sequence of five pairs. Moreover, the first three (ABC) lead to the fight as outcome, while the last three (CDE), with fight as onset, lead to the outcome as to the glove. The overall pattern seems convincing. Notice that the pivot (C) has the only initial pair of markers (So then). It is also the only stanza in which there is no alternation of participant: I, he; I, he; I, I; he, I; he, father. That seems to focus all the more on the teller as successful fighter.

The story appears as follows. It shows its profile.

A (a) When I was in fourth grade –   1
            no, it was in third grade –   2
               this boy he stole my glove.   3
   (b) He took my glove   4
            and said that his father found it downtown on the
                                                                    ground.   5
[And you fight him?]   6
B (a) I told him   7
            that it was impossible for him to find downtown   8
            cause all those people were walking by   9
               and just his father was the only one   10
                  that found it?   11
   (b) So he got all (mad).   12
C (a) So then I fought him.   13
   (b) I knocked him all out in the street.   14

D (a) So he say he give.   15
   (b) And I kept on hitting him.   16
E (a) Then he started crying   17
           and ran home to his father.   18
   (b) And the father told him   19
           that he ain't find no glove.   20

Leona's Narrative: Multiple Sequences from Michaels' Work in Boston

Classrooms continue to be a place in which unfamiliar pattern may be taken to be absence of pattern. This is especially likely when only one pattern is recognized, as when telling or writing of a story is understood only in terms of a certain traditional logic. It may be reasonable to expect children to learn the rhetorical patterns that prevail in the dominant culture. It is not reasonable to confuse being able to tell a story with being able to tell a story in a certain way. Only by accepting abilities to tell stories that children already have can one fairly judge their competence and connect what they have yet to learn with what they already know.

Sarah Michaels (1981; 1983) has made a valuable contribution to this concern through her study of 'sharing time' in classrooms in California and Boston. Children were expected to come forward and share an experience with the rest of the class. What follows draws on her account of work in a second-grade classroom in Boston as part of a project with Courtney Cazden (Michaels, 1983).[5]

The classroom Michaels studied had both white and African-American children. The teacher's expectation of what it meant to tell a story was such that white children were more likely to be recognized as telling a story, and allowed to finish one, than those who were African-American. Far more of the former told 'topic-centered' stories, stories with 'orienting information at the beginning and brief thematic elaboration which leads quickly to a resolution' (p. 32). Such a format fit the teacher's expectations, as shown by her questions when temporal clarity and spatial grounding were not explicit at the outset. When children used this approach, the teacher was quite successful at picking up on the child's topic and extending it through other kinds of questions and comments.

Some two-thirds of the African-American children's sharing time stories could not be so characterized (some three-fourths of those of the African-American girls). Their narratives had what Michaels calls a 'topic associating' style, a series of implicitly associated segments without explicit statement of overall theme or point. 'Temporal orientation, location and focus often shifted across segments, but the segments themselves were linked implicitly to a topical event or theme' (1983: 32).

By careful analysis of transcriptions, Michaels has been able to show that some of the stories told by African-American children had traditional patterning not recognized as such (1981; 1983). The story discussed below (1983, p. 33), seems to be more complex. To Michaels' recognition of lines and segments there can be added organization in ethnopoetic terms, terms which suggest further expressive richness. Let me first display the story (Leona's story) as it would appear if typed as a paragraph, and then as analyzed in lines and groups of lines.

Paragraphed typing of the story

On George Washington's birthday I'm goin' ice(?)[6] my grand-mother. We never um haven't seen her since a long time and she lives right near us. And she, and she's gonna, I'm gonna spend the night over her house. And every weekend she comes to take me, like on Saturdays and Sundays, away from home and I spend the night over her house. And one day I spoiled her dinner. And was having, we was, she paid ten dollars, and I got eggs and stuff, and I didn't even eat anything.

Lines according to intonation and pause (Michaels)[7]

On George Washington's bIRthday /	1
I'm goin' / ice / my grANDmother /	2
We never um / haven't seen her since a long tIMe /	3
and / ...she lives right nEAr us /	4
and /...she / and she's gonna /	5
I'm (acc.) gonna spend the night over her hóuse /	6
And /...every wEEkend / she comes to take mé /	7
like on Saturdays and Súndays	8
awA Y / from hOme /	
and (acc.) I spend the night over her hóuse. /	9
and one day I spOIled her dinner /	10
...um and was having UM, / we was / um	11
she paid ten dollars /	12
and I got eggs / . . . and stuff /	13
and I didn't even eat anything //	14

Much can be said about the narrative in terms of the form in which Michaels presents it. Still, there are puzzles. Why do some non-final boundaries count as the ends of lines, and not others? Why, that is, is there one such boundary with line 1, and three such boundaries with line 2? (All boundaries are non-final (/), until the end of the whole story (//).)

The characteristic high rising story-telling intonation, at or near the end of a line, distinguishes nine of the Michaels' lines. For the sake of the analysis, I relabel the candidates on this basis, distinguishing parts of 7 and 8(1, 2, 3, 4, 7b, 7c, 8b, 8c, 10, 11). High accent, at or near the end of a line is not mentioned in connection with lines by Michaels, but perhaps was used sometimes as a criterion. It is found in five candidates (6, 7b, 7c, 8a, 9).

Syntactic unity in relation to what precedes and follows is the only other criterion that could have been used to distinguish as whole lines sequences whose parts have non-final boundaries (5, 9, 12, 13). (Line 5 might be taken as going together with 6, because of the repetition of 'gonna', which seems to give three steps, two starts (and she/and she's gonna) and a completion (I'm gonna spend.). Evidently the change of subject pronoun from 'she' to 'I' made the latter seem disjunct, a new start.)

These criteria imply more lines than those numbered by Michaels. If the characteristic 'sharing time' intonation marks lines most of the time, why not also in what I have identified as 8b and 8c? If high accent can mark lines (6, 9), why not in 7c and 8a?

I suspect that Michaels gave priority to syntactic unity, whenever it conflicted with high rising intonation and high accent.

I suspect also that the narrative makes use of two levels, not one, in this regard. That the phrases marked as lines are indeed lines, and that the larger units, which have seemed to Michaels to make sense in the story, are most of the time what can be distinguished as verses.

From this standpoint, Michaels' first line (1) has a line that is a verse, or conversely, a verse that is a single line, as are her (6, 9, 10, 12, and 14). Her (2) is a verse that has three lines, as are her (5) and (11). Her (3) and (4) are verses that have two lines, as is (13).

Michaels' (7) and (8) are problematic. (7b) has a high rising intonation that precedes, not just a syllable, as at the end of (2, 4), or two syllables, and a hesitation, as at the end of (11) but an entire phrase, 'she comes to take me' (7c). It is a phrase, moreover, which is marked by high accent.

(8) begins with a line that ends with high accent ('like on Saturdays and Sundays'), and then has two lines (8b, 8c), each with the high rising intonation). I think that the high rising intonation, a defining feature of *sharing time* narratives, cannot be demoted as a marker without explanation, and that it is an indication of a verse. I think also that concentration of the high accent at the end of lines in the middle of the story is intentionally expressive. In short, I think that Leona, and other narrators, are usually consistent in their use of such markers.

The one exception called for by the patterning of the story overall is the back-to-back occurrence of the high rising intonation on 'away' and 'from home' in the middle of the story (Michaels', 8b, c). I think that this is expressive doubling, an intensification, or amplification, within a single level. Such a thing occurs in the Epistle of James, in which the address form, 'Brothers', marks major unit throughout, except when it occurs in short compass twice within a single figure of speech, as intensification. The Kalapalo material of Ellen Basso (1985: 46–7) also seems to have an example. If we were to count each occurrence here as a verse, it still would be an elaboration of a single part of the next higher level within its part (see below). Given the use of high accent as a line marker, then, I think that (8a) is distinct from (8a–8b). In terms of overall pattern (relations of three and five), I think that (8a–8b) together are a unit.

On these assumptions, the verses and lines of Leona's story can be shown as follows. To aid comparison, the numbers used by Michaels are retained as far as possible. Lines within verses are indented. Bold small capitals indicate the '*sharing time*' intonation. The spacing between parts of the story is implied by Michaels' analysis and is discussed below.

<u>O</u>n <u>G</u>eorge <u>W</u>ashington's **BIRTH**day /	1
I'm goin' /	
ice /	
my gr**AND**mother /	2
We never um/	
<u>h</u>aven't seen her since a long t**I Me**/	3
and/ . . .	
she lives right n**EAR** us /	4
And/ . . .	
she/	
and she's gonna /	5
I'm (acc.) gonna spend the night over her hóuse /	6
and/ . . .	
every w**EE**kend /	7
she comes to take mé /	8
like on Saturdays and Súndays /	9
aw**A Y** /	10
from h**O**me /	11
and (acc.) I spend the night over her hóuse. /	12
and one day I sp**OIL**ed her dinner /	13
. . . um and we was having **U M**, /	
we was/ um	14
she paid ten dollars /	15
and I got eggs / . . .	
and stuff /	16
and I <u>d</u>idn't <u>e</u>ven <u>e</u>at <u>a</u>nything //	17

As Michaels points out, the story has three parts. Parts are signalled by both wording and intonation. With regard to wording, the story makes use of expressions of time to mark the start of a new segment, as is common in oral traditions. There are three such time expressions here, on George

Washington's birthday (1); 'And. . .every weekend' (7); 'And one day' (13). Each introduces a unit. (I now use the line numbers just given).

Sharing time presentations are characterized by rising intonation, but not all lines have it. In this story the characteristic rising intonation occurs with the opening lines of a segment: 1, 2, 3, 4 in the first; what count as parts of the first and second lines for Michaels (her 7 and 8 = 7, 10, 11 now), in the second; and Michaels' 10, 11 (=13, 14) in the third.

Note that the second line of the second segment (8) has a time expression, 'on Saturdays and Sundays', expanding and doubling the time expression of its first line, 'every weekend'. Taking this into account, one can see that each segment begins with at least a *pair* of opening markers. The first segment (let us call it A) has two pairs of lines with rising intonation (1, 2; 3, 4); the second segment (B) has a pair of lines with time expressions (the first having also rising intonation), and a pair of lines with rising intonation (7, 8; 9, 10); the third segment (C) has a pair of lines with rising intonation (12, 13).

The ending of each segment is marked by intonation, but not by rising intonation. There is acceleration, beginning after the first word, in ending lines 6 and 11. (Cf. comment on these lines below).

Notice that low rise occurs with each of the first three words in the first line (indicated here by underlining the first letter). It occurs just once in the rest of the story (before 'haven't' in line 3), until line 16, where it occurs before all four words after the first . The only final boundary marker of the story occurs at the end of this line. This concentration of low rise in the first and last lines (1, 16) suggests that Leona used its multiple occurrence as a boundary marker.

Each segment thus is marked at both beginning and end. Notice also that each of the first two segments comes round to the same point: 'I'm gonna spend the night over her house.'[8] Such coming round is a frequent pattern in oral traditions, and sometimes a significant expression of pervasive theme (cf. discussion of 'The Crier' in Chapter 6 of Hymes, 1981.) Perhaps the third segment can be taken as addressing the same point. That seems the case on two levels.

In terms of the three segments, one can see that the first relates staying over as an upcoming event of importance to the narrator; the second places the event in terms of an important pattern; the third reports a notable occasion within that pattern.

Multiple Sequencing of Stanzas

On a close reading, the relationship of the segments needs further explication. On the face of it the first two segments contradict each other. To be sure, the initial time expressions are not themselves necessarily inconsistent. If 'George Washington's birthday' (A) was not on a weekend, then 'every weekend' (B) is an expansion of 'spend the night over her house', from 'I'm gonna (this particular time)' (A) to simply 'I (every weekend)' (B). But how can it be true that 'every weekend she comes to take me' (B), if it is true that 'we haven't seen her since a long time', though 'she lives right near us' (A)?

The crux and resolution would appear to lie in the third segment. It would appear that 'We haven't seen her since a long time' (A), because 'one day I spoiled her dinner' by not eating anything, although 'she paid ten dollars' (C). That Leona is going to go on George Washington's birthday (A), then, is news, and news that anticipates weekly visits (B). The actual temporal order is in effect something like (C) (A) (B).

Ambiguity as to the narrative time of (B), indeed, allows one to imagine (B) as central to the spoken story, and as pertinent to not one, but three points in the sequence of events alluded to in what is spoken. It is as if (B) is a variable that can be variously tensed, and marked or not marked for negation. The full implied sequence would appear to be (B) C (B) A (B): 'I [used to] spend the night over her house', [but] 'I spoiled her dinner', [so] 'I [did not] spend the night over her house', [but] 'on George Washington's birthday' 'I'm gonna spend the night over her house', 'and every weekend' 'I [will] spend the night over her house'.

(B) is central to this, and marked, I think, as the peak of the story. It is in (B) that an initial time expression is doubled ('every weekend', 'on Saturdays and Sundays'); that the characteristic rising intonation divides the story into finer lines than elsewhere, occurring on successive phrases, one a single word, framing 'away', 'from home'; that there occur three of the four instances of high accent (mé (7), Súndays (8), hóuse (9)). And the other instance immediately precedes (hóuse (6)).

Grouping of Lines Within Stanzas

Let me review and integrate consideration of the lines of the story, as given above, distinguishing Michaels' numbered lines with preceding M.

The M lines within each of the three segments, or stanzas, appear to be grouped into sets of three (pairs), four, and five verses, respectively. (1–2 form a sentence; 3–4 are two aspects of the point being made; 5–6 are parts of a single point. Pairs frequently enter into the organization of a stanza; cf. the text in Chapter 10 below).

In (A) rising intonation and time expression distinguishes M1, and rising intonation distinguishes M2, M3, and M4, while M5 and 6 show a three-step progression in formulation (she, and she's gonna, I'm gonna) characterized by acceleration at the end.

In (B) rising intonation and time expression distinguishes M7, time expression distinguishes M8, rising intonation distinguishes M9 and M10, while M11 is characterized by acceleration.[9]

In (C) rising intonation and time expression distinguish M12, rising intonation distinguishes M13, while M14–15–16 are characterized by a three-step progression (she paid, I got, I didn't) and acceleration at the end.

M7a and 7b have been distinguished (7b and 8 in the second presentation above) because of the high accent at the end of 7b. M8b and c have been distinguished because of the sharing time intonation in each (lines 10 and 11 in the second presentation). In consequence, each of the succeeding lines is numbered three units higher in the second presentation.

As already noted, these numbers actually identify verses, rather than lines. Some verses have more than one line. When numbers are reserved to identify lines as such, as is the usual practice with poetry, the text appears as follows. Only every fifth line is explicitly numbered.

Leona's story

<u>O</u>n <u>G</u>eorge <u>W</u>ashington's BIRTHday /   (A)
I'm goin' /
        ice/
             my grANDmother /
We never um/   5
      <u>h</u>aven't seen her since a long tI Me/
and/ . . .
      she lives right nEAR us /
And/ . . .
      she/   10
        and she's gonna /
I'm (acc.) gonna spend the night over her hóuse /

and/ . . .   (B)
      every wEEkend/
she comes to take mé /   15
like on Saturdays and Súndays/
awA Y /
      from hOme /
and (acc.) I spend the night over her hóuse. /

and one day I spOILed her dinner /   (C)   20
. . .um and we was having U M, /
        we was/ um
she paid ten dollars /
and I got eggs / . . .
      and stuff /   25
and I <u>d</u>idn't <u>e</u>ven eat <u>a</u>nything //

These relationships can be summarized in a profile. Lower case letters identify verses, and upper case letters identify stanzas.

A	a	1
	b	2–4 }
	c	5–6
	d	7–8 }
	e	9–11
	f	12 }
B	a	13–14
	b	15
	c	16
	d	17–18
	e	19
C	a	20
	b	21–22
	c	23
	d	24–25
	e	26

Conclusion

Building on Michaels' work, I have suggested that Leona's story has form and meaning to a finer point than previously recognized. There are not only segments, and lines within segments, but patterned groups of lines. When intonation and time expression markers are taken as consistent indicators of lines throughout, the organization of the story is found to use patterning based on relations of three and five. Such a principle is one of two so far known to be widespread in the world. Moreover, when the relations among units are examined in terms of the principle of arousal and satisfying of expectation, the story is expressively complex indeed. In a three-part sequence one is likely to find a rhythm of onset, continuation, and outcome (cf. Chapter 9 of this book, and Hymes, 1987a; 1987b; 1992a). As has been seen, Leona's story suggests, not one but three, such relationships. Not one sequence, in other words, but half of the six logically possible such sequences, given three elements. Nor do the three possibilities suggested appear to be random.

1 As the story is told, in the sequence of segments (ABC), the outcome (C) is the fact that 'one day I spoiled her dinner'. It stands as completion to an onset (A) of 'I'm gonna spend the night over her house' and as a continuation (B) of 'I spend the night over her house' (every weekend). Its implication appears to be 'even so I spend the night over her house'.

2   When the story is put in an inferred temporal sequence, (CAB), the outcome (B) is a hoped-for or expected recurrent state. (B) completes an onset of misbehaviour (C) that a continuation (A) shows to have been penalized, but now forgiven.

3   When the story is considered in the light of the likely inference that 'every weekend' had once been the case, then ceased to be so, (B) appears to figure as both onset and outcome in an implied longer sequence. (B) figures as onset (past) of a continuation (C) that had as outcome an end to 'every weekend' (negation of (B)). In short, BC(–B). That negation has had a continuation (A), however, that arouses expectation of reinstitution of the initial state (future) (B). In sum, BCB–AB, with B as starting point, negated as intermediate outcome, then expected as outcome again, as indicated above. (A) and (C) are links in B's chain. The concentration of expressive details in a few lines, again, suggests that this protean central stanza (B) is the story's expressive peak.[10]

As noted at the beginning of this section, this bit of *sharing time* shows a complexity not hitherto observed. That surface simplicity may disclose complexity should not surprise us. The point was made many years ago by the critic Edwin Burgum Berry about the lyric, and seems necessary to any consideration of elaboration or restriction of codes and texts (cf. Hymes, 1973c: 43). The present analysis further corroborates Michaels' point that 'structure was there of course, if one were expecting and listening for multiple segments' (p. 33), and suggests ethnopoetic relations likely to have been part of competence brought to bear by African-Americans who found the story 'well-formed, easy to understand, and interesting' (p. 33).

A major contribution of linguistics is to shed light on the relations between spoken and written uses of language, between oracy and literacy. When these problems came to the fore a decade or two ago, even some linguists were subject to the culture's inherited simple-minded dichotomy between the two, as if oracy and literacy had each an inherent nature everywhere and always the same. It is now more common to speak plurally of *literacies,* and to recognize the shaping forces of cultural tradition and social occasion. Ethnopoetics helps us to see more of what is there. It can bring to light kinds of organization in oral discourse not hitherto recognized. The vital point is that speech and writing may contrast, not only in terms of elementary units of composition, lines as opposed to sentences, but also in terms of larger units, verses and stanzas, as opposed to paragraphs. And where oral discourse shows only rudiments of such architecture, or presence of such architecture only in restricted circumstances, linguistics may offer evidence of social change and cultural loss. When schools seek to develop in students a personal voice in writing, they seek to reintroduce a capacity that through most of human history has come into being with mastery of speech itself.

Notes

1 This chapter is based on a working paper circulated by the Graduate School of Education, University of Pennsylvania (Hymes, 1987c), and subsequently revised (Hymes, 1991a) in a tribute to Susan Kaldor and her dedication to a linguistics in the service of society. The presentation of the last narrative (Leona's) has been corrected and amplified.

2 This story, and the one that follows, are cited by Cazden (1970) from Labov, *et al.* (1968: 298–9), and are to be found on pp. 300–1 of the reprinting of Cazden's article in Pride and Holmes (1970). In Labov (1972a), the stories are marked by letters at the same points, as shown below (a–j, a–n).

3 The omission of *b* here is no doubt a printing error. The corresponding line in Cazden (1970) is marked (appropriately in that context, being taken from Labov, *et al.*, 1968, with '2'.

4 Labov (1972a) has only 'Then' at the beginning of this line, whereas the earlier publication has 'So then'. Subsequent omission of 'So' is more likely than its earlier interpolation. Also, the emphasis of double particle marking (both 'So' and 'then') fits the role of being the start of the second part of the story.

5 A draft of the published paper was presented at the 81st Annual Meeting of the American Anthropological Association, December 3–7, 1982, in Washington, DC. Michaels thanks Michael Silverstein for comments on the draft: 'His sensitivity to the poetics of the children's stories has influenced my analysis' (p. 30, Note).

6 Michaels was not able to identify these sounds with confidence, and I can think of no likely interpretation.

7 Michaels follows work of John Gumperz and John Trim, dividing speech sequences first into tone groups or intonational phrases. A phrase can be marked by a minor, non-final boundary (/), indicating 'more to come', or a major or final boundary (//). Leona's narrative has just one final boundary at the end. Close-set dots indicate a break in timing, and spaced dots indicate a measurable pause. She also distinguishes low and high fall and low and high rise; high (´)and low (`) accented syllables in the tone group; and acceleration (acc.) and retarding of tempo.

I indicate low rise, because it appears to be structurally important in this text, but by underlining the first sound of the word before which it is marked by Michaels (who marks it by a preceding comma). High accented syllables also appear to be structurally important. They are marked by Michaels by a bold acute accent over the vowel, as distinct from high rise, marked by an acute accent that is not bold. Acceleration by line also appears to be structurally important, and I refer to it beside the lines in question.

Michaels does not mention the bold macron used over ice in her line 2, and 'she' in her line 5 (over the h). I guess that it is emphatic level tone or stress. She does not mention the underlining used with the first 'g' of 'eggs' in line 3. I take it again to be emphasis.

8 Michaels reports (p. 33) that when played side-by-side, these two phrases are indistinguishable.

9 Acceleration is indicated in the presentation of the story by '(acc.)'.

10 The narrative analyzed in Chapter 9, recorded from a young African-American in New York City, also turns out to have a centering, as well as a linear, organization.

Bernstein and Poetics

In the introduction to his first book, Basil Bernstein (1971) described one of the experiments he undertook as a teacher at the City Day College in London. The students were on one-day-a-week release from work as messenger boys or from various industries and the London Docks. Bernstein wrote:

> During the first two years I realized that the problem was, in Forster's phrase, 'Only connect'. Not being a born teacher, I had to learn by sensing that structure of meanings which were latent in the speech and writing. All this may seem to be an exaggeration. One day I took a piece of a student's continuous writing and broke it up into its constituent sentences and arranged the sentences hierarchically on the page, so that it looked like a poem. The piece took on a new and vital life. The gaps between the lines were full of meaning. I took a Bob Dylan ballad and produced a second version in which the lines were arranged continuously as in prose. I invited the students to read both versions. I then asked whether they felt there was any difference between the two versions. Yes, there was a difference. Poetry among other things has something to do with the hierarchical, and so spatial, ordering of lines. The space between the lines, the interval, allowed the symbols to reverberate against each other. The space between the lines was the listener or reader's space out of which he created a unique, unspoken, personal meaning. This may be bad aesthetics, but we experimented, putting together often weird or bizarre, sometimes unexpectedly beautiful series of lines, and exploring the symbolic nature of the space. I became fascinated by condensation; by the implicit. In my teaching I covered a range of contents and contexts, and yet, despite the variations, I felt that here was a speech form predicated upon the Implicit. (1971: 5–6).

Bernstein went on to say that he wrote an account that eventually became the two papers (originally 1958; 1959) that began the volume being introduced. He further recalled his discovery of Sapir, Vygotsky and Luria, and the development of a conception of speech as orienting and regulative, as a starting point for his theoretical and empirical contributions. The cited papers do not themselves present examples of the experiments with poetic form. I offer evidence that the intuition as to the presence of poetic form was correct. It appears that speakers of English, and of many other languages, have a tacit ability to shape what they say in terms of lines and groups of lines, in other words, in terms of poetic form. First, however, I say something about the conception of speech to which these experiences led, that of its implicit form.

Sapir and Implicit Relations

Bernstein's reference to Sapir points out the affinity of his work with a fundamental tradition in linguistic anthropology, as developed in the United States. Let me place it in that regard. The tradition is based on what might be called the 'cognitive unconscious'. Users of languages produce and interpret complex relationships of which they are mostly unaware. Two consequences follow: being out of awareness, hence out of reach of conscious manipulation, these relationships can influence their users in ways of which the users are unaware; others must discover what these relationships are.

The effective founder of the discipline, Franz Boas, singled out the unconscious character of linguistic phenomena as one of two reasons that linguistics was essential to anthropology (and the social sciences). One reason was that much of what people do cannot be grasped if one is unable to understand and analyze what they say (and write). The second reason he put this way:

> Language seems to be one of the most instructive fields of inquiry in an investigation of the fundamental ethnic ideas. The great advantage that linguistics offers in this respect is the fact that, on the whole, the categories which are formed always remain unconscious, and that for this reason the processes which lead to their formation can be followed without the misleading and disturbing factors of secondary explanations, which are so common in ethnology, so much so that they generally obscure the real history of the development of ideas entirely. (Boas, 1911: 70–1).

Whether Bernstein read Boas, I do not know, but Sapir, whom he did read, was recruited into anthropology by Boas and shaped by his outlook. Sapir's great book, *Language* (1921), still read and used in classes, refined and enriched the Boasian analytical conception of language in terms of the dimensions of grammatical categories and grammatical processes. Sapir's insightful essays on language and social life built on the thesis of unconscious patterning (cf. Sapir, 1927). He returned again and again to the antinomy between the relative autonomy of linguistic form and its inseparability from social life. He knew the lure of the study of linguistic form for its own sake, and he knew the need to understand what language is for those who use it.

Boas reconciled the tension by distinguishing between the short run and the long run. In the long run language responds to cultural need, but in the short run it can shape thought. That is a kind of autonomy for language, a mode of existence that makes it more than a pliable means, makes it a separate force. In the pioneering American Indian grammars that he wrote and guided, Boas stated the composite ideal of autonomous form and force: 'The grammar has been treated as though an intelligent Indian was going to develop the forms of his own thoughts' (Boas, 1911, p. 81).

In his own career Sapir emphasized first autonomy, then inseparability. Whorf's thesis of linguistic relativity is a development of Sapir's, who coined the term, a development even more trenchantly phrased and intently pursued (see discussion in Hymes (1966; 1970b); Silverstein (1981), and now the work of Lucy (1992a; 1992b)). It emphasized both short and long run. When a form of language and a form of life developed together over a period of time, patterns of language and conduct, of expression and expectation, would become congruent. The presence in a language of categories and of distinctions that must be made, if the language is used at all, the implicit patterning of so much of meaning, and the relative stability of language make language central to the transmission of such patterns to children.

Ideology and Equality

There is what could be called an 'ethnolinguistic theory of ideology'. What Bernstein has developed in the course of his work can be called a 'socio-linguistic theory of ideology'. The ethnolinguistic tradition, as it developed before the Second World War, thought in terms of a *language* and a *culture*. The world was implicitly taken to be a horizontal map: here a people, language, and culture; there a people, language, and culture. Difference was difference between separate, autonomous groups.

Bernstein, a sociologist working in a complex society, recognized both linguistic form and social relations, but necessarily in terms of a plurality of styles and social positions. Styles and social positions are only sometimes side by side. More often, they are superimposed, stratified. Some control others.

I write in this almost childlike way because this simple idea did not enter into the thinking of most critics of Bernstein's work. They might work in the largest cities of the world. The conception of differences among peoples, languages, and ways of life remained the traditional anthropological one of equivalence. Class position might be part of placing people, but not of assessing them. Differential access to resources there might be, but so far as ability was concerned, class had no cost (cf. Labov, 1970).

Bernstein has independently pursued a path parallel to that of Bourdieu (see, for example, 1991). Perhaps that is why Bourdieu has misrepresented Bernstein's work, stating (1991; 53) that Bernstein does not relate the elaborated code to social conditions of production and reproduction. Bernstein devoted at least 20 years of research to just such relations (Bernstein, 1990), and wrote the basis of his paper on 'Class and Pedagogies: Visible and Invisible' (1973/1977b) while visiting the Centre de Sociologie Européenne directed by Bourdieu!

Bourdieu is frequently cited in linguistic anthropology and sociolinguistics in the United States, but Bernstein is not. One reason may be that Bourdieu's writings are in an international idiom shared with other writers who have come to the fore in the last two decades and address social life in a broader way. Bernstein deploys a terminology and conceptual framework that has remained much his own, and his written use of it can be formal and severe. (Bernstein's oral presentations may be as engaging as Exodus, but the written theoretical statements can resemble Leviticus). Again, Bourdieu deals with issues of class in a way openly acknowledging Marxian tradition; Bernstein's Marx-like insights seldom mention that tradition. The fact that he places a fundamental analysis of social control in the context of Marx, Gramsci, and Foucault (Bernstein, 1990: 133–4) goes unnoticed (but cf. Hatlen, 1979). Neglect may be partly also because the immediate generation is in the habit of looking not to England, but to France, for social thought and writing about 'language'. The linguistic work of Michael Halliday and Ruqaiya Hasan, who have collaborated with Bemstein, has worldwide recognition but is almost never discussed in mainstream linguistics in the United States. If it were prominent, the relation with Bernstein would make his work better known to linguists as well.

The main reasons for neglect of Bernstein by linguists, and sociolinguists in particular, however, are two. First, he has been stereotyped, and misleadingly so. The fact that his work has steadily developed, that his theories have changed and grown, is not known. On the American scene he is understood (if 'understood' can be used) as someone who divides the world into two kinds of people, one of which is irrevocably linguistically inferior and likely to be black (as in the account of his work in Crystal (1987: 40). A young anthropologist recently told me that as a student she found Bernstein's account of restricted code to describe her own family but was told by a faculty member not to read him.

Indeed, it would be news to most of those who know his name to learn that much of his work has concentrated on the ideological role of the supposedly superior code, the elaborated code, and on the way in which pedagogy is central to reproduction of a social order, or that one of the most sensitive, well-balanced studies of white and black interaction is by a student he directed (Hewitt, 1986).

The case is like that of Whorf. A qualified and even nuanced view of the role of features and styles of language in shaping thought and behavior has been taken to be a simple-minded determinism. Neither Whorf nor Bernstein is ordinarily read carefully and completely. The case is like that of Whorf also with regard to the second main reason for neglect. If the view was properly understood, it would be not be welcome.

Both Whorf and Bernstein address the connection of language and social life in terms of constraint. The ways in which language is used constrain what is thought and done. That was plausible to a generation of anthropologists and associated linguists who understood differences among groups of people in terms of differences in culture. About 1960, however, the rise of transformational generative grammar to dominance carried with it, in Chomsky's formulation, a disdain of difference. The fundamental structures of language were considered to be innate, powerful, and operative early in the life of the child. Language was not learned, but acquired. Regularity came from within, not from without. There was no point to adding more data from different languages. The universal basis of all language was within reach, and introspection by the linguist as to his or her own language would suffice.

Whatever the degree of truth in this perspective, it has remained strong through various transmutations. It is not without rivals, now a number of them, but it has triumphed, if not in content, then in form. Formal, abstract analysis of the structure of language is identical with linguistic theory. In the 1950s, the linguists who had developed what has come to be called 'American structuralism' had a sense of having reached a plateau from which it would be good to look around. There was a surge of attention to the study of paralinguistics, kinesics, the psychiatric interview and cultural behavior. The kind of linguistic models being pursued were close enough to observable speech to be considered instruments of social and cultural investigation as well. That changed. The issues central to linguistic theory came to have to do with implicit rules and features, possibly innate. The issues were often internal to a model, only tangentially connected with behavior. The kinds of skill that would permit someone to transcribe speech and to analyze overt form in ways useful to others (including native speakers), became peripheral.

The goal of linguistic theory was stated to be an ideal speaker–listener member of a homogeneous community. In effect, linguistic theory adopted Feuerbach and rejected Marx. Language was to be understood in terms of human essence; members of a community were to be understood as related naturally, through a linguistic equivalent of Durkheim's mechanical solidarity and what A. F. C. Wallace later called a replication of uniformity. Marx's understanding of a community as an ensemble of social relations, Durkheim's organic solidarity, and what Wallace called an organization of diversity were effaced (see discussion in Hymes (1974: 47, 121–2).

This turning away from diversity and social constraint was widely shared with cognitive psychology and what has become cognitive science. To be sure, the very extremism of Chomsky's position helped stimulate the self-conscious development of sociolinguistics. What had seemed too obvious to mention (the importance of diversity with respect to language) became a position to be defended and developed. Concern for the maintenance of minority and ethnic languages has come to see Whorf's respect for diversity as a positive precedent. Work on semantic patterning and metaphor has taken on something of the character of cultural anthropology. Social constraint with regard to language has come to the fore in both linguistics and elsewhere through feminist scholarship. And a large number of scholars in the social sciences, some of them concerned with language, have taken up a concern with power.

It remains that even linguists who study diversity and power may be unwilling to acknowledge inequality. External inequality, yes. Speakers of a certain variety may be discriminated against. A variety of speech may be restricted in its use. Perhaps the variety cannot now express certain meanings or be used in certain activities. It remains that it could be developed to do so. All normal human beings are equivalent in general linguistic ability, and all human languages can be developed to express new meanings and serve new needs.

There is a fundamental truth to that. It is the truth of the potential equality of languages. If English is now a world language, Anglo-Saxon was not. If circumstances had been different, Irish or Frisian or Catalan might have the place that English now has. This liberal position was enunciated by Boas (1911), that in the long run a language could do what its culture and community required. It is a liberal position that stands against a variety of kinds of prejudice. In justifying respect for all languages, it also justifies attention to all by scholars.

The difficulty is that potential equality is taken as equivalent to actual equality (see discussion in Hymes,1993a; Chapter 10 in this book). It is as if history, like class, had no consequences. Let one language become an instrument of technical invention and research, explicit logic, schooling, and a multitude of metalinguistic activities. Let another language be restricted to the home and life in a local area. What can be done in the two will not be the same. But fear of giving aid and comfort to prejudice has inclined many linguists to ignore the obvious. What if only some languages are now world languages of science, and few if any will join that club? If country after country relegates some of its languages to a permanently local, limited role, what will be used and taught in different levels of schooling, and what money will be available for development of materials? What if many users of a world language do not acquire much of its resources? If even where a language of marvelous structure survives, no one can perform myths and rituals, use it in once elaborated ways? What if children of immigrant workers end up with only impoverished command of two languages; that of their parents and that of their present country (for example, Moroccan children in The Netherlands)?

The practice of most linguists in the United States is not to draw conclusions from such facts. The notion of effective equality of all languages and speakers is too highly valued as a weapon against prejudice and a justification of uniform practice. To be sure, exceptions increase. Adequate study of pidginization and creolization must take for granted that languages, and those who use them, change in what they are able to do (see Hymes, 1993a; Mühlhäusler, 1986; Romaine, 1988). The subject of obsolescent languages has been opened up, and an important literature is emerging (see Dorian, 1989, 1994).

The study of oral narrative can extend understanding of potential equality and at the same time deepen understanding of forces at work in shaping actual competence. The attractive result of discoveries in ethnopoetics is that human beings generally have ways of giving shape and point to narratives, ways that seem almost inherent in language (cf. Hymes, 1991b). At the same time opportunity for developing and using such patterning is dependent on social circumstance. It may not be recognized and, in a given language, it may not survive. The patterning is mostly out of awareness, and it is different from kinds of patterning to which speakers, teachers and scholars attend. It is a matter of relations among lines.

It is commonplace in social science today to present what speakers say in lines. What is almost never attempted, is to look for relations among the lines. Again and again, however, what speakers say in recounting experience can be found to be given shape by patterns of relations among lines. Much of local meaning and larger significance are implicit in such patterning. Yet such accounts are usually heard or read as newspaper articles and prose stories. Information is sought; examples of already determined categories are sought. What is uncommon is to look for signals of form, to expect what has been said to display a close covariation of form and meaning, to be an expression of a narrative competence that can be said to be poetic in the sense of implicit form. (An exception is Hatlen (1979, p. 154) who argued for the poetic character of working-class speech in terms of a high degree of concreteness and perceptual precision, an important cognitive and stylistic trait that is missed by those who argue that such speech is as abstract as any other. Hatlen saw himself as building on Bernstein (and Whorf) in this regard.)

A Text from South-Central Harlem

Let me show how Bernstein's early insight into the poetic character of line-by-line oral expression can be realized by this perspective. I do this by considering a text analyzed by Labov. In the course of his pioneering research into sound change in New York City, Labov studied narratives as well, notably ough not exclusively) narratives by young African-Americans, and eloped an influential framework for narrative analysis.

Labov's Approach

Labov defined narrative first of all in terms of clauses that are temporally ordered. A change in the order of the clauses would change the temporal order. Not every way of recapitulating past experience is narrative, but only that way in which the order of inferred events is matched by the order of clauses (Labov, 1972a, p. 360). Labov mentioned syntactic embedding and the past perfect as alternatives.

What we are to call stories that use other ways is not said. The problem does really arise (cf. Leitch, 1986: 12, 16–17). Use of 'narrative' for temporally *oriented* stories, however arranged (Leona's story in Chapter 8; Laurence Sterne's *Tristram Shandy*) does usually prevail, but the purely temporal order singled out by Labov requires a modifier. Perhaps 'linear narrative' would serve.

A minimal narrative is a sequence of two such temporally ordered clauses (Labov, 1972a: 360-1). Narratives might consist only of temporally relevant clauses, but of course many do not. Labov focused on a contrast between narrative progression and 'evaluation' (in which narrative progression is suspended (p. 374)). There may be an absence of evaluation, that is, of personal relation to what is recounted. There may be a richness of evaluation, as in the story studied here, such that devices conveying evaluation occur in a variety of places.

All this is part of an adaptation and extension of categories from traditional rhetoric. A famous text of the time (Brooks and Warren, 1949: 312) had distinguished four categories: Exposition, Complication, Climax, and Denouement. Labov and his co-workers recognized six categories: Abstract, Orientation, Complicating Action, Evaluation, Resolution, and Coda. These six are said to constitute a fully formed narrative.

Briefly put, an Abstract summarizes the story; an Orientation identifies time, place, participants, and activity or situation; a Complicating Action evidently need be no more than a second action following a first. (That is a way to make sense of the remark made by Labov (1972a, p. 363) that 'complicating action has been characterized in the preceding section 1', and the remark that 'Only c, the complicating action, is essential if we are to recognize a narrative, as pointed out in section 1' (p. 376). (The term 'complicating action' itself is not used in section 1).)

Evaluation has to do with point. Codas signal a close and bridge the gap between the time of the narrative and the present.

The five main dimensions can be seen as answers to questions (Labov, 1972a p. 370):

Abstract: What was this about?
Orientation: Who, when, what, where?
Complicating action: Then what happened?
Evaluation: So what?
Result: What finally happened?

Whose Questions and Answers?

Labov presented these categories as universal, as in effect a universal description or definition of fully formed narrative. They have often been accepted as such. A recent book concerned with literature for children accepts them in just this way (Hurst, 1990: 95–7). The categories and the questions to which they are taken to be answers are taken to be, in effect, a definition of narrative as an ideal type.

The general difficulty with such definitions has been stressed by a leading folklore scholar (Ben-Amos, 1992). In the Native-American and English language narratives I have analyzed, it is true that something usually can be found to fit these categories. That is not the same as finding the categories illuminating. Finding something to fit the categories is not proof that the associated questions fit. A story may answer questions specific to a tradition of which it is a part.

For example, many Native American stories of the trickster–transformer are not answers to these abstract questions, but meditations on the question: What is the nature of this fundamental figure? In Chinookan narratives and some others, the narrative answer is in terms of two cultural dimensions – being smart and being proper. To be smart is to be alert to what is happening and to interpret it realistically. To be proper is to know norms and maintain them. What happens is to be understood in terms of the relation of a principal actor to these dimensions: one who is both smart and proper succeeds, thus giving the story a happy, perhaps heroic ending; one who is neither fails, usually a numskull held up as a comic object lesson; one who is proper, but not smart, invites tragedy; or one who is smart, but not proper, can at best return to what had been before or start again.

When the trickster–transformer is both smart and proper, in the sense of serving the nature and interests of others as well as himself, he succeeds for both. When what he takes to be an interest is against the nature and interest of others, he fails. Sometimes a narrator chooses sides, as it were, underscoring respects in which Coyote is to be condemned, or highlighting respects in which Coyote is to be condoned and enjoyed. Occasionally one discovers a set of narratives in which aspects of Coyote's nature seem to be explored for their own sake (cf. Hymes, 1987a; 1995a; 1995b).

Let me indicate two ways in which effects associated with evaluation in Labov's analysis work differently in narratives from the Chinookan-speaking peoples of the Columbia river in Oregon and Washington, and many other

Native-American peoples. These narratives do usually begin with a conventional form of orientation: Some one (or more) was somewhere. In Chinookan often a second element says that someone always did a certain thing. That element tags the character in question as good or bad and thereby predicts the corresponding element of the outcome. A woman who is always out digging roots (obtaining food) will not come to ill. A boy described as mean to his playmates will in the end be deprived. Such initial evaluation is not emotional and is not embedded in the narrative proper (cf. Labov, 1972: 372ff). It does not suspend the action, but occurs before it begins.

Suspension of action is identified with evaluation in Labov's material. In Native-American narratives a line of action may be suspended without evaluation, and without a break in succession of temporal clauses. What happens is that realization of a formal expectation is delayed. The main line of action is amplified.

In Simpson's 'The Deserted Boy' (Hymes (1981: 142–83; 1994), the boy fishes five times. The outcome of the first four times is given succinctly. Each time there is one more fish. Each time is parallel in form: a single set of lines, or verse, beginning 'Now then. . .Now again. . .Now again. . .Now again . . .'. The fifth time parallel form is maintained, but the lines do not say what is caught.

> Now again did he go to fish for the fifth time,
> now five times the boy had fished,
> now he had become a grown man.

This fifth verse, concluding the scene of which it is a part, uses 'now' in a summative way, not only about fish, but about the deserted boy. Now he had become a grown man. That implies some power had taken pity on him and entered into a relationship. Who it is, and what he receives, are both held over to a separate scene, a double outcome to be resolved there.

The boy examines his line and finds a cooking trough brimful with special food, huckleberries and salmon. The daughter of a power living in the river has taken pity on him and has given it, implying there are other blessings to come. He sings again and again in celebration (cf. Hymes, 1981: Chapter 4).

I call this device *extraposition*. What is expected at one point is extracted and placed outside that sequence. Another example occurs in a Zuni narrative. Coyote learns a song from Old Lady Junco, loses it, and comes back for it. The fourth time (the Zuni pattern number is four) she sees him coming, and at the point in the scene at which one would expect the outcome of the fourth time, the narrator says instead that Old Lady Junco put a rock inside her blouse. The outcome of the fourth time is a scene in itself, a scene (the fourth) longer than any of the others. In it Coyote's fourth request is made six times. When Old Lady Junco twice does not answer at all, he threatens her and counts out loud four times, then jumps at her and breaks his teeth on the rock. Again, immediate outcome is delayed for sake of an extended finale. This is dramatic suspense – evaluation, one might say – of the dramatic importance of what happens, but there is no break in succession of temporal clauses (cf. Hymes, 1982; Chapter 6 of this book).

Examples such as these show that oral narratives have more than a single level of successive action and have groupings of lines that answer to expectations of form other than those posed by Labov's questions. Still, many have accepted the Labov model, as if in order to grasp the meaning of a narrative it is enough to grasp it as an answer to the questions cited earlier. Acceptance of the model sometimes has carried with it an assumption that in order to grasp the form of a narrative it is enough to segment it according to these categories. Hurst (1990) appears to act as if this were so.

The difference between categories such as those developed by Labov and the approach taken here is one of being both more inductive and more theoretical. Finer relations and further architecture are both sought and expected. The seeking can involve several stages of attention to the verbal details of the story, such that one seeks not only to segment it, but also to discover its rhythms and repetitions. The expectation is grounded in a body of experience in the last two decades as to the range of formal relations and resources narrators may deploy, in finding again and again that the deployment constitutes a coherent whole; and in discovering unanticipated themes and concerns through the formal relations.

On such an expectation, two short narratives from Labov's (1966) monograph were found to have ethnopoetic patterning (Hymes, 1991a, revised as Chapter 8 above), one indeed having an evaluative point where none had been seen. (I shared these analyses with Labov some years ago.) The three stories presented in an important paper of 1982 (quoted later) also have such patterning. Here I examine a story from the major study of 1972 – one prominent in Labov's exposition (Labov, 1972a: 358–9), and used by Hurst (1990: 95–7) to illustrate Labov's approach. Let me exhibit the story first, then say more about an ethnopoetic approach in connection with its characteristics. The lines are taken from Labov. The relations among the lines, the shape shown, and indicated by markers, have been gradually discovered. Italics are as in Labov's presentation. Underlining is added to indicate significant repetition that is not line-initial.

'Well, one was with a girl. . .'
Told by John L.

What was the most important fight that you remember, [i] (A)
    one that sticks in your mind...

Well, one was with a girl   (B)
Like I was a kid, you know,

And she was the baddest girl,   5
    the baddest girl in the neighborhood.
If you didn't bring her candy to school,
    she would punch you in the mouth;
And you had to kiss her when she'd tell you.

This girl was only about 12 years old, man,   (C)   10
    but she was a killer.
She didn't take no junk;
She whupped all her brothers.

And I came to school one day   [ii]   (A)
    and I didn't have no money.   15
My ma wouldn't give me no money.

And I played hookies one day   (B)
[She] put something on me.

I played hookies, man,   (C)
so I said, you know,   20
    I'm not gonna play hookies no more
    'cause I don't wanna get a whupping.

So I go to school   [iii]   (A)
and this girl says, 'Where's the candy?'

I said, 'I don't have it.'   (B)   25
She says, powww!

So I says to myself,   (C)
    'There's gonna be times my mother won't give me money
        because a poor family
    And I can't take this all, you know   30
        every time she don't give me money'.
So I say,
    'Well, I just gotta fight this girl.
    She gonna hafta whup me.'
I hope she don' whup me   35

And I hit the girl, powww!   (D)
    and I put something on it.
I win the fight.

That was one of the most important.   (E)

Analysis of John L.'s Story

Labov (1972a) identified the lines of the story with successive letters of the alphabet; each such line counted as a narrative clause. He found the story to have all five of his categories, except the first (abstract), for which no identifying letter was given. The sequence of categories and lines, then, is orientation (a–p), complicating action (q–t), evaluation (v–y), resolution (z–bb), coda (cc) (1972b, p. 375).

A summary of the assignment of lines to parts has what must be an inadvertent slip: 'John L.'s narrative therefore fits the paradigm of Figure 9.1, with a long orientation section a–p, complicating action q–u, evaluation v–y, resolution z–bb, and coda cc' (p. 375). The discussion preceding this identifies a sequence of narrative events with q, r, s, t, and a set of five evaluative clauses with u–y. The evaluative section is also separately identified as u–y (p. 372). In the quoted sentence q–u . . . v–y must be a slip for q–t . . . u–y.

These letters correspond to line numbers in my presentation as follows:

a–p	(orientation)	3–22
q–t	(complication)	23–26
u–y	(evaluation)	27–35
z–bb	(resolution)	36–38
cc	(coda)	39

Here is a profile of the story as presented above, analyzed in terms of relations among lines that reveal an implicit architecture of several levels.

Profile

Scenes/Stanzas/Verses/			Lines	Features	Contexts
[i]	A	a	1–2	*Turn*	[Framing question]
	B	abcde	3, 4, 5–6, 7–8, 9	*Well*	[the girl]
	C	abc	10–11, 12, 13	*man*	[the girl]
[ii]					[Ma and me]
	A	ab	14–15, 16	*And, one day, no money*	
	B	ab	17, 18	*hookies, one day*	
	C	ab	19, 20–22	*hookies, man, said*	
[iii]					[Girl and me]
	A	ab	23, 24	*So, turn*	[he, she]
	B	ab	25, 26	*turn, turn*	[he, she] [first round]
	C	ab	27–31, 32–35	*So+turn, So+turn*	[deliberation] [he as to she$_1$, he as to she$_2$]
	D	(ab)c	36, 37, 38	*And I . . .*	[second round]
	E	a	39		[answer]

As said, the lines are taken from Labov, and indeed predicate clauses are often distinct lines in narrative traditions. The differences result from the kind of competence narrators are assumed to have. Narrators are understood to proceed in terms of expectations as to content (Labov's questions) and also expectations as to form. The narrative may be understandable as an answer to the question Labov posits as fundamental: So what? It will also be understandable as an answer to the question: What is satisfying (interdependence of) shape? In a word, not only 'What?' but also 'How?' A narrator is understood to proceed in terms of a double-edged competence, integrating sequences of incident, event, and image and sequences of appropriate form.

What Happens First?

Note that Labov did not assign a letter to the initial question. The narrative, however, responds to it. There are indeed three responses: an immediate answer, 'Well, one was with a girl'; a summative answer at the end, 'That was one of the most important'; and the narrative as a whole of which these are a part. An initiating question and a summative answer enclose the rest.

The event includes the talk of two participants, then, and indeed the question appears to be a part of the pattern of the opening scene, the first of three sets of lines. For the scene to have three sets of lines is in keeping with 3- and 5-part relations throughout the rest of the narrative. I conjecture that John L. had a sense of the question as part of an evolving discourse, and so it entered into the shape he gave to what he himself said. (On the shape that stories take in conversation as interactively organized, see Goodwin, 1990: 236–7, 279, and cf. Duranti and Goodwin 1992. On conversational narrative generally, see Goodwin, 1990: 231 ff.).

Where Does Narrative Begin?

If what John L. said had ended with line 13, one could consider the opening question as having been answered. The most important fight, one that sticks in the mind, does so because it was with a girl, and not just any girl, but the girl described.

Labov (1972a) assigned these lines and the rest of the lines through 22 to a single category and section: Orientation. On the present analysis, these lines are not one, but two sections. If the first of these is background to what happens, the second is certainly use of temporal clauses to enact past experience and as such a part of the story proper. Lines 3–3 are 'an elaborate portrait of the main character. . .*the baddest girl in the neighborhood*' (p. 364), to be sure. But what about lines 14–22?

Labov says that the 'first *narrative* clause [line 23] brings John L. and the girl face-to-face in the schoolyard' (p. 364; emphasis added). That is, the immediately preceding lines, 4–22, are *not* narrative clauses, not part of the story proper. This is to overlook the fact that lines 14–22 do not go with the lines that precede them; they do not directly follow. There is discontinuity. Lines 14–22 do have continuity with other lines, but with lines that succede them. Lines that Labov describes as beginning the narrative proper, lines 23ff., follow directly on lines 14–22. Lines 14–22 explain why the narrator is at school, lines 23ff. what happens at school.

Indeed, the opening lines of each of these sets (14ff.; 23ff.) are parallel. Both have the narrator going to school. Such change of location is a common way of indicating the opening of a new narrative scene, and both sets of lines have it. If line 23, bringing John L. and the girl face-to-face in the courtyard, is a narrative clause, so is line 14, bringing John L. to school in a recounted event, and lines 14–22 twice have time reference ('one day' in lines 14, 17). Time reference is also a common mark of a beginning of action. There is parallelism of ending point as well. Lines 14–22 end with desire not to get a 'whupping' from the mother. Lines 23–35 end with desire not to get a 'whupping' from the girl.

Each set of lines is a three-step series that is part of the point of the narrative, as an aspect of self-presentation. Each provides context for what happens next and support for the kind of person the narrator is, one who makes a courageous proper decision, and does so twice (not play hookies, just gotta fight this girl).

Such parallelism and proportion of words, theme, and placement is characteristic of oral narrative. It bespeaks organization not reducible to sequences of clauses, propositions, or actions. One and the same such sequence can be shaped in more than one way, to more than one effect. Such ethnopoetic organization is marked by parallelism and repetition (cf. Tannen, 1989: 97ff) and by implicit patterns of expectation.

Speech Acts Do Not a Difference Make

It should be noted that Labov subsequently revised his earlier conception. Much of previous work, he wrote:

> focussed on the elaboration of narrative beyond the fundamental sequence of narrative clauses. The main thrust of this discussion is in the other direction: to reduce the narrative to its skeletal outline of narrative clauses, and to outline the generating mechanism that produces the narrative backbone (1982: 227).

He concluded that:

> Though there are tying relations between sentences – anaphoric, elliptic – the coherence of discourse is not established at this level but a more abstract level of representation. Ultimately, the cohesion of the three narratives that we are examining does not depend on the sequence of narrative clauses but on the sequences of speech acts and actions that the narrative presents. (1982: 233).

Attention to a level of speech acts does not alter his basic conception of a narrative as a composite of that which advances the narrative line (the backbone) and that which does not. There is a single level of organization.

There is a limitation inherent in all such approaches. By focusing on the what of narrative, and neglecting the how, implicit architecture as a way of shaping of meaning is missed. (For an example in relation to the approach of Levi-Strauss, see Hymes, 1985a).

Ethnopoetic Dimensions

On what is implicit architecture based? Briefly put, on three considerations. The first is that oral narrative begins not with sentences, but with lines. One or more spoken lines are normally marked by certain intonation contours or tone groups as units that can be called verses. When contours are not available, implicit relations and lines can often be inferred from certain types of marker, repetition and parallelism.

The second consideration is that the relations among lines are governed not by sequence alone, but by equivalence (Jakobson, 1960). In traditional poetry we are used to meter and rhyme marking lines as equivalent. In oral narrative, lines commonly do not have meter to mark them internally or rhyme to match them. Rather, the verses that they constitute are grouped according to a few implicit possibilities. In American English the usual possibility is a sequence of three or five (cf. Hymes, 1991b; 1993b). In languages generally there appear to be two types of possibility; three and five, on the one hand, two and four, on the other (cf. Hymes, 1987a; 1991b; 1992a). Against the background of one of these patterns, a part of a narrative may be marked by recourse to the other, providing emphasis or intensity. Sometimes the two types of pattern have social meaning, as when relations of two and four are associated with women, three and five with men in narratives from the Tillamook Salish tradition of Clara Pearson (Hymes, 1993b). John L.'s narrative is organized in terms of relations of three and five throughout, making use in the section involving his mother of a common option, three pairs.

When there is only a transcription with which to work, as in this case, and not intonational contours, clauses, as noted, are close equivalents to what are usually spoken lines. Turns at talk are always verses (cf. the three verses of lines 23–26). Time expressions and particles, especially at the beginning of lines, commonly indicate verses. In John L.'s narrative, the first stanza begins with a marker much used in English, 'Well'. Three groups of the scene with the fight are marked initially by 'So', which does double duty as a formal marker and a semantically apt one, conveying consequence at this culminating point. Initial 'and' twice indicates parallelism within a sequence (lines 14, 17, and 36, 37). The address term 'man' is part of the signaling of lines 10 and 19 as new stanzas, and indeed 'man' occurs in a parallel position within the two scenes: They are the third and last stanzas of their scenes. Notice also that the opening words of line 10 – 'This girl' – indicate a new sequence through explicit resumption of the subject. In this first scene each of the two stanzas by the narrator (3–9; 10–13) begin with 'girl' succeeded by 'she'.

A set of verses that constitutes a stanza often enough has internal repetition. Notice the repetition of 'no money' in the first stanza of scene ii (lines 15, 16) and the interlocking repetition in the first lines of each pair of verses in the scene: 'one day' (14, 17) and 'played hookies' (17, 19). Again, the three verses of iii A (21–24) are each a turn with a form of 'say'. (Labov remarked that objects that make noises are said to 'say X', rather than 'go X' (1972a, p. 372, n. 9); in this context 'powww!'), framed by 'says', is evidently not only a noise, but a communication).

Change in location or participants commonly goes together with change of scene. There is close covariation of form and meaning in this regard in John L.'s story. Scene i introduces the girl at length, the narrator barely (line 4). Scene ii concerns the mother and the narrator. Scene iii tells the decisive encounter between the girl and the narrator. Scenes ii and iii each begin with change of location (came to school, go to school).

A stanza or scene may be marked internally by a grammatical feature, such as tense. Scene ii is in the past tense throughout. Scene iii goes into the present tense for almost all its first three stanzas (23, 24, 26, 27, 32; cf. Hymes, 1993a; Wolfson, 1982). (Lines 23–26 might be taken to have four verses, one for each line, but the internal makeup seems to be controlled by the three steps marked by 'says', 'said', 'says' (24, 25, 26). The first line in each of the sequences introduced by 'So' (22, 27, 32) appears to be introductory to what is said.)

A stanza can be expected to be coherent internally in terms of topic. It is no accident that the five verses beginning with 'Well' ([i] (B)) develop the theme of the *baddest girl*, and no accident, perhaps, that explicit elaboration of the theme, the 'baddest girl in the neighborhood', comes in the third verse. In a sequence of five units, the third and the fifth are the usual places of culmination. In this stanza the first three verses (1, 4, 5–6) appear to fit a common 3-step pattern leading to the emphatic culmination, the twice-repeated 'baddest girl'. At the same time this third verse can be seen as initiating a second, interlocking 3-step sequence, with the next two verses (7–8, 9) providing details. (Cf. the relations among the five stanzas of scene iii, discussed below.)

The next three verses are a separate stanza, indicated by the address marker 'man' and ending with a point that recurs at the end of each of the first three sequences, a boy being whupped: 'She whupped all her brothers' (13); 'cause I don't wanna get a whupping' (21); 'I hope she don' whup me' (35). Often enough a narrator brings successive sequences around to share a theme as an ending point. John L. does this with dramatic effect. When being 'whupped' comes around the third time, it is not a final ending point, but an intermediate one, followed by the fight and victory, five steps in all.

These kinds of effect are examples of the third consideration that informs ethnopoetic patterning – 'arousal and satisfying of expectation' (Burke, 1925). Those who are party to a tradition of narrative form are sensitive to things coming around at a third or fifth step, if that is the tradition, or a second or fourth, in the other type. Some aspects of a tradition are consciously known. If there are a series of sisters, or a series of events, people will be able to remark that one can expect four, or five, as the case may be. People do not remark on such expectations at the levels of verse and stanza. These pervasive relations are like much of syntax in this regard.

Doubling

Labov introduced the story with these words (1972a, p. 358):

> Among the young adults we interviewed in our preliminary exploration of southcentral Harlem, John L. struck us immediately as a gifted story teller; the following is one of many narratives that have been highly regarded by many listeners.

I hope to have shown that the gift involves more than the disposition of the categories of orientation, complicating action, evaluation, or resolution (and abstract and coda). The gift involves a skill specifically linguistic and literary, a skill in the disposition of lines among local relations that enter into larger levels of organization. In particular, in addition to the shaping of stanzas and scenes, the story shows a pointed shaping of emphasis in terms of doubling.

The entire event is in a sense a sequence of questions and answers. Within that context John L. gives both an immediate and a summative answer. In the first and second scenes the third and final stanza of each begins with a line ending in the address form, 'man'. Within the second scene the three stanzas are linked by the overlapping doubling of 'one day' and 'I played hookies'. The second and third scenes open in tandem with 'And I came to school one day', 'So I go to school'. The third stanza of each ends with not wanting a 'whupping'.

Here John L.'s skill with larger form is especially evident. The third stanza of the third scene is a point of culmination, but only of local culmination. It is the end of one sequence of three stanzas and the beginning of another. (This interlocking within sequences of five is common in traditions that use relations of three and five. Recall the five verses of scene i (B). For an example from Philadelphia, see the next chapter).

The first desire not to have a whupping was within the narrator's power; his decision was enough to avoid it. The second desire and decision was not in itself enough. The rest of the scene, taking the desire now as the beginning point of a three-verse sequence, shows the successful outcome in the fight. The third stanza in effect resolves the issue of what the narrator will do (stanzas ABC), and initiates the resolution of the relation with the girl as a whole (CDE).

This third stanza in the third scene is highlighted by the doubling of the initial marker 'So'. 'So' is often a major marker of stanzas in English narratives. Ordinarily one would take each occurrence here (lines 27, 32) as beginning a new stanza. There are two reasons not to do so. First, all the preceding stanzas of narrative action proper ([ii] ABC; [iii] AB) have consisted of pairs of closely related verses. The doubling of 'So' as initial particle here continues a pattern of pairing. That does not jar, given the limited use of 'So' elsewhere in the story. At this point it has occurred just twice (in the third stanza of [ii] (line 20), and at the beginning of the first stanza of this third scene (line 27). And the pair of verses so paired are closely related also. Both are reflections, spoken by John to himself. The first recalls the situation at home, as to his mother and money. The second considers the immediate situation, facing and fighting the girl. Each leads to a moral decision.

Herein is the second reason for taking the pair together as a stanza. Not to do so would disrupt the pattern of relations of three and five that has been maintained throughout the story. The result would be that the last line would be a sixth verse, standing outside the story. Yet it responds to the first line, which has been found to fit within the story's first scene, as the first of three steps. When the two verses of reflection, marked with 'So', are taken as a pair in a single stanza, the last line fits within the last scene, as the last of five steps.

Such reasoning gives John L. the benefit of the doubt, as to maintenance of pattern, and indeed, for ingenious symmetry. And it is to find the moral center of the story formally centered (see below).

In connection with the outcome, notice that doubling of the one expressive particle in the story underscores the question and answer to which the story may be seen as an answer, doubled from John L.'s standpoint: 'Am I the kind of person who can make the right decision, even when it requires courage? Yes.'

The first 'powww!' is the girl hitting John (26), unanswered. It echoes, recapitulates (doubles), the long initial account of her prowess. The second 'powww!' (36) is an answer, a reversal, John hitting the girl.

Expressive Alternatives

Labov noted in his analysis of the story that the two lines, 36 and 37, are not (in his terms) in narrative sequence. What they do, of course, is twice double the power of the blow, first lexically within a line (hit...powww!), then syntactically with a parallel line:

> 'And I hit the girl, powww!
> and I put something on it.'

Perhaps as a sequence of actions the order is indifferent, but expressively a different order has a different effect. Compare:

> 'And I put something on it,
> and I hit the girl, powww!'

The first order states and dramatizes the action, following it with a con-firming gloss. The second order signals an intention, confirming it with the final particle.

The proper way to consider these two lines probably is together with the third line with which on this analysis they form a stanza. Let me expand each alternative sequence of the first two lines in such a context. There is an implicit syllogism in each order.

> a   And I hit the girl, powww!
> and [because] I put something on it.
> [therefore] I win the fight.
> b   And [because] I put something on it
> [when] I hit the girl, powww!
> [therefore] I win the fight.

Alternatively,

> b   And I [really] put something on it.
> [so when] I hit the girl, powww!
> [therefore] I win the fight.

In the (b) form of these three-step formulations, the sequence of three lines fits a common pattern for three steps, onset, ongoing, outcome. The (a) form does not. The second line is a condition of the first, not something that follows it.

The difference does not depend upon three lines instead of two, or upon logical expansion (in brackets). The same relation holds if just the first two lines are considered. The alternative sequence (b) permits an inter-pretation in terms of temporal sequence, the first does not. But the first is the sequence actually spoken.

Given what John L. actually said, it is clear, I think, that temporal sequence is not intended, indeed, not wanted. What is intended is an outcome of a different kind. The essential step toward winning the fight is not a punch, but an intention: 'and I put something on it'. Moral resolve, the carrying out of resolve, is the key. And it is not a separate step, but part of a pair (body and spirit together, one might say).

Narratives answer to two elementary functions of language, presentational as well as propositional (cf. Hymes, 1979a). John L. has used presentational possibilities (of order) to establish what he wants to say. Moreover, the expressive pair makes the scene's four narrative stanzas (ABCD) consistent as a sequence of temporal pairs. The fifth stanza, of course, is the final line, a response to the initiating line of the whole.

Circles

The narrative has yet another kind of relation. The question that prompts the story and its explicit answer enclose the rest. The question is followed by the account of the girl as a fighter, and the answer is preceded by the actual fight with the girl; together, those two accounts constitute a second enclosure. At their center is the account of playing hookies and being punished by his mother. (I owe the observation of the three circles to Scott Johnson) .

These three spheres fit the three scenes of the story, an organization arrived at earlier and on other grounds. In one sense, the second scene is a step on the way toward the third. There is a sequence commonly found with a series of three: onset (background), ongoing (development), outcome, each having a relation to whupping (the end of the third stanza in each). In another sense, the second scene is a center, formally and thematically.

The centrality of the second scene is more than a matter of counting. It is this scene that initiates grouping verses in pairs. (There are two sets of pairs, the three of scene [ii] and the three that begin scene [iii]. It is this scene that has three pairs of verbal repetition (one day, no money, played hookies). Both are modes of intensification. Thematically, the second scene establishes John L.'s moral resolve in relation to his mother.

These relations, moreover, are repeated within the third scene, another doubling. The central stanza of the third scene is to it what the second scene is to the story as a whole. The central stanza is uniquely intensified (initial 'So' twice), and doubles the theme of moral resolve, recalling first the mother, then thinking of the girl. John L. enhances his victory at the end by enhancing his opponent at the beginning, but the will to fight has his mother at its heart.

In terms of shape and artistry, then, John L.'s story is, of course, a sequence of actions, as Labov's method can show. It is also a sequence of doublings, and a series of enclosing circles.

Conclusion

Labov has done much to call attention to oral narratives and to urge that they be treated with respect. Ethnopoetics, understood as the study of the ways in which oral narratives are organized as culturally modeled groups of lines, makes it possible to connect oral narrative with linguistics in terms of the study of discourse markers and organization and competence generally. Such a conjunction is in the spirit of Labov's own efforts to connect his findings about variation with formal studies of phonology.

But if ethnopoetics is to contribute to an understanding, not only of stories, but of those who tell them and hear them and of what happens to narrative competence, to storytelling itself, it must draw on Bernstein's realistic grasp of the complex communities and institutions of urban life.

The range of what happens to stories in the Bible, for example, from Sunday School classes to sermons to scholarly exegesis, within and across groups, can be articulated in terms of Bernstein's dimensions of framing and classification. In some churches, the one who reads the lesson from the Old Testament or Epistles begins by framing in his or her own words the point of what the congregation is about to hear. In other churches, the one who reads does not, and may even take on the voice of, say, Isaiah. What is the distribution in region and class of the two practices? In what Sunday School classes do children hear the original story (in what translation?), and where do they hear a teacher's retelling? Where does the story remain a story, discussed as such? Where is it transformed into a set of questions and answers about isolated facts? Why are some churches and television the same in this regard? Neither trusting others with the words of their source; both feeling called on to make the shape of telling their own, transforming genres in the process.

Such mediation in terms of institutional culture by local personnel is the focus of Bernstein's book on pedagogy. We are probably all aware of the pervasiveness of such mediations. A number of linguists have come to recognize the necessity of studying them. It would be just and instructive to realize that Bernstein began exploring them more than 30 years ago and is a pioneer in the study of language in recognizing class as not just a diagnostic attribute, but an active, specifiable force.

Chapter 10

Inequality in Language: Taking for Granted[1]

Preface

I will focus on social meaning as it is involved in evaluation of languages and of what can be said in them, more particularly, with the dialectic between actual and potential ability.

Many address these issues, not least those concerned with literacy and bilingual education, with language policy, the official English movement, and the like. Recent experiences have brought this aspect of social meaning home to me anew. I want to suggest that we are not always entirely frank and consistent. Let me consider three aspects of inequality in turn. Each involves a kind of taking for granted.

One aspect has to do with potential equivalence. A second has to do with equating what is potential with actual ability. A third has to do with oral narrative.

I will talk in terms of 'language'. Most people do, including linguists, and the issue of inequality is historically associated with the notion of 'language'. The true subject, of course, is not 'language' alone, but repertoire – the mixes of means and modalities people actually practise and experience. Study of communicative repertoires makes the question of inequality all the more salient, if only because repertoires inescapably involve choices among alternatives. Much of what I say is a recollecting of things already known, but often enough, it seems, left out of account.

Potential Equality

Linguists tend to take for granted that languages, and varieties of language, are (*potentially*) equal. That users of any have a right to life, liberty (autonomy) and the pursuit of meaning. This assumption is foreign to many outside the field. That foreignness is clear to those who work with and on behalf of minority languages. Within theoretical linguistics, the matter is not likely to arise. If it does, the focus is on potentiality. That has a history.

Linguistics is rather recent as a separate discipline. The Linguistic Society of America was founded only in 1924. Many of its founders were conscious of a need to dispel misconceptions about language. They were conscious of working against popular, even learned, conceptions about language, conceptions which relegated many languages, especially unwritten ones, to primitive status, as lacking sufficient vocabulary, even regularity of grammar, or at least as deficient in some respect. Much of the general linguistics of the time was a projection of acquaintance with the languages of one region, Europe. To combat such preconceptions was an important part of the mission of linguistics itself. Boas, Bloomfield, Sapir, Whorf and others took it as part of their mission.

Their egalitarian perspective extended to varieties within a language. It was clear that many notions of correctness had grown up, even been invented, in the course of instructing an aspiring middle class in verbal manners. Seen against the history of the language, and beside other languages around the world, many preferences of pronunciation, or construction, were arbitrary. Many explanations of preferences were secondary rationalizations. The choice of a standard had little to do with intrinsic qualities, much more to do with politics, class and location.

In sum, such differences among languages were not to be ranked on a scale of superiority. Differences within a language had social meaning for its users, and might be ranked by them, but such rankings were not intrinsic to the linguistic features themselves. They were the result of secondary association. One and the same pronunciation of 'bird' [bəid] might be stigmatized in New York City, admired in Charleston. Diversity of structure went together with equivalence of function.[2]

The great, liberating consequence of this was to sever the age-old connection between verbal trappings and personal worth. Character does not come in one accent alone; intelligence has many voices.

We take this so for granted within linguistics that we may forget to teach it. I remember some years ago, in an anthropology course at Penn, when a question revealed that a student had just those notions about 'primitive' languages that, one assumed, the labors of Boas, Bloomfield and Sapir had driven from the land. I had said nothing about them in class. Were it not for a chance question, that student (and others?) would have passed through the class with such notions intact.

The truth is that we must never take for granted that what we take for granted is known to others. *Elementary assumptions of linguistics can be liberating for those to whom they are unknown.* The task of confronting misconceptions about the status of languages, as languages, may never be over. A victory which may seem to have been won by those such as Boas and Sapir and

Bloomfield will continue to need to be won. In the United States there are people, progressive in outlook, who are surprised to meet or hear of someone who studies Indian languages. Are they really 'languages', our daughter was asked by such a person. With regard to the languages of the Aborigines in Australia, Blake (1991) reports: 'Even among highly educated people the question is still asked, "Do these people have real, full languages" (vii). His book is intended to illustrate that this is the case, and to encourage further inquiry.

Wherever there is a variety of English that differs from a certain standard, there will be those who will see it, not as different, but as deficient. Yet the burgeoning creativity of those in Africa and Asia and the Pacific, replanting English, cross-breeding English, their novel integrations of resources, add color and beauty to the world, to those who can see them as configurations of their own (cf. Kachru, 1990).

The task may continue to be true indefinitely with what can be called the 'hidden injuries of accent'. I have argued in the past that there are those with a vested interest in bemoaning the decline of the language, and that even if everyone spoke a recognizably standard English, they would create a hierarchy, say, of adverbs, and continue to lament. At present we are far from so esoteric a condition.

Students may come to a class in sociolinguistics, believing their normal speech intrinsically inferior, and leave with that sense of stigma never having become known.

Recently one spring my wife, Virginia, taught a large undergraduate class in sociolinguistics. The size of the class was frustrating, the students mostly anonymous faces. She decided to ask each student to write a journal, which she would read and respond to. The journals disclosed personal experiences and beliefs as to difference and deficiency, right and wrong, that would otherwise have been invisible. The journals disclosed effects of the course as well. Learning about diversity from the standpoint of linguistics made a difference to some, who could now separate what was socially necessary for them to use from prejudice against other forms of speech, including their own. It made a difference to one student just to learn that what she and her family spoke was called 'Highland Southern'. That it had a name. A name added identity, a degree of legitimacy.

Linguistic assumptions may come to be taken for granted without our realizing it. This was brought home to me recently by a colleague who works in the Caribbean. He stressed continuing prejudice in education there against Jamaican Creole, the continued dominance of the view that only standard English counts, how that affects what is done and who can do it. That should not have surprised me, but study of pidgin and creole languages has grown immensely. Thirty years ago there were only a few scholars, a few significant studies. Now even a specialist can hardly keep track of the literature, and it influences other branches of linguistics. Languages once of interest to few are accepted as worthy of study by all. Even a specialist can forget that such legitimacy once had to be fought for even within the field, and, outside, still does.

In our own classes there are likely to be students with kinds of misconceptions we tend to forget, and for whom common practices of teaching and evaluation may be harmful. Indeed, we may have to face in our society an increasing authoritarianism, as in England. Here, as there, there may not only be practised, but mandated, the costly policy of teaching a single standard that Harold Rosen protests in a recent essay, 'The Nationalisation of English' (1991). Diversity of accent may be accepted in principle; so may appropriateness of different styles to different situations. Yet the practice may be oppressive, Rosen argues, if there is no allowance for contestation and negotiation.

Insofar as the issue is the primacy of (standard) English there is really no issue except a symbolic one, or perhaps a covert one. Students do recognize their social system, and that in it one language, and a version of that language, not their own, is firmly in place, with a socal meaning for others that may not be their own (Edelsky, 1991, Chapter 2). Still, it makes a difference if one recognizes the circumstances, does not misrecognize them, understands that they might be otherwise.[3]

In this context one should note the widespread assumption that a brain has room for only one language. If that were true for Americans, they would have to be classed as biologically deficient, since multilingualism is normal in most of the world. Note the frequent opinion that difference of language is divisive. Difference of language is not itself divisive; it can become a symbol of conflict in certain economic and political circumstances. A good way to make a language a symbol of conflict is to repress it.

Actual Inequality

As linguists, we often act as if the kind of equality just discussed is the whole of the story, as if the potential is the actual. Rankings of languages, and of features of languages, are secondary and arbitrary. Where differences exist, what matters is a) relativity, and b) potential equality (or equivalence). As to abilities, the preferred image, the representative anecdote, is that of Chomskian theory, the amazing unfolding ability of the growing child.

All this involves an equation of the potential with the actual. The ideal picture is poignant, given the realities of our world, where pregnant women may not have enough to eat, and where judgments of subordination can be enforced.[4]

We may shut out findings that suggest actual inequality. A methodological relativism – all languages are equal in the sight of science – is translated into the ideology that all languages are equal in the sight of humankind, or should be. Of course they should be, when evaluation is based on unfamiliarity or prejudice. But people often know perfectly well that they can accomplish some things in one language or variety that they can not in another. Sometimes the reason is a secondary prejudice, a matter of acceptability. Even then knowledge that the privileging of one pronunciation or style over another is arbitrary does not remove the privilege. And sometimes the reason is truly matter of what can be done. Any language has the potential to become a language in which scientific medicine is practised. Most languages do not now have the vocabulary, discourse patterns and texts.

The projection of actual equality echoes an older time and the rise of linguistics in the nineteenth century. The origin and history of peoples was a nineteenth-century preoccupation. Linguistics rose to intellectual prominence through its success in tracing common origins backward, subsequent diversification forward. The implicit picture was of the peopling of the world by groups marked each by a single, autonomous language.

This implicit picture has continued well into this century. It was the unstated premise of earlier discussions of linguistic relativity. The Hopi language could shape the Hopi view of the world because, it was implied, it was the only language the Hopi learned and used. The language was autonomous. Whatever came to expression in it, or did not, had its origin and explanation among the Hopi.

We know that the world in which we live is actually one in which communities with a single, autonomous language are scarce. Since the emergence of what Immanuel Wallerstein calls 'the world-system', the great process affecting languages has not been separation and diversification, but contact and reintegration. Of course there has always been multilingualism, and, within a monolingual group, a plurality of styles or registers. Ways of using language have always been defined in relation to each other, have always been potentially in competition with each other. All this has become the general case. Not only varieties, but most languages themselves are probably now alternatives within a repertoire. Most are not autonomous. What they can express is partly a function of their niche within the cultural ecology of a community and larger society, influenced by policies and funding for schools, resources for printing, and the like.

When I entered linguistics, the rightness of the equality of all languages was so certain that it was believed, and argued, that one could express anything in any language, translate anything into any language, that all languages were equally complex. Not that one had evidence. The statements were simply consistent with elaborations of an insurgent and triumphant world view.[5]

These statements were felt consistent with a belief in the cognitive relativity of languages. In effect, different structures, different styles, but equivalence of function. One took delight in differences, in surprises, in the wonderful way another language might do something.[6]

Another world view has become dominant, so that for some, it can be believed and published that there are no cognitive differences worth considering, that differences are superficial and without significant effect.

Linguistic relativity, which had seemed obviously true, came for many to seem obviously wrong. Whorf, whose name became attached to the notion, had seemed important and interesting, if not necessarily right; now he came to seem naive (and to some still does).

One of the rewards of surviving in the same line of work is that people rediscover their youth. The study of metaphor and cognitive bases for grammar and language now lends a certain respect to Whorf (Lakoff, 1987; Langacker, 1987; 1990; 1991; Lucy, 1991). Insofar as difference might imply incapacity, emphasis on difference once made Whorf seem bad – to Joshua Fishman and others. Now an emphasis on difference is seen to reinforce respect for minority languages, and Whorf has a role to play (Fishman, 1982). Peter Mühlhäusler and Rom Harré (1990) find it perfectly obvious that Whorf's claims are true for the individual who internalizes particular kinds of social meaning in learning the person-marking of a language.[7]

Perhaps one can live long enough to see the core of linguistics accept the consequences of a world of only partly-autonomous languages, and varieties of language, a world in which the development of a given language or variety for a certain purpose may have a cost which will not be met. In which it is recognized that the same language name does not entail the same means and abilities. In which it is recognized that the dimensions which govern the development of pidginization and creolization govern the development of all languages.

The historically derived character of *any* language has to do with:[8]

a scale of linguistic means, having regard both to outer form (simplification, complication) and inner form (reduction, expansion) in the various levels and domains;
b provenience of linguistic means, that is, confluence of traditions;
c scope of social role (restricted, extended), having to do with use within a group as primary or secondary means of communication, and between groups as well.
d contexts, with regard to selection and channeling of use; motivation and identification on the part of persons involved; the communicative repertoires of the persons involved; relations to other linguistic norms (Hymes, 1971: 83).

Contact and integration within a repertoire entail change in one or more of these dimensions. Since the emergence of a world-system, hardly any language has escaped such change. Some have expanded, some contracted, in use and consequently in means as well. A wide range of processes – standardization, pidginization, creolization, obsolescence – are aspects of a common history. It will take some time to develop adequate pictures for all this, an understanding comparable to that achieved for 'genetic' diversification. At least it is clear that potential equivalence is not adequate.

The social meaning of a language, in other words, is a function not only of immediate context, but also of *persistent* context. Over time some possibilities of meaning, expressive as well as referential, poetic as well as pragmatic, will have been cultivated, others not. Means are at hand for indicating and shaping some kinds of meaning, not others. Some kinds of expression have a cost that others do not. In short, means of speech can be evaluated in terms of characteristics that are not secondary, but *intrinsic*.

This is so even under conditions of community primacy and autonomy. Languages, varieties, verbal repertoires adapt and evolve, developing some means and meanings and not others. In an important sense Navajo over time became a language better suited for dealing with the American Southwest, not so apt for snow, more fit for maize, more fluent for the kind of cosmology expressed in Pueblo tradition. Translators know that there are things done in one language which cannot be done in another. Only if one divorces meaning from form can one claim that there is completeness of translation. Given pages enough and time, a meaning or an effect that takes one line in the original can be explained. Still the meaning is not the same. Meaning is partly a matter of means. Elaboration and explanation substitute or insert the meaning of a different genre. What was funny or trenchant or compelling in the profile of a single line is not so as a disquisition. The hearer or reader is made a student of the text, no longer a participant in immediate recognition. Intrinsic difference is all the more the case when a language or variety is socially constrained.[9]

As everyone knows in daily life, and especially those in the work of education, it is a fallacy to equate the resources of a language with the resources of (all) users. English is rich in vocabulary, but knowing it may still leave a user inferior as a narrator to someone in a Native American or African-American language tradition. Every community is diverse in relative command of the possibilities of the language(s) available. When one considers literacy, we are likely to live in a world in which almost everyone will be 'literate' in some sense, yet command of literacy cruelly stratified – often because the conditions under which people are introduced to literacy perpetuate inequality (Hymes, 1987d), sometimes because the kind of literacy expected may alienate them from their communities (Edelsky, 1991: Chapter 8, 'Risks and Possibilities of Whole Language Literacy: Alienation and Connection').

One must be willing to recognize that lack of equivalence is endemic to the world. Stigmatizing those who call attention to it (such as Whorf and Bernstein) is not a help. The kind of help that is needed is to describe and compare such cases, to recognize and analyze recurrent types of case, and to address what can be done. An important part of such help can come from those in education who necessarily address the actual inequalities of minority languages and language learners. If human beings are not only language-using animals, but also goaded by the spirit of hierarchy, as two elements of Kenneth Burke's definition of human beings would have it, then there will never be a lack of need for such work.

Oral narrative

These two aspects of any language situation, potential and actual, come together in narrative. Every community has narrative. Evidently it rests on an ability inherent in human nature, perhaps as an aspect of the ability for language itself.

Like much of language, much of the organization of oral narrative is out of awareness. Nessa Wolfson made a pioneering contribution in this respect, tracing use of the historical present in conversation. Many speakers are aware that in English a change into the present tense may dramatize what is said, convey immediacy: instead of 'And then I saw. . .', 'And then I see. . .'. What may not be realized is that there are occurrences in narrative that cannot be explained that way. That whatever else may be the case, switching into and out of the historical present may mark the beginning and end of a part of what is being said. The changing itself segments. It may organize narrative, unconsciously so.

Some years ago Virginia Hymes and I independently analyzed a narrative Nessa had noted down. We did so in the light of other forms of unconscious patterning that we had found in Native American languages. Nessa encouraged us in this. I would like to share now an analysis of one of her favorite examples (Wolfson, 1982: 25–7; 1989: 140). We refer to it by its first line, 'She's a widow' (see pp. 223–228 for text of narrative).

This analysis has passed through several stages. Narratives may follow an obvious pattern, but many do not. They will make use of principles shared with other stories, but in an individual way, having rhythms partly their own, a shape that varies and emerges. One has to live with such a story for a while, becoming sensitive to its details and themes, trying alternative ways of being true to both. A given analysis may prove to be one of a series of approximations. This analysis does seem to recognize detail, to be consistent, to show coherent development of themes.

To discover the patterning of oral narratives, one must start with lines and the ways in which lines constitute verses. One must go on to recognize relations among verses that constitute larger rhetorical forms. The second is a step that few so far have taken.

The story is presented in two forms. The first is the form in which it was published as part of the evidence for the conversational historical present – a continuous sequence of prose (Wolfson, 1982: 25–7; 1984: 140) . The second shows the story as a sequence of lines.[10]

The shape of the sequence is indicated by certain conventions. The first (or only) line of a *verse* is flush left. Verses go together in what can be called a *stanza*, and between stanzas there is a space. One or more stanzas constitute what can be called a *scene*, and a scene is identified by lower case Roman numbers at the margin.

There appear to be two basic types of organization. In many cases, the unmarked, or default, relation among elements is that of sets of two and four. For many other traditions, the unmarked relation is that of sets of three and five. English-speaking communities are not uniform. Some traditional story-tellers from the British Isles use two and four. English-language storytellers in the United States appear to use three and five.

At first it seemed that 'She's a Widow' might use relations of two and four, and have four scenes overall. Possible parallels in the opening stanzas suggested as much. Then it became clear that relations of two and four relations would twice separate parts of a conversational exchange; that two lines which initial capitalization and final period indicated should be taken as verses had not been recognized as such; that parallel remarks about making everything up should be recognized as ending points of parallel sections. All this fell into place when the narrative was seen as having five scenes and as using relations of three and five.

In traditions whose unmarked pattern is three and five, there is often a striking rhetorical relation, one of *interlocking*. It occurs in widely separated languages, in Chinookan and other Native American languages of the Pacific Northwest, in songs in the Kalevala tradition of Finnish, in northeast Philadelphia English. In a sequence of five elements the first three will go together as one sequence of action, and the last three go together as another. The third element is a pivot, simultaneously ending the one sequence and beginning the other. In the arithmetic of such narratives, $3 + 3$ can equal 5.

Interlocking holds throughout 'She's a Widow'. At the level of the story as a whole, the five scenes interlock. The first three report a situation, then an opportunity and strategy, then an outcome, acceptance of a bid. At the same time the third scene initiates three steps of acceptance: of a price, of certificates, of a date of settlement.

Each of the last three scenes thus involves a common theme, and a parallel outcome (acceptance); the third and fourth do so indeed in parallel fashion. Such coming round to a recurrent ending point is decisive for analysis (cf. the ending points of the last three sections of Part I of the story collected by Amy Shuman in Chapter 7).

The three scenes that have five stanzas also are linked internally by inter-locking. (The five lines of the first scene are a single stanza, and the last scene has three stanzas). In the second scene the first two stanzas (AB) are marked initially in terms of summertime, and the last two (DE) are marked finally by variants of 'making up a lot of things/everything'. The first pair bring in the realtor and the narrator; the last pair bring in the narrator's wife in conversation with the realtor. The two pairs are linked by a pivot (C). In this pivotal stanza the narrator finds out the actual amount bid for the house. The discovery is outcome to the stanzas in which he has become involved in an effort to buy the house, and onset of the stanzas in which he initiates a possible plan. In sum, stanza (C) is at one and the same time outcome of one series of three stanzas (ABC), and onset of another (CDE).

The third and fourth scenes both consist of pairs of conversational exchange. In each there are four pairs of exchange, followed by a paired call and acceptance. In each scene the third pair is a pivot. Someone states a condition (the narrator's wife in iii, the narrator in iv). The condition is an outcome of what has so far occurred, and an onset of the conclusion to follow. In both scenes the next (fourth) exchange has the realtor say the widow will not go for it. The final (fifth) pair, as said, is a call and acceptance. Again, AB(C)DE.

The fifth scene does not use interlocking, perhaps because its dramatic focus is different. There is demand and refusal, followed by acceptance, but not an abrupt shift. Perhaps pairs facilitate such a climax in the third and fourth scenes. In any case, the fifth scene does not have the realtor say she will not go for it, followed immediately by a call and acceptance. It has the narrator succeed in a protracted struggle over dates, or deadlines.

The three stanzas seem to be organized with a focus on their successive ending points. The first ends with the widow wanting October, and the narrator intending to get January. The second ends with the realtor going to her, and this time getting, not a call of acceptance, but rejection of January (reported in two verses, not one). The third stanza opens with three dates in a row (December, November, November 18th) in a first verse, returns to that third date in a fourth verse, and ends with a fifth deadline in the last, fifth verse, a deadline with a twist, for the narrator himself.[11]

The last verse returns the story to the present. No more widow, realtor, cousin or wife, or house to be bought, but suddenly, a house to be sold. In the last verse the deadline of three weeks perhaps echoes the deadline of forty-five days in the first verse. In any case the lines address the hearer, changing what is said from a story to a conversation of which the story is part. Perhaps it is not an accident that the lines rhyme ('now'-'now'), as if a closing couplet, or an analogue to formal words that return a Native American myth to the present. Nor an accident that all four of the verses, after the extended opening, are pairs of lines, as if the steady balancing of pairs of lines were a way of settling into a close.

On Alternation of Tenses

Verse analysis of the narrative gains further point and support by attention to the use of tenses. Use of the conversational historical present in relation to past and general present was indeed the focus of Wolfson's treatment of the narrative. This story from Philadelphia is one source of her conclusion that neither tense need be marked in itself, that what is marked is the switch, and that indeed the past may become the marked tense. Discovering the organization of the story in terms of verses, stanzas and scenes underscores this observation.

The short introductory scene begins with the general present (twice) and then has the past (twice). The second scene is entirely in the past for its first stanza (A), in the past, general present and past for the second stanza (B), and in the past, general present and past for the third stanza (C). The fourth stanza (D) begins in the past (twice) and then introduces a convention of the narrator, namely, *communicative acts are present tense* ('calls', 'figure' (followed by quoted thought), 'gets on the phone', 'says').

The exceptions are at points of structural emphasis. The third and fifth verses of the stanza, that is, *intermediate and closing culminations*, are marked with past tense ('told', 'made up'). The fifth stanza (E) has two verbs of saying, then like the fourth culminates in the past (made up).

The central scene [iii] has five pairs of verses. Its first four pairs are verbal exchanges between the realtor and the narrator's wife. All use present tense 'says'. The fifth pair is the outcome, the first of what are to be three outcomes for the theme of acceptance, and these two culminating verbs are also in the past ('got', 'was accepted').

The fourth scene follows the model of the third. There are four pairs of verbal exchange, all in the present, and then a fifth pair for the outcome, acceptance. Here the fifth pair is also in the present ('get a call', 'okay, she's accepted'). The present tense of '*get* a call' contrasts with 'got a call' at the end of the preceding scene. Possibly the local specialization of present and past tenses is presupposed, and the present tense of 'get' can be expressive because in its position of culmination the past has been used.

Alternatively, the present tense may have become so much the unmarked tense that now it carries through the whole scene and into the next. The fifth scene begins by repeating 'get', followed by non-communicative verbs now also in the present: 'do', 'picks up', 'take', 'goes', 'walk in', 'sign' as well as 'says'. These seem to be the two possibilities: a localized double reversal of marking, or a run.

In the fifth scene the present tense continues up to the culminating brace of verses of the second stanza (B), save one verb (line 120). Wolfson (1982: 36) says that the verb here expresses the real estate agent's astonishment when he discovers that the date was changed ('all of a sudden he looked at the agreement'). In short, the string of present tenses have come to be the background, amidst which a single past tense is expressive.

The remainder of the story is in the past tense. It follows the last assertive demand ('Deal's off' (line 128)). This ultimatum parallels the final demand in the preceding two scenes [iii, iv]. In those scenes the demand comes at the end of the fourth stanza. Here it comes just before the end of the second.

What follows again has to do with acceptance, but in scenes [iii] and [iv] acceptance was surprisingly sudden, short and sweet. Here the surprise is complication, a last minute suspension of resolution. The culmination is expressed, not by tense change, but by elaboration. In its first verse stanza (C) reports five moves in five lines (my date, her date, my date, we got it (she agrees), she backs off). For two verses the narrator then states his expectation that she would agree nevertheless, and then (fourth verse) he is proven right. The story of what the widow will accept is over.

The past tenses in these lines can be taken as equivalent to the concluding past tense of scene [iii]. In the arc of the last three scenes, then, the end of stanza [iv] stands apart. Perhaps its present tense is indeed expressive, not part of a continuity of line, a *sostenuto* as it were, but a *sforzando*, presupposing a perhaps personal convention that ending points are to be noticed in relation to each other.

Notice that the twist of the last verse is a twist in tense. Its present tense is neither expressive nor conventional (for communicative acts). What is said *is* in the present.

All this indicates that the expressive or evaluative role of tense change should be interpreted in relation to specific narrators, even specific narrations. There is good reason to doubt that any one calculation of the significance of the historical present will serve all occasions. (Cf. now the account of two tellings of a Scottish story by Leith, 1995).

Johnstone (1990: 82–3) notes Schiffrin's claim (1981), as against Wolfson, that the historical present is inherently expressive and specifically an evaluative device, and advances the hypothesis that in her own data from Fort Wayne Indiana, there is an evaluative role restricted to 'the say/go system' (that is, to the use of certain verbs in attributing dialogue).' She cites a story in which, whenever there is a tense difference in attributing discourse, it is the authority figure (police officer) whose words have the marked form, non-past for a past event. The nonauthority figure has always the unmarked form, the past tense.

Such a use is not limited to Fort Wayne. It appears in a long auto-biographical narrative by a man now working in New York City on Madison Avenue, recounting interaction between himself, as a student, and a woman flight instructor (Gallina, 1992: 7). Gallina's finding is part of an analysis into lines, verses and stanzas, and Johnstone's published Fort Wayne narratives lend themselves to such analysis as well. Interpretation of the narrative significance of the historical present in narrative generally is likely to be illuminated by knowledge of such relationships.

Overview

We see in this conversational narrative a thoroughgoing shaping of personal experience. A mode of shaping, which, in a myth by the last Kathlamet Indian able to recount myths, undergirds and articulates a wrenching vision of the end of a people. A mode of shaping which, perceived, gives point and proportion to what seemed to lack it, revealing meaning through implicit relations.

Perhaps more than anything else, oral narrative is an indication of the relation between potential and actual in language, the dialectic between potential equality and actual inequality. Every normal child may be born with the potentiality for such shaping, but not every community gives such shaping the same place. Oral narrative is central to a traditional Native American community, marginal perhaps to ours. Evidence there of the nature and shaping of the world, here something that can be dismissed as anecdote. Even when languages survive, there may be no one who any longer has the old skills, or is encouraged to develop them anew. In this aspect of language, many communities may have been richer before Columbus than they and many of us are now.

Too little is known of the life of oral narrative to say very much. All one can say is that it appears likely that language carries with it everywhere the possibility of giving experience the form of story, richly shaped, by means of equivalences and internal relations that make it a kind of poetry. The one universal definition of poetry is organization in terms of lines. That is what we see in this narrative recorded by Nessa Wolfson, and in many other narratives in English. When it comes to the possibility of poetry, Homer walked with the Macedonian swineherd, Li Po with the headhunting savage of Assam.[12] Recognition of this dimension of narrative may make it possible to find more meaning in, give more weight to what is sometimes dismissed as gossip or anecdote, yet is the only articulate form some experiences and lives achieve. Recognition of this dimension shows narratives from Native American communities, dismissed by some as repetitively dull, to be works of art. The working out of this dimension of narratives recorded in the past can be part of repatriation (Hymes, 1991c). Where a tradition has been lost, we can at least bear witness to what has been lost and help redeem its worth for its descendants.

We can indeed enable participants in traditions to take up such analysis themselves. Such analysis depends upon a linguistic perspective, a close attention to linguistic features and relations, to covariation of form and meaning, but it is a use of linguistic perspective that can be shared, that can be given away. To notice tone groups and intonation contours, to notice recurrence of particles, to notice groupings of turns at talk, to build up a ground sense of how resources such as these are deployed – to do that does not require a graduate degree, but a degree of training.

In sum, there lies ahead a vast work, work in which members of narrative communities can share, the work of discovering forms of implicit patterning in oral narratives, patterning largely out of awareness, *relations* grounded in a universal *potential*. whose *actual* realization varies. To demonstrate its presence can enhance respect for and appreciation of the voices of others.

Such discovery does not guarantee that what is said is true or admirable, but it continues the tradition of discovering in the oral what had not been recognized – relationships, order, and values thought to be restricted to the written. Oral varieties have not only grammar and regularity of change; their narratives have shape, often a thoroughgoing architecture.

Elementary Linguistics

The possibility of sharing brings up again the opening suggestion that a program in linguistics, socially concerned, should attend to the dialectic of potential and actual. There are many established varieties of linguistics. I would like to suggest one more.

One often thinks of branches of linguistics in terms of the study of groups of languages: Germanic, Romance, Chinese, Finno-Ugric, Athapaskan, Niger-Congo (including Bantu), etc. Sometimes one thinks of the study of types of language, such as tone languages, ergative languages, pidgins and creoles, or the study of aspects of language, such as phonology, semantics or historical linguistics. If there is any simple contrast, probably it is that between *theoretical linguistics* and *applied linguistics*.

These two labels can be misleading. Those who work with practical situations do not merely apply findings of theoretical linguistics, for the simple reason that theoretical linguistics does not take into account much of what needs to be known. It abstracts from social life altogether, or, if it models social life, abstracts from its actual patterns, often in an *a priori* way. Practical situations require a knowledge of language in use, and in terms of the situation itself. They require description of features of language and features of social life together. Application is not a matter merely of implementation, but a matter of acquiring new knowledge. Practical problems are a point of integration, of emergent configurations, if you will, on which an adequate theory of language in use will depend. Beyond this contrast between theoretical and applied, there is what one might call *elementary linguistics*. It is the linguistics someone needs, not to write a grammar, but to read one. To recognize that two transcriptions of a word in a language of concern are not significantly different. To discern that something has recurred in a conversation or a narrative. It is the linguistics that every student of human life should know, that one would like everyone to know, the linguistics that should be part of general education, indeed, of elementary education.

Such a linguistics would be equivalent to elementary literacy in linguistics. It would give a grasp of the sounds and forms of language in general. It would enable those not linguists to make use of material of concern to them.[13] It would enable them to recognize in narratives points of recurrence and relations of shape. It would enable students at leading universities to understand that when someone says 'fightin', they have not dropped a 'g', but substituted one sound for another, an alveolar nasal for a palatal velar. It would mean not having to start over again from scratch in every course about language at a leading university. It would mean not having to explain the term 'aspect' to speakers of a language (English) in which it is pervasive. It is a linguistics that would enable people who can recognize and name so much of what is around them to recognize and name the elements of that which makes naming possible, language itself. And to approach the many social aspects of language, literacy, bilingualism, ethnic identity, and the like, in realistic terms.

Such an elementary linguistics would involve values that have been earned by experience: understanding the potential equality of all languages; understanding the secondary origin of most social meaning and evaluation of varieties of language; understanding as well that disparate historical circumstances shape languages differently, affecting what can actually be done with their resources now.

Elementary linguistics is ultimately a contribution to the well-being of linguistics itself, no doubt, but first of all a contribution to society. It is where linguistics is undertaken to contribute to society that one can most hope for that contribution to be made.

Linguistics is so fascinating that it is easy to forget its connections with the world around it. It is where linguistic work is connected with practical problems and the circumstances of actual communities that one is most likely to realize the need to stress the potential equality/equivalence of all languages, grounded in human nature, to recognize the actual inequalities that obtain, and to be brought face-to-face with the difference it can make to share with others understandings linguists may take for granted.

Many branches of linguistics are in such a position. Their day-to-day experience can be linked to a general good, a humanistic goal, the understanding of the actual life of language and the sharing of that understanding with others.

Notes

1   This paper is based on a lecture in memory of Nessa Wolfson, sponsored by the Wolfson family and the Graduate School of Education of the University of Pennsylvania. The lecture was given October 25, 1991, and that text has appeared in the *Working Papers in Educational Linguistics*, prepared by graduate students in the Educational Linguistics program of the School, **9**, (1) (Hymes, 1992c). A revised version was presented at the Georgetown University Round Table in Languages and Linguistics in the spring of 1992, and published in the proceedings (Hymes, 1993a). The analysis of 'She's a Widow' in that version (pp. 32–33) has been revised, and the text of the story, omitted there, is provided.
2   Cf. discussion in the opening pages of Hymes (1966).
3   Cf. Bourdieu (1991), Part II, 'The Social Institution of Symbolic Power', especially Chapter 3, 'Authorized Language: The Social Conditions for the Effectiveness of Ritual Discourse', developing Marx's observations on false consciousness and fetishism of commodities (Marx 1912 [1867]: 83; cf. Lichtheim, 1967: 43-6).
4   These points about the Chomskian representative anecdote, and its poignancy, first came to me in preparing a paper in 1967 for a conference on language and education at Yeshiva University. See now Hymes, 1984.

5   Such statements continue to be made. A manuscript I read in December 1991 had several, including the claim that 5-year-old children arrive at school knowing 95 per cent of the rules of their language. Is there an agreed-upon count of the number of rules of English – of any language? A book that assumes equivalence between potential and actual equality has just had a second edition (Aitchison, 1990). It does so in the name of equality. My point is that we cannot expect to achieve greater equality by claiming as true what no one knows, and denying actualities of which many have experience.

6   An explicit statement is found at the end of Sapir and Swadesh (1946).

7   For extended discussion of the current state of the subject, see Lucy (1991, 1992a; 1992b, 1992c).

8   What follows generalizes to all languages the characteristics of pidginization and creolization, as indicated by a survey of information two decades ago (Hymes 1971b: 83). It was a point of that essay that pidgins and creoles were complex configurations of processes more widely shared.

9   For example, the obsolescent language, East Sutherland Gaelic, closely studied by Nancy Dorian (1981); Cf. Dorian (1989). Cf. also what Bloomfield reported about the Menomini, White Thunder (Hymes, 1974, Chapter 3: 71ff). The example is taken up more fully in the original article of 1967 and in somewhat different form as the beginning of Chapter 2 of my *Toward Linguistic Competence* (1984).

10 Neither Virginia nor I have heard the tape of the narrative. We have worked from the text as presented in Nessa's dissertation, and as published in her monograph of 1982 (Wolfson: 25–7), and in a later article (1989: 140). In doing so, Virginia has paid particularly scrupulous attention to the details of the transcription. Commas, periods, and capitalization have been consistently used as indications of verses in the light of her experience with a variety of English oral narratives. The few exceptions are due to my sense of overall pattern.

11 In the account of the story in an earlier version of this study (Hymes, 1992; 1993), I thought that the fifth scene had five stanzas, the last three each a pair of verses. That now seems dumb. The overriding signal of organization in the scene is initial, 'So (then)', correlated with changes in participants – the narrator and his cousin in (A), the narrator and the realtor in (B), the narrator and the widow in (C). As to the internal organization of each: Stanzas (A) and (B) each end with a verse beginning with 'So', (C) with a verse with a twist. The verse in (A) without 'So' begins with a time marker ('In October'). The two verses without 'So' in (B) are turns at talk (as is the preceding verse having 'So'). The intermediate verses in (C) are not marked initially, but each is distinguished in Wolfson's transcription by a final period.

      If one considered initial 'So' to outrank turns of talk as an indication of organization in this stanza, then (B) could be taken as having three verses (abc). Within (b) one would distinguish three subordinate turns at talk as (b–1) (b–2) (b–3). Such a distinction of levels within a stanza can be necessary in situations in which a unit parallel with other single units is internally elaborated. In this case internal elaboration is not apparent, but rather narrative sequence, and I take the stanza as having five verses, as shown.

12 To adapt Sapir's well known sentence about linguistic form (1921: 219).

13 Recently (1991) I received a letter from Coos Bay, Oregon, from the man in charge of cultural heritage for the Confederated Tribes of Coos, Lower Umpqua and Siuslaw Indians. He knew that almost 40 years ago I had sought out the last

speakers of those languages, and learned something at least of Siuslaw. We drove down. He himself (Donald Whereat) was of Coos descent, and knew nothing of the language, but was systematically gathering together everything that had been done and was known about the language, including correspondence among those who had studied it. He was without illusions or ideology. He simply wanted help in understanding what he had gathered – to begin with, the differences in the symbols used by two linguists at different times to write the language.

Virginia undertook to provide him first with an understanding of the sounds of his own English, and then, through that, with an understanding of the respects in which the sounds of Coos were different. He could have learned those symbols, the logic of their presentation in a chart, and the descriptive terms, at any time in his life. It was almost an accident that he reached someone to share the information with him. There must be many such instances of alienation from knowledge of one's own heritage for lack of elementary linguistics.

Text of Narrative from Nessa Wolfson (1982, pp. 25–27)

The following story, given in its entirety, is a typical example of the way in which a speaker may dramatically structure his story through the use of performance features. Thee speaker had just announced that he had 'made a very good deal' on the purchase of a new house. The addressee who had seen the house in question, expressed astonishment and asked how the house had come to be sold for such a low price. The answer was the following:

A. 'What happened?'

B. 'She's a widow. She's a widow, she put the house up originally during the winter for forty-five – with Langsdorf. She couldn't move it. Came summertime, she handed it over to Larry Snyder at – thirty-seven five. So they had a couple people in – the bids were – she had a bid for thirty-five and got stubborn and didn't take it. So as the summer sent, she got sick, and she's in the hospital now, and she's living in an apartment and uh – they – when I went to see it, the guy says to me, says, 'We got a bid for thirty-three – thirty-four,' says, 'If you bid thirty-five,' he says, 'You'll get it.' I said, 'Okay, let me think it over.' And I went home and I called up my wife's cousin who's a realtor. Well, his partner knows Snyder very well, so he called him up. The bid was for twenty-seven, five! So I figured they could do the same thing I was going to do. So he calls me up the next day and I figure, 'Look, I could always bid a little higher than the guy and work my way up.' So he calls me the next day and I told my wife exactly what to say. So he gets on the phone and so my wife ways, 'Look, we're not talking land, we're talking house. The house isn't worth it and it needs a lot of work.' You know, and we made up a lot of things . . . 'We have to paper and paint it.' So he says, 'That you have to do in any house.' So she says, 'Yes, we have to lay down new floors, the rugs are no good (the rugs happen to be in good shape), we have to – there's too much shrubbery, we have to tear out some of the shrubs.' (The shrubbery around the house is magnificent if it's done right, if it's done right.) So really we made up everything. So he says to my wife, he says, 'Well, what would you bid?' So she says, 'It's stupid for me to talk,' she says, 'You got a bid for thirty-three, thirty-four,' she says. 'Why should I even talk to you? It ain't gonna be anywheres near.' So he says to her, he says, 'Well,' he says, 'the person at thirty-four backed out.' So she says, 'Oh yeah?' He says, 'Yeah,' he says. 'What would you bid?' So she says, 'Twenty-eight.' He says, 'Oh,' he says, 'No, that she'll never go for.' So she says, 'Okay, that's my bid, Mr. Smith. You want it, fine; you don't, fine.' Got a call that afternoon. It was accepted! So I go to see the house – I go to sign the contract, I look at the contract and I says, 'I ain't signing this.' He says, 'Why?' I says, 'I want a plumbing certificate, I want an air conditioning certificate, I want a heating certificate and I want a roof certificate!' So he says, 'Really, we won't guarantee . . .' I says, 'I don't want a guarantee, I want certificates, from certified people that it's in good shape, and I want the right to bring in any of my guys.' So he says, 'She won't go for it . . . this, that . . .' So I says, 'Aah, don't be silly,' I says, 'Look, you just take it to her.' So I get a call back about a day later, 'Okay, she's accepted.' So then I get a – now what I do is, I pick up this thing, I take it to my cousin, he goes to someone, he says, 'Settlement's no good. She's got us for forty-five days.' In October she wanted to settle. So I says, 'Okay, I'll try to get January and I'll play around with that.' So I walk in and I sign a check for twenty-eight hundred dollars and I says to him, I says, 'Now,' I says, 'take this back to her.' So he picked up the agreement – all of a sudden he looked at the agreement. he says, 'Well,' he says, 'This uh date was changed.' I says, 'That's right. Settlement.' I says, 'Now you take and show her the check. She wants to play around fine. Deal's off!' So he took it back to her and she called the deal off. She wouldn't accept January. So then my next date was December and she went to November and I finally pushed her to November 18th and that's where we got it, and uh, she did back off. I didn't expect her to back off, though, with a check of twenty-eight hundred dollars. Cause she knew it was settled, you know, the deal was there. She finally went – we settle at November 18th. And I got to sell my house now – three weeks now.'

She's a Widow

[i] ['She's a widow']

She's a widow.
She's a widow,
     she put the house up originally during the winter for forty-five –
       with Langsdorf.
She couldn't move it.

                                               5

[ii] [Opportunity, strategy]
(A)
Came summertime,
    she handed it over to Larry Snyder at –
        thirty-seven five.
So they had a couple people in –
      the bids were –   10
she had a bid for thirty-five
      and got stubborn
      and didn't take it.

So as the summer went,   (B)
    she got sick,   15
      and she's in the hospital now,
        and she's living in an apartment
          and uh – they –
when I went to see it,
    the guy says to me,   20
      says, 'We got a bid for thirty-three – thirty-four',
      says, 'If you bid thirty-five', he says,
        'You'll get it.'
I said, 'Okay, let me think it over.'

And I went home   (C) 25
    and I called my wife's cousin who's a realtor.
Well, his partner knows Snyder well,
so he called him up.
The bid was for twenty-seven, five!

So I figured   (D) 30
    they could do the same thing I was going to do.
So he calls me up the next day
    and I figure,
      'Look, I could always bid a little higher than the guy
      and work my way up.'   35
So he calls me the next day,
    and I told my wife exactly what to say.
So he gets on the phone
    and so my wife says,
      'Look, we're not talking land,   40
        we're talking house.
      The house isn't worth it
      and it needs a lot of work.'
You know,
    and we made up a lot of things. . .   45
      'We have to paper and paint it.'

So he says,   (E)
    'That you have to do in any house.'
So she says,
    'Yes, we have to lay down new floors;   50
        the rugs are no good'
        (the rugs happen to be in good shape).
    'We have to –
        there's too much shrubbery,
        we have to tear out some of the shrubs.'   55
        (The shrubbery around the house is magnificent
            if it's done right,
            if it's done right).
So we really made up everything.

                                  [iii] [bid accepted]
So he says to my wife, he says,   (A)   60
    'Well, what would you bid?'
So she says,
    'It's stupid for me to talk,' she says,
    'You got a bid for thirty-three, thirty-four,' she says,
        'Why should I even talk to you?   65
        It ain't gonna be anywheres near.'

So he says to her, he says,   (B)
    'Well,'he says,
        'the person at thirty-four backed out.'
So she says, 'Oh yeah?'   70

He says,   (C)
    'Yeah,' he says,
        'What would you bid?'
So she says, 'Twenty-eight.'

He says, 'Oh,' he says,   (D)   75
    'No, that she'll never go for.'
So she says,
    'Okay, that's my bid, Mr. Smith.
    You want it,
        fine.   80
    You don't,
        fine.'

Got a call that afternoon.   (E)
It was accepted!

                              [iv] [certificates accepted]

So I go to see the house –   (A)   85
I go to sign the contract,
    I look at the contract
        and I says, 'I ain't signing this.'

He says, 'Why?'   (B)
I says, 'I want a plumbing certificate.   90
    I want an air conditioning certificate,
    I want a heating certificate,
    and I want a roof certificate.'

So he says, 'Really, we won't guarantee. . .'   (C)
I says, 'I don't want guarantee,   95
    I want certificates,
        from certified people that it's in good shape,
    and I want the right to bring in any of my guys.'

So he says, 'She won't go for it. . .this, that. . .'   (D)
So I says, 'Aah, don't be silly,' I says,   100
    'Look, you just take it to her.'

So I get a call back about a day later,   (E)
'Okay, she's accepted.'

                [v] [Settlement date accepted]
So then I get a –   (A)
    now what I do is,   105
        I pick up this thing,
        I take it to my cousin,
            he goes to someone,
            he says, 'Settlement's no good.
                She's got us for forty-five days.'   110
In October she wanted to settle.
So I says, 'Okay, I'll try to get a January and I'll play around with that.'

So I walk in   (B)
    and I sign a check for twenty-eight hundred dollars,   115
    and I says to him, I says,
        'Now,' I says,
        'Take this back to her.'
So he picks up the agreement –
    all of a sudden he looked at the agreement.   120
        He says, 'Well,' he says,   }
        'This uh date was changed.'
I says, 'That's right.
    Settlement.'

```
I says, 'Now you take it                                                    125
            and show her the check.
        She wants to play around fine.
        Deal's off!'                                        }
So he took it back to her
        and she called the deal off                                         13
She wouldn't accept January.                               }

So then my next date was December                          (C)
        and she went to November,
            and I finally pushed her to November 18th
                and that's where we got it,                                 135
                    and, uh, she did back off.
I didn't expect her to back off, though,
        with a check of twenty-eight thousand dollars.
Cause she knew it was settled, you know,
        the deal was there.                                                 140
She finally went –
        we settled at November 18th.
And I got to sell my house now –
        three weeks now.
```

Profile

Scene Stanza verse line Features

[i]	A	a	1	She's a widow
		b	2–4	She's a widow. . . (triad)
		c	5	She couldn't move it (ending point)
[ii]	A	a	6–8	Came summertime
		b	9–10	So they. . . – . . . –
		c	11–13	she. . . 'didn't take it' (triad)
	B	a	14–18	So as the summer went. . .and uh. . . – they – (quintad)
		b	19–23	when I went to see it 'you'll get it' (quintad)
		c	24	I said, '. . .'
	C	a	25–26	And I went home / and
		b	27–28	Well. . ., so he called him up
		c	29	twenty-seven, five!
	D	a	30–31	So I figured
		b	32–35	So he calls me. . . / and I figure, '. . .'
		c	36–37	So he calls me/ and I
		d	38–43	So / and so '. . .'
		e	44–46	You know / made up a lot of things/ '. . .'

	E	a	47–48	So he says
		b	49–58	So she says
		c	59	So we really made up everything
[iii]	A	a	60–61	So he says to my wife
		b	62–66	So she says, you've got
	B	c	67–69	So he says to her. . .at 'thirty-four' backed out
		d	70	So she says
	C	e	71–73	He says
		f	74	So she says, 'twenty-eight'
	D	g	75–76	He says
		h	77–82	So she says
	E	i	83	Got a call that afternoon
		j	84	It was accepted!
[iv]	A	a	85	So I go
		b	86–88	I go, look, says '. . .' (triad)
	B	c	89	He says
		d	90–93	I says
	C	e	94	So he says
		f	95–98	I says
	D	g	99	So he says
		h	100–101	So I says
	E	i	102	So I get a call
		j	103	'accepted'
[v]	A	a	104–110	So then/now '. . .'
		b	111	In October
		c	112–113	So 'January'
	B	a	114–118	So I walk in. . . '. . .' (three pairs)
		b	119–122	So. . . '. . .' }
		c	123–134	'. . .'
		d	125–138	'. . .' }
		e	129–131	So
		f	131	January }
	C	a	132–136	So then (quintad)
		b	137–138	
		c	139–140	
		d	141–142	
		e	143–144	

229

In brief: [i] abc   she (the widow)
          [ii] AB(C)DE   narrator + realtor/wife + realtor
          [iii] ab cd (ef) gh ij   wife and realtor
          [iv] ab cd (ef) gh ij   narrator and realtor
          [v] ABC   narrator and cousin
                                    narrator and realtor
                                    narrator and she (the widow)

References

ABBOTT, L.M, Jr. (1968) 'Considerations of Language and Culture for a Social Survey', paper for Anthropology 528, Philadelphia, PA: University of Pennsylvania.

ABRAHAMS, R. (1972) 'The Training of the Man of Words in Talking Sweet', *Language in Society*, **1** (1), pp. 15–29.

ABRAHAMS, R. and SZWED, J. (1975) 'Black English: A Review of the Work', *American Anthropologist*, **77**, pp. 329–35.

ADAMS, K.L. and BRINK, D.T. (Eds) (1990) *Perspectives on Official English: The Campaign for English as the Official Language of the USA*, Berlin: Mouton de Gruyter.

AITCHISON, J. (1990) *Language Change: Progress or Decay?* (2nd ed.) Cambridge Approaches to Linguistics, Cambridge University Press.

ALBERT, E. (1972) 'Rhetoric', 'Logic' and 'Poetics' in Burundi: Cultural Patterning of Speech Behavior', in GUMPERZ, J.J. and HYMES, D. (1972) *Directions in Sociolinguistics*, pp. 72–105.

ALCALA, C.N., RIVERA, H. and THAYER, B. (1974) 'The Legal Significance of Lau vs. Nichols', in REICHERT, J. and TRUJILLO, M. (Eds), *Perspectives on Contemporary Native American and Chicano Educational Thought*, Davis, CA: D.Q.U. Press, pp. 90–111.

ALLEN, J.R. (1992) 'I Will Speak, Therefore, of a Graph: A Chinese Metalanguage', *Language in Society*, **21**, pp. 189–206.

ANDERSON, E.N., Jr. (1973) 'The Life and Culture of Ecotopia', in Hymes, D. (1973b) *Reinventing Anthropology*, pp. 264–83.

ANDRESEN, J.T. (1990) *Linguistics in America 1769–1924: A Critical History*, London: Routledge.

APPEL, R. (1983) 'Minority Languages in the Netherlands: Relations Between Sociopolitical Conflicts and Bilingual Education', in BAIN, B. (1983) *The Sociogenesis of Language and Human Conduct*, pp. 517–26.

ATKINS, J.D.C. (1888) 'Correspondence on the Subject of Teaching the Vernacular in Indian Schools', Washington, DC: Government Printing Office, pp. 187–8.

ATKINSON, P., DAVIES, B. and DELAMONT, S. (Eds) (1995) *Discourse and Reproduction: Essays in Honor of Basil Bernstein*, Cresskill, NJ: Hampton Press.

BAIN, B. (Ed.) (1983) *The Sociogenesis of Language and Human Conduct*, New York: Plenum.

231

BARON, D. (1990) *The English-only Question: An Official Language for Americans?*, New Haven, CT: Yale University Press.

BASSO, E.B. (1985) *A Musical View of the Universe: Kalapalo Myth and Ritual Performance*, Philadelphia, University of Pennsylvania Press.

BASSO, K. (1974) 'The Ethnography of Writing', in BAUMAN, R. and SHERZER, J. (1974) *Explorations in the Ethnography of Speaking*, pp. 423–32.

BASSO, K. and ANDERSON, N. (1973) 'The Painted Symbols of Silas John: A Western Apache Writing System', *Science*, **180** [4090], pp. 1013–22. Also in Basso, K. (1990) *Western Apache Language and Culture*, Tucson, AZ: University of Arizona Press, Chapter 3.

BAUGH, J. (1983) *Black Street Speech: Its Structure, History, and Survival*, Austin, TX: University of Texas Press.

BAUMAN, R. (1974) 'Speaking in the Light: The Role of the Quaker Minister', in BAUMAN, R. and SHERZER, J. (Eds), *Explorations in The Ethnography of Speaking*, Cambridge and New York: Cambridge University Press, pp. 144–160.

BAUMAN, R. and SHERZER, J. (Eds) (1974) *Explorations in the Ethnography of Speaking*, Cambridge and New York: Cambridge University Press.

BELTRAMO, A.F. (1981) 'Profile of a State: Montana', in FERGUSON, C.A. and HEATH, S.B. (Eds) *Language in the USA*, pp. 339–80.

BEN-AMOS, D. (1992) 'Do We Need Ideal Types (in Folklore)? An Address to Lauri Honko', *NIF Papers* 2, Turku, Finland, Nordic Institute of Folklore.

BERGEN, J.J. (Ed.) (1990) *Spanish in the United States: Sociolinguistic Issues*, Washington, DC, Georgetown University Press.

BERNSTEIN, B. (1971) *Class, Codes and Control, Vol. 1: Theoretical Studies Towards a Sociology of Language*, London: Routledge & Kegan Paul.

BERSTEIN, B. (1972) 'A Critique of the Concept of "Compensatory Education"' in CAZDEN, C., JOHN-STEINER, V. and HYMES, D. (Eds), *Functions of Language in the Classroom*, New York: Teachers College Press.

BERNSTEIN, B. (1973) *Class, Codes, and Control, Vol. 2: Applied Studies Towards a Sociology of Language*, London: Routledge, Kegan Paul.

BERNSTEIN, B. (1977a) *Class, Codes and Control, Vol. 3: Towards a Theory of Educational Transmissions* (2nd rev. ed.). London: Routledge & Kegan Paul.

BERNSTEIN, B. (1977b) 'Class and Pedagogies: Visible and Invisible', in BERNSTEIN, B. (1977a) *Class, Codes and Control*, pp. 116–56.

BERNSTEIN, B. (1990) *Class, Codes and Control, Vol. 4: The Structuring of Pedagogic Discourse*, London: Routledge.

BERRY, J.W. (1983) 'The Sociogenesis of Social Sciences: An Analysis of the Cultural Relativity of Social Psychology', in BAIN, B. (Ed.) *The Sociogenesis of Language and Human Conduct*, New York: Plenum, pp. 449–58.

BISSERET, N. (1979) *Education, Class Language, and Ideology*, London: Routledge & Kegan Paul.

BISSEX, G. (1968) 'The Harvardization of Michael', Unpublished term paper, Harvard University.

BLACKALL, E.A. (1959) *The Emergence of German as a Literary Language*, Cambridge: Cambridge University Press.

BLAKE, B.J. (1991) *Australian Aboriginal Languages: A General Introduction* (2nd ed.) St. Lucia: University of Queensland Press.

BLOOMFIELD, L. (1933) *Language*, New York: Holt, Rinehart and Winston.

BLU, K.I. (1967) 'Kinship and Culture: Affinity and the Role of the Father in the Trobriands', *Southwestern Journal of Anthropology*, **23**, pp. 90–109. [Reprinted in DOLGIN, J.L. and KEMNITZER, D.S. (Eds) *Symbolic Anthropology*, New York: Columbia University Press, (1977) pp. 47–62].

BOARDMAN, P.C. (Ed.) (1987) *The Legacy of Language. A Tribute to Charlton Laird*, Reno, NV: University of Nevada Press.

BOAS, F. (1911) 'Introduction', in BOAS, F. (Ed.), *Handbook of American Indian languages*, **1**, Bureau of American Ethnology, Bulletin 40, Part 1, Washington, DC: Smithsonian Institution, pp. 1–18.

BOAS, F. (1920) 'The Classification of American Languages', *American Anthropologist*, **22**, pp. 367–76.

BODINE, A. (1975) 'Androcentrism and Prescriptive Grammar: Singular "they", and Sex-indefinite "he" and "he or she" ', *Language in Society*, **4**, 2, pp. 129–46.

BOLINGER, D.L. (1946) 'Visual Morphemes', *Language*, **22**, pp. 333–40.

BOLINGER, D.L. (1977) *Meaning and Form*, London and New York: Longman.

BOURDIEU, P. (1991) *Language and Symbolic Power*, THOMPSON, J.B. (Ed.) Oxford, Polity Press; Cambridge, MA., Harvard University Press.

BOYARIN, J. (Ed.) (1992) *The Ethnography of Reading*, Berkeley and Los Angeles, CA: University of California Press.

BRANDT, E. (1970) 'On the Origins of Linguistic Stratification: The Sandia Case', *Anthropological Linguistics*, **2**, 2, pp. 46–50.

BRIGGS, C. (1988) *Competence and Performance: The Creativity of Tradition in Mexicano Verbal Art*, Philadelphia, PA: University of Pennsylvania Press.

BRIGHT, W. (1984) *American Indian Linguistics and Literature*. The Hague: Mouton.

BROOKS, C. and WARREN, R.P. (1949) *Modern Rhetoric*, New York: Harcourt, Brace.

BROWN, P. and LEVINSON, S. (1978) 'Universals in Language Usage: Politeness Phenomena', in GOODY, E.N. (Ed.) *Questions and Politeness*, New York: Cambridge University Press, pp. 56–289.

BRUNER, J. (1981) 'The Social Context of Language Acquisition', Paper presented at the Sixth Annual Boston University Conference on Language Development, Boston. ('Formats of language acquisition', *American Journal of Semiotics* (1982), 1).

BRUNOT, F. (1947) *La Propagation du Français en France jusqu''a la fin de l'Ancien Régime*, in his *Histoire de la Langue Française des origines `a 1900*, VII, 2nd ed., Paris, Colin.

BURKE, K. (1925) 'Psychology and Form', *The Dial*, **79**, 1, pp. 34–46. Also in his *Counterstatement*, (1931) New York: Harcourt Brace; (1957) Chicago: University of Chicago Press; (1968) Berkeley and Los Angeles: University of California Press.

BURKE, K. (1941) 'Semantic and Poetic Meaning', *The Philosophy of Literary Form* Baton Rouge, LA: Louisiana State University Press. Also 1973 (3rd ed.) Berkeley and Los Angeles, CA: University of California Press.

BURKE, K. (1945) *The Grammar of Motives*, Englewood Cliffs, NJ: Prentice Hall. Reissued 1955, New York: George Braziller; (1962) Cleveland, World; (1974, 2nd ed.) (Berkeley and Los Angeles, CA: University of California Press.

CAMERON, D., FRAZER, E., HARVEY, P., RAMPTON, M.B.H. and RICHARDSON, K. (1992) *Researching Language: Issues of Power and Method*, London and New York: Routledge.

CARBAUGH, D. (Ed.) (1990) *Cultural Communication and Intercultural Contact*, Hillsdale, NJ: Lawrence Erlbaum Associates.

CARNOY, M. (Ed.) (1972) *Schooling in a Corporate Society: The Political Economy of Education in America*, New York, McKay.

CARNOY, M. (1974) *Education as Cultural Imperialism*, New York: McKay.

CARROLL, J.B. (1956) *Language, Thought and Reality: Selected Writings of Benjamin Lee Whorf*, New York: John Wiley; Cambridge, Technology Press.

CASSIRER, E. (1961) [1942] *The Logic of the Humanities*, New Haven, CT: Yale University Press. [Translated from *Zur Logik der Kulturwissenschaften*, Goteborg.]

CAZDEN, C. (1970) 'The Situation: A Neglected Source of Social Class Differences in Language Use', *Journal of Social Issues*, **26**, 2, pp. 35–60. Reprinted in PRIDE, J. and HOLMES, J. (Eds) *Sociolinguistics*, London: Penguin, pp. 294–313.

CAZDEN, C.B. (1992) *Whole Language Plus. Essays on Literacy in the United States and New Zealand*, New York: Teachers College Press.

CAZDEN, C.B. and DICKINSON, D.K. (1981) 'Language in Education: Standardization Versus Cultural Pluralism', in FERGUSON, C.A. and HEATH, S.B. (Eds) *Language in the USA*, pp. 446–68.

CAZDEN, C.B. and HYMES, D. (1978) 'Narrative Thinking and Story-telling Rights: A Folklorist's Clue to a Critique of Education', *Keystone Folklore*, **22**, 1–2, pp. 21–36. [Chapter 5 in this book].

CAZDEN, C.B., JOHN, V. and HYMES, D. (Eds) (1972) *Functions of Language in the Classroom*, New York: Teachers College Press.

CHALFEN, R. (1987) *Snapshot Versions of Life*, Bowling Green, OH: Bowling Green State University Press.

CHOMSKY, N. (1965) *Aspects of the Theory of Syntax*, Cambridge, MA: MIT Press.

CHOMSKY, N. (1966) *Cartesian Linguistics*, New York: Harper and Row.

CHOMSKY, N. (1971) *Problems of Knowledge and Freedom*, New York: Pantheon Books.

CHOMSKY, N. and HALLE, M. (1968) *Sound Pattern of English*, New York: Harper and Row.

CICOUREL, A.V. (1974) 'Ethnomethodology', in SEBEOK, T.A. (Ed.) *Current Trends in Linguistics* **12**, The Hague: Mouton, pp. 1563–605.

CICOUREL, A.V. (1981) 'Language and Medicine', in FERGUSON, C.A. and HEATH, S.B. (Eds) *Language in the USA*, pp. 407–29.

CLECAK, P. (1974) *Radical Paradoxes: Dilemmas of the American Left, 1945-1970.* New York: Harper & Row.

CMIEL, K. (1990) *Democratic Eloquence: The Fight over Popular Speech in Nineteenth Century America*, New York: William Morrow.

COATES, J. and CAMERON, D.O. (Eds) (1988) *Women in Their Speech Communities*, London and New York: Longman.

COFFIN, W.S. (1993) *A Passion for the Possible: A Message to US Churches*, Louisville, KY: Westminster/John Knox Press.

COLE, M., GAY, J., GLICK, J.A., SHARP, D.W. (1971) *The Cultural Context of Learning and Thinking*, New York: Basic Books.

CORSON, D.J. (1993a) 'Discursive Bias and Ideology in the Administration of Minority Group Interests', *Language in Society*, **22**, pp. 165–92.

CORSON, D.J. (1993b) *Language, Minority Education and Gender: Linking Social Justice and Power*, Clevedon and Philadelphia, PA: Multilingual Matters.

COUPLAND, N., COUPLAND, J. and GILES, H. (1991) *Language, Society and the Elderly: Discourse, Identity and Ageing*, Oxford: Blackwell.

COUPLAND, J., COUPLAND, N. and ROBINSON, J.D. (1992) '"How are you?": Negotiating Phatic Communion', *Language in Society*, **21**, pp. 207–30.

CRADDOCK, J.R. (1981) 'New World Spanish', in FERGUSON, C.A. and HEATH, S.B. (1981) *Language in the USA*, pp. 196–211.

CRAWFORD, J. (Ed.) (1992) *Language Loyalties: A Source Book on the Official English Controversy*, Chicago, IL: Chicago University Press.

CRYSTAL, D. (1987), *The Cambridge Encyclopedia of Language*, Cambridge & New York: Cambridge University Press.

DANIELS, H.A. (Ed.) (1990) *Not only English: Affirming America's Multilingual Heritage*, Urbana, IL: National Council of Teachers of English.

DARNELL, R. (1971) 'The Bilingual Speech Community: A Cree Example', in DARNELL, R. (Ed.) *Linguistic Diversity in Canadian Society*, Edmonton, Alberta: Linguistic Research, pp. 155–72.

DARNELL, R. (1972) 'Prolegomena to Typologies of Speech Use', *Texas Working Papers in Sociolinguistics*, Austin, TX: University of Texas, Department of Anthropology.

DARNELL, R. and FOSTER, M. (Eds) (1988) *Native North American Interaction Patterns*,

Ottawa, Canada: Canadian Museum of Civilization, National Museums of Canada.

DE TERRA, D. (1983) 'The Linguagenesis of Society: The Implementation of the National Language Plan in West Malaysia', in BAIN, B. (Ed.) *The Sociogenesis of Language and Human Conduct*, New York: Plenum, pp. 527–40.

DICKINSON, D., WOLF, M. and STOTSKY, S. (1993) 'The Interwoven Development of Oral and Written Language' in GLEASON, J.B. (Ed.) *The Development of Language* (3rd Ed.), New York: Macmillan, pp. 369–420.

DIDERICHSEN, P. (1974) 'The Foundation of Comparative Linguistics: Revolution or Continuation?', in HYMES, D. (Ed.) *Foundations in Sociolinguistics*', pp. 277–306.

DITTMAR, N. (1983) 'Descriptive and Explanatory Power of Rules in Sociolinguistics', in BAIN, B, (Ed.) *The Sociogenesis of Language and Human Conduct*, pp. 225–55.

DORIAN, N.C. (1981) *Language Death: The Life Cycle of a Scottish Gaelic Dialect*, Philadelphia, PA: University of Pennsylvania Press.

DORIAN, N.C. (Ed.) (1989) *Investigating Obsolescence: Studies in Language Contraction and Death*, Cambridge, Cambridge University Press.

DORIAN, N.C. (1994) 'Varieties of Variation in a Very Small Place: Social Homogeneity, Prestige Norms and Local Variation', *Language*, **70**, 4, pp. 631–96.

DUNDES, A. (1994) *The Cockfight. A Casebook*, Madison: University of Wisconsin Press.

DURANTI, A. and GOODWIN, C. (Eds) (1992) *Rethinking Context: Language as an Interactive Phenomenon*, Studies in the Social and Cultural Foundations of Language **11**, Cambridge & New York: Cambridge University Press.

EDELSKY, C. (1991) *With Literacy and Justice for all: Rethinking the Social in Language and Education*, London: The Falmer Press.

ELIOT, T.S. (1943) *Four Quartets*, New York: Harcourt Brace.

ENGELS, F. (1941) [1886] *Feuerbach and the Outcome of Classical German Philosophy*, New York: International Publishers.

EVERSON, W. (1968) *The Residual Years: Poems 1934–1948*, New York: New Directions.

FALK, J.S. (1994) 'The Women Foundation Members of the Linguistic Society of America', *Language* **70**, pp. 455–90.

FERGUSON, C.A. (1966) 'National Sociolinguistic Profiles', in Bright, W. (Ed.) *Sociolinguistics*, The Hague: Mouton, pp. 309–24.

FERGUSON, C.A. (1991) 'Diglossia Revisited', in HUDSON, A. (Ed.) 'Studies in Diglossia', *Southwest Journal of Linguistics*, **10**, 1, pp. 214–34.

FERGUSON, C.A. and HEATH, S.B. (Eds) (1981) *Language in the USA*, New York: Cambridge University Press.

FINEGAN, E. (1980) *Attitudes towards English Usage*, New York: Teachers College Press.

FISHMAN, A. (1988) *Amish Literacy*, Portsmouth, NH: Heinemann.

FISHMAN, J.A. (1966) *Language Loyalty in the United States*, The Hague: Mouton.

FISHMAN, J.A. (1972) *The Sociology of Language*, Rowley, MA: Newbury House.

FISHMAN, J.A. (1974) 'The Sociology of Language', in SEBEOK, T.A. (Ed.) *Current Trends in Linguistics* **12**, The Hague: Mouton, pp. 1629–1784.

FISHMAN, J.A. (1982) 'Whorfianism of the Third Kind: Ethnolinguistic Diversity as a Worldwide Societal Asset', *Language in Society*, **11**, pp. 1–14.

FISHMAN, J.A. (1989) *Language and Ethnicity in Minority Sociolinguistic Perspective*, Clevedon and Philadelphia, PA: Multilingual Matters.

FISHMAN, J.A. (1991) *Reversing Language Shift: Theoretical and Empirical Foundations of Assistance to Threatened Languages*, Clevedon and Philadelphia, PA: Multilingual Matters.

FISHMAN, J.A. and LEUDERS-SALMON, E. (1972) 'What has the Sociology of Language to say to the Teacher? (on Teaching the Standard Variety to Speakers of Dialectal or Sociological Varieties)', in CAZDEN, C., JOHN, V. and HYMES, D. (Eds) *Functions of Language in the Classroom*, pp. 67–83.

FOWLER, R., HODGE, B., KRESS, G., TREW, T. (1979) *Language and Control*, London: Routledge & Kegan Paul.

GALINDO, R. (1994) 'Amish Newsletters in *The Budget*: A Genre Study of Written Communication', *Language in Society*, **23**, pp. 77–105.

GALLINA, S.N. (1992) 'Bringing it all back to life', paper for Ethnopoetics (English 333), Charlottesville, VA: University of Virginia, Spring semester.

GARCIA, O. and OTHEGUY, R. (Eds) (1989) *English Across Cultures/Cultures Across English: A Reader in Cross-cultural Communication*, Berlin: Mouton de Gruyter.

GARVIN, P. and RIESENBERG, S. (1952) 'Respect Behavior on Ponape: An Ethno-linguistic Study', *American Anthropologist*, **54**, pp. 201–20.

GASTIL, R.D. (1975) *Cultural Regions of the United States*, Seattle, WA: University of Washington Press.

GEE, J.P. (1989) 'Literacy, Discourse and Linguistics. Essays by James Paul Gee', *Journal of Education*, **171**, 1.

GEE, J.P. (1991) 'A Linguistic Approach to Narrative', *Journal of Narrative and Life History*, **1**, pp. 15–40.

GEE, J.P. (1992) *The Social Mind: Language, Ideology and Social Practice*, Series in Language and Ideology, Macedo, D. (Ed.) New York: Bergin and Garvey.

GEERTZ, C. (1972) 'Deep Play: Notes on the Balinese Cockfight, *Daedalus*, **101**, pp. 1–37.

GEERTZ, C. (1976) ' "From the Native's Point of View": On the nature of anthropological understanding', in BASSO, K.H. and SELBY, H.A. (Eds) *Meaning in Anthropology*, Albuquerque, NM: University of New Mexico Press, pp. 221–37.

GEERTZ, H. and GEERTZ, C. (1975) *Kinship in Bali*, Chicago, IL: University of Chicago Press.

GILBERT, G. (Ed.) (1971) *The German Language in America*, Austin, TX: University of Texas Press.

GILBERT, G. (1981) 'French and German: A Comparative Study' in FERGUSON, C.A. and HEATH, S. B. (Eds) *Language in the USA*, pp. 257–72.

GILES, H. and COUPLAND, N. (1991) *Language: Contexts and Consequences*, Pacific Grove, CA: Brooks/Cole.

GOFFMAN, E. (1956) 'The Nature of Deference and Demeanor', *American Anthropologist*, **58**, pp. 473–502.

GOFFMAN, E. (1978) 'Response Cries', *Language*, **54**, pp. 787–815.

GOODENOUGH, W.H. (1956) 'Residence rules', *Southwestern Journal of Anthropology*, **12**, pp. 22–37.

GOODWIN, M.H. (1990) *He-said-she-said: Talk as Social Organization among Black Children*, Bloomington, IND: Indiana University Press.

GOULDNER, A.W. (1975–76) 'Prologue to a Theory of Revolutionary Intellectuals', *Telos*, **26**, pp. 3–36.

GRAVES, R. (1958) *The Poems of Robert Graves*, Garden City, NY: Doubleday, Anchor Books.

GREENBERG, J. (1968) *Anthropological Linguistics*, New York: Random House.

GREER, C. (1972) *The Great School Legend: A Revisionist Interpretation of American Public Education*, New York: Basic Books.

GRIMSHAW, A.D. (1989) *Collegial Discourse: Professional Conversation among Peers*, Norwood, NJ: Ablex.

GRIMSHAW, D. (1990) *Conflict Talk*, Cambridge: Cambridge University Press.

GRIMSHAW, A.D. (Ed.) (1994) *What's Going on Here? Complementary Studies of Professional Talk (Volume Two of the Multiple Analysis Project)*, Norwood, NJ: Ablex.

GUMPERZ, J.J. (1982a) *Discourse Strategies*, Cambridge: Cambridge University Press.

GUMPERZ, J.J. (1982b) *Language and Social Identity*, Cambridge: Cambridge University Press.

GUMPERZ, J.J. and HYMES, D. (Eds) (1972) *Directions in Sociolinguistics*, New York: Holt, Rinehart and Winston. Reprinted Oxford: Basil Blackwell (1986).

HABERMAS, J. (1970a) *Toward a Rational Society: Student Protest, Science and Politics*, Boston, MA: Beacon Press. (Translated by SHAPIRO, J.J. from essays in *Technik und Wissenschaft als 'Ideologie'* (1968), and *Protestbewegung und Hochschulreform*, (1969), Frankfurt, Suhrkamp.)

HABERMAS, J. (1970b) 'Toward a Theory of Communicative Competence', in Dreitzel, H.P. (Ed.), *Recent Sociology*, **2**, New York: Macmillan, pp. 115–48.

HABERMAS, J. (1971) *Knowledge and Human Interests*, Boston, MA: Beacon Press.

HABERMAS, J. (1973) *Theory and Practice*, Boston, MA: Beacon Press. (Translated from *Theorie und Praxis*, Frankfurt, Suhrkamp (1971), 4th edition, with an additional chapter by Viertel, J.).

HALE, K. (Ed.) (1992) 'Endangered Language', *Language*, **68**, (1), pp. 1–42 (seven essays).

HALL, R.A. Jr (1975) 'Review of J. Vachek, Written Language: General Problems and Problems of English', *Language*, **51**, pp. 461–5.

HALLIDAY, M.A.K. (1977) *Learning how to Mean*, New York: Elsevar North-Holland.

HALLIDAY, M.A.K. (1978) *Language as Social Semiotic: The Social Interpretation of Language and Meaning*, Baltimore, MD: University Park Press.

HANKS, W.F. (1991) *Referential Practice: Language and Lived Space among the Maya*, Chicago, IL: Chicago University Press.

HANKS, W.F. (1995) *Language and Communicative Practices*, Boulder, CO: Westview Press.

HARRIS, R.A. (1993) *The Linguistics Wars*, New York: Oxford.

HARRIS, Z.S. (1951) 'Review of Selected Writings of Edward Sapir', *Language*, **27**, pp. 288–333.

HATLEN, B. (1979) 'The Quest for the Concrete Particular, or, do Poets have Something to say to Sociolinguists?', in BROWN, R.L., Jr and STEINNMAN, M., Jr (Eds), *Rhetor 78: Proceedings of Theory of Rhetoric: An Interdisciplinary Conference*, Minneapolis, MN: University of Minnesota Center for Advanced Studies in Language, Style and Literary Theory.

HAUERWAS, S. and JONES, L.G. (Eds) (1989) *Why Narrative? Readings in Narrative Theology*, Grand Rapids, MI: Wm. B. Eerdmans.

HAUGEN, E. (1953) *The Norwegian Language in America: A Study in Bilingual Behavior*, Philadelphia, PA: University of Pennsylvania Press. (Reissued, Indiana University Press, 1969).

HAUGEN, E. (1956) *Bilingualism in the Americas: A Bibliography and Research Guide*, American Dialect Society, **26**, University, Alabama, University of Alabama Press.

HEATH, S.B. (1982a) 'What no Bedtime Story Means: Narrative Skills at Home and School', *Language in Society*, **11**, 2, pp. 49–76.

HEATH, S.B. (1982b) 'Questioning at Home and at School: A Comparative Study', in SPINDLER, G. (Ed.) *Doing the Ethnography of Schooling: Educational Anthropology on Action*, New York: Holt, Rinehart & Winston.

HEATH, S.B. (1983) *Way with Words: Language, Life and Work in Communities and Classrooms*, Cambridge, Cambridge University Press.

HELLER, M. (1988) *Codeswitching: Anthropological and Sociolinguistic Perspectives*, Berlin: Mouton de Gruyter.

HERNANDEZ-CHAVEZ, E., COHEN, A.D. and BELTRAMO, A.F. (Eds) (1975) *El lenguaje de los Chicanos*, Arlington, VA: Center for Applied Linguistics.

HEWITT, R. (1986) *White Talk Black Talk: Inter-racial Friendship and Communication Amongst Adolescents*, Cambridge, Cambridge University Press.

HILL, J. and IRVINE J.T. (Eds) (1993) *Responsibility and Evidence in Oral Discourse*, Cambridge: Cambridge University Press.

HIMLEY, M. (1991) *Shared Territory: Understanding Children's Writing as Works*, New York/Oxford: Oxford University Press.

HINSON, G. (1995) *Fire in my Bones: Inviting Annointment in African-American Gospel*, Philadelphia, PA: University of Pennsylvania Press.

HODGEN, M.T. (1964) *Early Anthropology in the Sixteenth and Seventeenth Centuries*, Philadelphia, PA: University of Pennsylvania Press.

HOGAN, D. (1980) Review of Bisseret (1979), *Language in Society*, 9, pp. 393–8.

HOGAN, H.M. (1971) 'An Ethnography of Communication among the Ashanti', *Penn-Texas Working Papers in Sociolinguistics*, 1, Austin, TX: University of Texas, Department of Anthropology.

HOGGART, R. (1957) *The Uses of Literacy*, London: Chatto & Windus.

HOGGART, R. (1971) Introduction to the French edition of Hoggart 1957, translated by PASSERON, J.C., *Working papers in cultural studies*, Birmingham: Centre for Contemporary Cultural Studies, University of Birmingham, pp. 120–31.

HOIJER, H. (Ed.) (1954) *Language in Culture*, Chicago, IL: University of Chicago Press.

HOOVER, M. (1978) 'Community Attitudes toward Black English', *Language in Society*, 7, pp. 65–87.

HORVATH, B. and VAUGHAN, P. (1991) *Community Languages: A Handbook: Studies of Languages used in Predominantly English-Speaking Countries*, Clevedon and Philadelphia, PA: Multilingual Matters.

HUCK, G.J. and GOLDSMITH, J.A. (1995) *Ideology and Linguistic Theory*, London: Routledge

HURST, M.J. (1990) *The Voice of the Child in American Literature: Linguistic Approaches to Fictional Child Language*, Lexington, KY: The University Press of Kentucky.

HYMES, D. (1953) 'Two Wasco Motifs', *Journal of American Folklore*, 66, pp. 69–70.

HYMES, D. (1964) 'Introduction: Toward Ethnographies of Communication', in GUMPERZ, J.J. and HYMES, D. (Eds), *The Ethnography of Communication*, Washington, D.C.: American Anthropological Association, pp. 1–34.

HYMES, D. (1966) 'Two Types of Linguistic Relativity: Some Examples from American Indian Ethnography', in Bright, W. (Ed.), *Sociolinguistics*, The Hague: Mouton, pp. 114–67.

HYMES, D. (1967a) 'Why Linguistics Needs the Sociologist', *Social Research*, 34, 4, pp. 632–47. Also in HYMES, D. (1974) *Foundations in Sociolinguistics*, Chapter 3.

HYMES, D. (Ed.) (1967b), *Studies in Southwestern Ethnolinguistics*, The Hague: Mouton.

HYMES, D. (1967c) 'Models of the Interaction of Language and Social Setting', *Journal of Social Issues*, 23, 2, pp. 8–28.

HYMES, D. (1967d) 'On Communicative Competence', in *Research Planning Conference: On Language Development in Disadvantaged Children, June 1966*, New York: Yeshiva University, pp. 1–16. (=Hymes, 1971c).

HYMES, D. (1968) 'Linguistic Problems in Defining the Concept of "Tribe" ', in HELM, J. (Ed.), *Essays on the Problem of Tribe*, Seattle, WA: University of Washington Press for the American Ethnological Society.

HYMES, D. (1970a) 'Linguistic Aspects of Comparative Political Research', in HOLT, R.R. and TURNER, J.E. (Eds), *The Methodology of Comparative Research*, New York: The Free Press, pp. 295–341.

HYMES, D. (1970b) 'Linguistic Method in Ethnography', in GARVIN, P.L. (Ed.), *Method and Theory in Linguistics*, The Hague: Mouton, pp. 249–311.

HYMES, D. (1971a) 'Lexicostatistics and Glottochronology in the Nineteenth Century (with Notes Toward a General History)' in DYEN, I. (Ed.) (1971) *Lexicostatistics in Genetic Linguistics*, The Hague: Mouton, pp. 122–76. Also in HYMES, D. (1983) *Essays in the History of Linguistic Anthropology*, pp. 59–114.

HYMES, D. (1971b) 'Introduction to Part III' in HYMES, D. (Ed.), *Pidginization and Creolization of Languages*, London and New York: Cambridge University Press, pp. 65–90.

HYMES, D. (1971c) 'On Linguistic Theory, Communicative Competence, and the Education of Disadvantaged Children', in WAX, M. L., DIAMOND, S.A., GEARING,

F. (Eds), *Anthropological Perspectives on Education*, New York: Basic Books, pp. 51–66.

HYMES, D. (1972a) 'Introduction', *Language in Society*, 1, 1, pp. 1–14.

HYMES, D. (1972b) 'Models of the Interaction of Language and Social Life', in GUMPERZ, J.J. and HYMES, D. (1972) *Directions in Sociolinguistics*, pp. 35–71. Also revised in HYMES, D. (1974) *Foundations in Sociolinguistics*, Chapter 2.

HYMES, D. (1973a) 'The Scope of Sociolinguistics', in SHUY, R.W. (Ed.) *Report of the 23rd Annual Round Table Meeting on Linguistics and Language Study; Sociolinguistics*, Washington, D.C: Georgetown University Press, pp. 313–33. Also in HYMES, D. (1974) Foundations in Sociolinguistics, Chapter 10.

HYMES, D. (Ed.) (1973b) *Reinventing Anthropology*, New York: Pantheon.

HYMES, D. (Ed.) (1973c) 'Speech and Language: On the Origins and Foundations of Inequality Among Speakers', *Daedalus*, 102, 3 (Summer), pp. 59–86. [Chapter 3 in this book].

HYMES, D. (1974) *Foundations in Sociolinguistics*, Philadelphia, PA: University of Pennsylvania Press.

HYMES, D. (1977) 'Qualitative/Quantitative Research Methodologies in Education: A Linguistic Perspective', *Anthropology and Education Quarterly*, 8, 3, pp. 165–76.

HYMES, D. (1978a) 'What is Ethnography?', *Working Papers in Sociolinguistics*, 45. Austin, TX: Southwest Educational Development Laboratory. Also in GILMORE, P. and GLATTHORN, A. (Eds) (1982) *Children in and out of School: Ethnography and Education*, Language and Ethnography Series, 2, Washington, DC: Center for Applied Linguistics, pp. 21–32. [Chapter 1 in this book].

HYMES, D. (1978b) Review of Bolinger, 'Meaning and Form,' *Lingua*, 45, pp. 175–92.

HYMES, D. (1979a) 'Foreword', in Basso, K.H. *Portraits of The Whiteman*, New York: Cambridge University Press.

HYMES, D. (1979b) 'Sapir, Competence, Voices', in Fillmore, C.J., KEMPLER, D. and WANG, W. S-Y. (Eds), *Individual Difference in Language Ability Language Behavior*, New York: Academic Press, pp. 33–45.

HYMES, D. (1979c) 'Ethnography Monitoring', in BRIERE, E.J. (Ed.) *Language Development in a Bilingual Setting*, Los Angeles: National Dissemination and Assessment Center, pp. 73–88. Reprinted in Hymes (1980b), pp. 104–118.

HYMES, D. (1980a) 'Educational Ethnology', *Anthropology and Education Quarterly*, 11, pp. 3–8. [Chapter 2 in this book].

HYMES, D. (1980b) *Language in Education: Ethnolinguistic Essays*, Washington, DC: Center for Applied Linguistics.

HYMES, D. (1981) *In Vain I Tried to Tell You: Essays in Native American Ethnopoetics*, Philadelphia, PA: University of Pennsylvania Press.

HYMES, D. (1982) 'Narrative Form as Grammar of Experience: Native American and a Glimpse of English', *Journal of Education*, 164, 2, pp. 121–42. [Chapter 6 in this book].

HYMES, D. (1983a) *Essays in the History of Linguistic Anthropology*, Amsterdam and Philadelphia: John Benjamins.

HYMES, D. (1983b) 'Report from an Underdeveloped Country: Linguistic Competence in the United States', in BAIN, B. (Ed.) *The Sociogenesis of Language and Human Conduct* pp. 189–224. [Chapter 4 in this book].

HYMES, D. (1983c) 'Victoria Howard's 'Gitskux and His Older Brother': A Clackamas Chinook Myth', in SWANN, B. (Ed.), *Smoothing the Ground: Essays on Native American Oral Literature* (Berkeley and Los Angeles, CA: University of California Press, pp. 129–70.

HYMES, D. (1984) *Vers la Competence de Communication* (Langues et Apprentissages des Langues), Paris: Hatier-Credif.

HYMES, D. (1985a) 'Language, Memory and Selective Performance: Cultee's Salmon's Myth as Twice told to Boas', *Journal of American Folklore*, 98, (390), pp. 391–434.

HYMES, D. (1985b) 'Some Subtleties of Measured Verse', in HESCH, J.L. (Ed.) *Proceedings 1985*, 15th Spring Conference, Niagara Linguistics Society, Buffalo, NY: The Niagara Linguistics Society, pp. 13–57.

HYMES, D. (1985c) 'Towards Linguistic Competence', *Revue de l'AJLA*, **2**, pp. 9–23.

HYMES, D. (1986) ' Discourse: Scope Without Depth', *International Journal of the Sociology of Language*, **57**, pp. 48–89. Extract from HYMES, D. (1982b) *Ethnolinguistic Study of Classroom Discourse*, Final report to the National Institute of Education. Philadelphia, PA: University of Pennsylvania, Graduate School of Education.

HYMES, D. (1987a) 'Anthologies and Narrators', in SWANN, B. and KRUPAT, A. (Eds), *Recovering the Word: Essays on Native American Literature*, Berkeley, CA: University of California Press, pp. 41–84.

HYMES, D. (1987b) 'A Theory of Irony and a Pattern of Chinookan Verbal Humor', in VERSCHEUREN, J. and BERTUCELLI-PAPI, M. (Eds), *The Pragmatic Perspective: Selected Papers from the 1985 International Pragmatics Conference*, Amsterdam/Philadelphia, PA: John Benjamins, pp. 293–338.

HYMES, D. (1987c) 'A Note on Ethnopoetics and Sociolinguistics', in MICHEAU, C. (Ed.), *Working Papers in Educational Linguistics*, **3**, 2, pp. i–xxi. Philadelphia, PA: Graduate School of Education, University of Pennsylvania. [Chapter 8 in this book].

HYMES, D. (1987d) 'Foreword', in WAGNER, D. (Ed.), *The Future of Literacy in a Changing World*, Oxford, New York: Pergamon Press, pp. xi–xvii. [Reprinted, revised, 1996].

HYMES, D. (1987e) 'Communicative Competence', in AMMON, U., DITTMAR, N. and MATTHIAS, K.J. (Eds) *Sociolinguistics*, Berlin: Walter de Gruyter, pp. 219–29.

HYMES, D. (1990) 'Epilogue to "The Things we do with Words" ' in CARBAUGH, D. (Ed.) *Cultural Communication and Intercultural Contact*, Hillsdale, NJ: Lawrence Erlbaum, pp. 419–29.

HYMES, D. (1991a) 'Ethnopoetics and Sociolinguistics: Three Stories by African-American Children', in MALCOLM, I.G. (Ed.) *Linguistics in the Service of Society*, Perth, Australia: Institute of Applied Language Studies, Edith Cowan University, pp. 155–70. [Chapter 8 in this book].

HYMES, D. (1991b) 'Is Poetics Original and Functional?', *Language and Communication*, **11**, (112), pp. 49–51.

HYMES, D. (1991c) 'Custer and Linguistic Anthropology', *Journal of Linguistic Anthropology*, **1**, pp. 5–11.

HYMES, D. (1992a) 'Using all There is to Use', in SWANN, B. (Ed.), *On the Translation of Native American Literatures*, Washington, DC: Smithsonian Institution.

HYMES, D. (1992b) 'Helen Sekaquaptewa's "Coyote and the birds": Rhetorical analysis of a Hopi Coyote story', *Anthropological Linguistics*, **34**, 1–4, pp. 45–72.

HYMES, D. (1992c) 'Inequality in Language: Taking for Granted', in DELORME, R.S., RITTER, I. and SILVER, R.E. (Eds), *Working Papers in Educational Linguistics*, **8**, 1, pp. 1–30. Philadelphia, PA: Graduate School of Education, University of Pennsylvania. [Chapter 10 in this book].

HYMES, D. (1992d) 'The Concept of Communicative Competence Revisited', in PUTZ, M. (Ed.) *Thirty Years of Linguistic Evolution*, Amsterdam: John Benjamins, pp. 31–57.

HYMES, D. (1993a) 'Inequality in Language: Taking for Granted', in ALATIS, J.E. (Ed.) *Language, Communication and Social Meaning*, Georgetown University Round Table 1992, Washington, DC: Georgetown University Press, pp. 23–40. [Chapter 10 in this book].

HYMES, D. (1993b) 'In need of a Wife: Clara Pearson's "Split-His-Own-Head" ' in Mattina, A. and Montler, T. (Eds) *American Indian Linguistics and Ethnography in Honor of Laurence C. Thompson*, University of Montana Occasional Papers in

Linguistics, 10, Missoula, MT: University of Montana, Department of Anthropology, pp. 127–62.

HYMES, D. (1994) 'Ethnopoetics, Oral-formulaic Theory and Editing Texts', *Oral Tradition*, **9**, pp. 330–70.

HYMES, D. (1995a) 'Bernstein and Ethnopoetics', in ATKINSON, P., DAVIES, B. and DELAMONT, S. (Eds) (1995) *Discourse and Reproduction: Essays in Honor of Basil Bernstein*, Cresskill, NJ: Hampton Press, pp. 1–24. [Chapter 9 in this book].

HYMES, D. (1995b) 'Coyote, Master of Life, True to Life', in SWANN, B. (Ed.) *Coming to Light, Contemporary Translations of Native American Literatures of North America*, New York: Random House & Vintage Books, pp. 286–306.

HYMES, D. (1995c) 'Seal and her Younger Brother lived There', in SWANN, B. (Ed.) *Coming to Light, Contemporary Translations of Native American Literatures of North America*, New York: Random House and Vintage Books, pp. 307–10.

HYMES, D. (1996) 'Oral Patterns as a Resource in Children's Writing: An Ethnopoetic Note', in SLOBIN, D.I., GERHARDT, J., KYRATZIS, A. and GUO, J. (Eds) *Social Interaction, Social Context and Language: Essays in Honor of Susan Ervin-Tripp*, Hillside, NJ: Lawrence Erlbaum Associates. [Chapter 7 in this book].

HYMES, D. (1996) 'Thinking about the News about Coyote', in ARNOLD, J. (Ed.) *American Identities*, Charlottesville, VA: The University of Virginia Press.

HYMES, D. and FOUGHT, J. (1981), *American Structuralism*, The Hague: Mouton.

HYMES, V. (1995) 'Experimental Folklore Revisited', in ABRAHAMS, R.D. (Ed.), *Fields of Folklore: Essays in Honor of Kenneth Goldstein*, Bloomington, IN: The Trickster Press.

IBN KHALDUN (1967) [1381] *The Muqaddimah*. Translated from the Arabic by Frany Rosenthal. Abridged and edited by N.J. Dawood. Princeton: Princeton University Press.

ILLICH, I. (1983) 'Vernacular Values and Education', in Bain, B. (1983) *The Sociogenesis of Language and Human Conduct*, pp. 461–95.

JACOBS, M. (1959) *Clackamas Chinook Tests, Part II*, Research Center in Anthropology, Folklore and Linguistics, Publication 11, Bloomington, IN: Indiana University.

JAQUITH, J. (1983) 'The Alphabet Revisited' (Ms).

JAKOBSON, R. (1960) 'Concluding Statement: Linguistics and Poetics', in SEBEOK, T.A. (Ed.) *Style and Language*, Cambridge, MA: MIT Press, pp. 350–77.

JEFFERSON, G. (1974), 'Error Correction as an Interactional Resource', *Language in Society*, **3**, pp. 181–200.

JONES, R.F. (1953) *The Triumph of the English Language*, Stanford, CA: Stanford University Press.

JOOS, M. (1961) 'Linguistic Prospects in the United States', MOHRMANN, C., SOMMERFELT, A. and WHATMOUGH, J. (Eds), *Trends in European and American Linguistics 1930–1960*, Utrecht and Antwerp: Spectrum, pp. 11–20.

KACHRU, B. (1990a). *The Alchemy of English: The Spread, Functions, and Models of Non-native Englishes*. Champaign, IL: University of Illinois Press. (First published, Oxford: Pergamon, 1986).

KACHRU, B. (1990b) 'World Englishes and Applied Linguistics. Learning, Keeping, and Using Language'. *Selected Papers from the Eighth World Congress of Applied Linguistics, Sydney, 16–21 August 1987*, Amsterdam/ Philadelphia: John Benjamins, pp. 203-29.

KATZ, M. (1968) *The Irony of Early School Reform: Educational Innovation in Mid-Nineteenth Century Massachusetts*, Cambridge, MA: Harvard University Press.

KATZ, M. (1971) *School Reform: Past and Present*, Boston, MA: Little, Brown.

KATZ, M. (1975) *Class, Bureaucracy and Schools: The Illusion of Educational Change in America*, New York: Praeger.

Keenan, E.O. (1973) 'A Sliding Sense of Obligatoriness: The Polystructure of Malagasy Oratory', *Language in Society*, **2**, 225–43.

241

KJOLSETH, R. (1972) 'Making Sense: Natural Language and Shared Knowledge in Understanding', in Fishman, J.A. (Ed.) *Advances in the Sociology of Language, 2: Selected Studies and Applications*, The Hague: Mouton, pp. 50–76.

KOCHMAN, T. (1972) *Rappin' and Stylin' out: Communication in Urban Black America*, Urbana, IL: University of Illinois Press.

KOKTOVA, F. (1995) 'Decentering Linguistics: A Review of the Encyclopedia of Language and Linguistics', *Journal of Pragmatics*, **24**, 5, pp. 35–56.

KRAMARAE, C., SCHULZ, M. and O'BARR, W.M. (1984) *Language and Power*, Beverly Hills, CA: Sage.

KRAMER, M.P. (1992) *Imagining Language in America: From the Revolution to the Civil War*, Princeton: Princeton University Press.

KRESS, G. and HODGE, R. (1979) *Language as Ideology*, London: Routlege & Kegan Paul.

KROSKRITY, P. (1993) *Language, History and Identity. Ethnolinguistic Studies of the Arizona Tewa*, Tucson: University of Arizona Press.

KUIPERS, J.C. (1990) *Power in Performance: The Creation of Textual Authority in Weyewa Ritual Speech*, Philadelphia, PA: University of Pennsylvania Press.

LABOV, W.A. (1966) *The Social Stratification of English in New York City*, Washington, DC: Center for Applied Linguistics.

LABOV, W.A. (1970) 'The Logic of Non-standard English', in ALATIS, J.E. (Ed.) *Report of the Twentieth Round Table Meeting on Linguistics and Language Studies*, Washington, DC: Georgetown University Press, pp. 1–29. Reprinted (1972b).

LABOV, W.A. (1972a) 'The Transformation of Experience in Narrative Syntax', in LABOV, W.A. *Language in the Inner City*, Philadelphia, PA: University of Pennsylvania Press, pp. 354–96.

LABOV, W.A. (1972b) 'The Logic of Non-standard English', in LABOV, W.A., *Language in the Inner City: Studies in the Black English Vernacular*, Philadelphia, PA: University of Pennsylvania Press, pp. 201–240.

LABOV, W.A. (1972c) *Language in the Inner City. Studies in the Black English Vernacular*, Philadelpha, PA: University of Pennsylvania Press.

LABOV, W.A. (1972d) *Sociolinguistic Patterns*, Philadelpha, PA: University of Pennsylvania Press.

LABOV, W.A. (1982) 'Speech Actions and Reactions in Personal Narrative', in TANNEN, DEBORAH (Ed.) *Analyzing Discourse: Text and Talk*, Georgetown University Round Table on Languages and Linguistics, 1981, Washington, DC: Georgetown University Press, pp. 219–47.

LABOV, W.A., COHEN, P., ROBINS, C. and LEWIS, J. (1968) *A Study of the Non-standard English of Negro and Puerto Rican Speakers in New York City*, Report on Co-operative Research Project 3288, New York: Columbia University.

Labov, W.A. and Waletzky, J. (1967) 'Narrative Analysis', in Helm, J. (Ed.) Essays on the Verbal and Visual Arts, Proceedings of the American Ethnological Society, Seattle, WA: University of Washington Press, pp. 12–44.

LAIRD, C. (1970) *And Gladly Teche: Notes on Instructing the Natives in the Native Tongue*, Englewood Cliffs, NJ: Prentice-Hall.

LAKOFF, G. (1987) *Women , Fire, and Dangerous Beings: What Categories Reveal about the Mind*, Chicago: University of Chicago Press.

LANGACKER, R.W. (1987) *Foundations of Cognitive Grammar, Vol. I: Theoretical Prerequisites*, Stanford: Stanford University Press.

LANGACKER, R.W. (1990) *Concept, Image, and Symbol. The Cognitive Basis of Grammar*. Berlin and Hawthorne, NY: Mouton de Gruyter.

LANGACKER, R.W. (1991) *Foundations of Cognitive Grammar, Vol. II: Descriptive Application*, Stanford: Stanford University Press.

LANHAM, R.A. (1974) *Style: An Anti-textbook*, New Haven, CT: Yale University Press.

LASCH, C. (1973) 'Inequality and Education', *New York Review of Books*, May 17, pp. 19–25.

LAVANDERA, B. (1974) 'On Sociolinguistic Research in New World Spanish', *Language in Society*, **3**, 2, pp. 247–92.

LEAP, W. (1974) 'On Grammaticality in Native American English: The Evidence from Isleta', *International Journal of the Sociology of Language*, **2**, pp. 79–80.

LEAP, W. (1981) 'American Indian languages', in FERGUSON, C.A. and HEATH, S.B. (1981) *Language in the USA*, pp. 116–44.

LEAP, W. (1993) *American Indian English*, Salt Lake City, UT: University of Utah Press.

LEE, D. (1992) *Competing Discourses: Perspectives and Ideology in Language*, London: Longman.

LEEDS-HURWITZ, W. (1989) *Communication in Everyday Life: A Social Interpretation*, Norwood, NJ: Ablex.

LEEDS-HURWITZ, W. (1993) *Semiotics and Communication: Signs, Codes, Cultures*, Hillsdale, NJ: Lawrence Erlbaum Associates.

LEITCH, T.M. (1986) *What stories are. Narrative theory and interpretation*. University Park, PA: Pennsylvania State University Press.

LEITH, D. (1995) 'Tense Variation as a Performance Feature in a Scottish Folklore', *Language in Society*, **24**, pp. 53–77.

LEONARD, S.A. (1929) *The Doctrine of Correctness in English Usage, 1700–1800*, University of Wisconsin Studies in Language and Literature, 25, Madison, WI: University of Wisconsin. (Reprinted, New York: Russell and Russell, 1962.)

LICHMAN, S. (ca. 1980), 'On Gloucestershire Mumming Tradition', unpublished manuscript, Philadelphia, PA: University of Pennsylvania, Department of Folklore and Folklife.

LICHTHEIM, G. (1967) *The Concept of Ideology and Other Essays*, New York: Vintage Books.

LUCY, J.A. (1991) 'Empirical Research and Linguistic Relativity'. Symposium, 'Rethinking Linguistic Relativity' (May 3–11, 1991) sponsored by Wenner-Gren Foundation for Anthropological Research.

LUCY, J. (1992a) *Language Diversity and Thought: A Reformulation of the Linguistic Relativity Hypothesis*, Studies in the Social and Cultural Foundations of Language, **12**, Cambridge and New York: Cambridge University Press.

LUCY, J. (1992b) *Grammatical Categories and Cognition: A Case Study of the Linguistic Relativity Hypothesis*, Studies in the Social and Cultural Foundations of Language, **13**, Cambridge and New York: Cambridge University Press.

LUCY, J. (Ed.) (1992c) *Reflexive Language: Reported Speech and Metapragmatics*, Cambridge: Cambridge University Press.

MCCONNELL-GINET, S., BORKER, R. and FURMAN, N. (Eds) (1980) *Women and Language in Literature and Society*, New York: Praeger.

MCDAVID, R.I. (1966) [Comment], in Bright, W. (Ed.) *Sociolinguistics*, The Hague: Mouton, p.321.

MCDERMOTT, R. (1974) 'Achieving School Failure: An Anthropological Approach to Literacy and Social Stratification', in SPINDLER, G.D. (Ed.) *Education and Cultural Process: Toward an Anthropology of Education*, New York: Holt, Rinehart & Winston, pp. 82–118.

MCDERMOTT, R. (1977a) 'The Cultural Context of Learning to Read', in WANAT, S.F. (Ed.) *Issues in Evaluating Reading*, Linguistics and Reading Series, **1**, Arlington, VA: Center for Applied Linguistics, pp. 10–18.

MCDERMOTT, R. (1977b) 'The Ethnography of Speaking and Reading', in SHUY, R. (Ed.) *Linguistic Theory: What Can It Say About Reading*, Newark, Delaware: International Reading Association.

MALCOLM, I.G. (1991) 'The Relevance of the Ethnography of Communication to the Language Teacher' in MALCOLM, I.G. (Ed.) *Linguistics in the Service of Society*, Perth, Australia: Institute of Applied Language Studies, Edith Cowan University, pp. 175–190.

MANDELBAUM, D.G. (Ed.) (1949) *Selected Writings of Edward Sapir*, Berkeley and Los Angeles, CA: University of California Press. (2nd ed., 1985.)

MARX, K. (1912) [1886] *Capital: A Critique of Political Economy, Vol. 1*, Translated from the 3rd German edition by MOORE, S. and AVELING, E. and edited by ENGELS, F., Chicago, IL: Charles H. Kerr.

MASCALL, E.L. (1968) *Words and Images*, London: Darton, Longman and Todd.

MAESMANN, V.L. (1983) 'Cultural Reproduction in the Bilingual Classroom', in Bain, B. (1983) The Sociogenesis of Language and Human Conduct, New York: Plenum, pp. 541–51.

MAYNARD, D.W. and CLAYMAN, S.B. (1991) 'The Diversity of Ethnomethodology', Annual Review of Sociology, 17, pp. 35–418.

MEHAN, H. (1972) 'Language using Abilities', Language Sciences, 22, (October), pp. 1–10.

MERLAN, F. and RUMSEY, A. (1991) Ku Waru. Language and Segmentary Politics in the Western Nebilyer Valley, Papua New Guinea, Cambridge: Cambridge University Press.

METCALF, G.J. (1974) 'The Development of Comparative Linguistics in the Seventeenth and Eighteenth Centures: Precursors to Sir William Jones', in Hymes, D. (1974) Foundations in Linguistics, pp. 233–57.

METCALF, P. (1989) Where are You Spirits: Style and Theme in Berawan Prayer, Washington, DC: Smithsonian Institution.

MICHAELS, S. (1981) ' "Sharing Time": Children's narrative Styles and Differential Access to Literacy', Language in Society, 10, pp. 423–42.

Michaels, S. (1983) 'Influences on Children's Narratives', The Quarterly Newsletter of Comparative Human Cognition, 5, 2, pp. 30–4.

MILROY, L. and MIROY, J. (1992) 'Social Network and Social Class: Toward an Integrated Sociolinguistic Model', *Language in Society*, **21**, pp. 1–26.

MINAMI, M. and McCABE, A. (1991) '*Haiku* as a Discourse Mechanism: A Stanza Analysis of Japanese Children's Personal Narratives', *Language in Society*, **20**, pp. 577–99.

MITCHELL-KERNAN, C. (1972) 'Signifying and Marking: Two Afro-American Speech Acts' in GUMPERZ, J.J. and HYMES, D. (1972) Directions in Sociolinguistics, pp. 161–79.

MORGAN, L.H. (1870) Systems of Consanguinity and Affinity of the Human Family, Washington, DC: Smithsonian Institution.

MORGAN, L.H. (1877) Ancient Society: Researches in the Lines of Human Progress from Savagery through Barbarism to Civilization, New York: Henry Holt.

MUELLER, C. (1973) The Politics of Communication: A Study in the Political Sociology of Language, Socialization and Legitimation, New York: Oxford.

MÜHLHÄUSLER, P.(1986) *Pidgin and Creole Linguistics*, Oxford: Basil Blackwell.

MÜHLHÄUSLER, P. and HARRÉ, R. (1990) *Pronouns and People: The Linguistic Construction of Social and Personal Identity*, Oxford: Basil Blackwell.

MURRAY, D.A. (1988), 'The Context of Oral and Written Language: A Framework for Mode and Medium Switching', *Language in Society*, 17, pp. 351–73.

MYERS-SCOTTON, C. (1993) *Duelling languages: Grammatical Structure in Code-switching*, Oxford: Clarendon.

NADER, L. (1973) 'Up the Anthropologist: Perspectives Gained from Studying up', in HYMES, D. (1973b), *Reinventing Anthropology*, pp. 284–311.

NEUSTUPNY, J.B. (1974), 'The Modernization of the Japanese System of Communication', *Language in Society*, **3**, pp. 33–48.

NEUSTUPNY, J.B. (1979) Post-Structural Approaches to Language: Language Theory in a Japanese Context, Tokyo, Japan: University of Tokyo Press.

NEWMEYER, F.J. (1986) *The Politics of Linguistics*, Chicago, IL: University of Chicago Press.

NUYTS, J. and VERSCHEUREN, J. (1987) *A Comprehensive Bibliography of Pragmatics*, Amsterdam/Philadelphia, PA: John Benjamins. 4 volumes.

O'BARR, W.M. (1981) 'The Language of the Law', in FERGUSON, C.A. and HEATH, S. (1981) *Language in the USA*, pp. 386–406.

O'BARR, W.M. (1982) *Linguistic Evidence: Language, Power and Strategy in the Classroom*, New York: Academic Prress.

OCHS, E. (1988) *Culture and Language Development: Language Acquisition and Language Socialization in a Samoan Village*, Cambridge: Cambridge University Press,

ONG, W. (1988) [1982] *Orality and Literacy: The Technologizing of the Word*, London: Routledge. [London, Methuen].

PARAIN, B. (1969) *Petite Métaphysique de la Parole*, Paris: Gallimard. Translated as *A Metaphysics of Language*, Garden City, NY: Doubleday, Anchor Books, 1971.

PARKER, I. (1983) 'The Rise of the Vernaculars in Early Modern Europe: An Essay in the Political Economy of Language', in BAIN, B. (1983) *The Sociogenesis of Language and Human Conduct*, pp. 323–51.

PAULSTON, C.B. (1981) 'Bilingualism and Education', in FERGUSON, C.A. and HEATH, S.B. (1981) *Language in the USA*, pp. 469–85.

PAULSTON, C.B. (1994) *Linguistic Minorities in Multilingual Settings: Implications for Language Policies*, Amsterdam and Philadelphia, PA: John Benjamins.

PETTY, Sir W. (1927) [1686] 'Queries Concerning the Nature of the Natives of Pennsylvania', in the Marquis of Lansdowne (Ed.) *The Petty Papers: Some Unpublished Writings of Sir William Petty* (from the Bowood Papers), London: Constable, Vol. II, pp. 125–9.

PHILIPS, S. (1983) (A) 'Self-concept and Sexism in Language'; (B) 'Sexism and Self-concept in the Language of Children: A Middle Childhood Survey' in BAIN, B. (1983) *The Sociogenesis of Language and Human Conduct*, pp. 131–51.

PHILIPS, S (1972) 'Participant Structure and Communicative Competence: Warm Springs Children in Community and Classroom', in CAZDEN, J. and HYMES, D. (1972) *Functions of Language in the Classroom*, pp. 370–94.

PHILIPS, S. (1974) 'Literacy as a Mode of Communication on the Warm Springs Indian Reservation', in LENNEBERG, E.H. and LENNEBERG, E. (Eds) *Foundations of Language Development*, New York: Academic Press, **2**, pp. 367–82.

PHILIPS, S. (1983) [1974] *The Invisible Culture: Communication in Classroom and Community on the Warm Springs Indian Reservation*, New York: Longman. Reissued with changes, Prospect Heights, IL: Waveland Press, 1993, based on *The Invisible Culture*, unpublished doctoral dissertation, University of Pennsylvania, 1974.

PHILIPS, S., STEELE, S. and TANZ, C. (Eds) (1987) *Language, Gender and Sex in a Comparative Perspective*, Cambridge: Cambridge University Press.

PIKE, K.L. (1965) *Language in Relation to a Unified Theory of the Structure of Human Behavior*, The Hague: Mouton.

POMERANTZ, A.M. (1989) 'Epilogue', *Western Journal of Speech Communication*, **53**, 2 (issue devoted to 'Sequential Organization of Conversational Activities', (Ed.) BEACH, W.A.)

PRUCHA, J. (1983) 'Using Language: A Sociofunctional Approach', in Bain, B. (1983) *The Sociogenesis of Language and Human Conduct*, pp. 287–95.

RAMSEY, I.T. (1957) *Religious Language*, New York: Macmillan.

ROBINS, R.H. and UHLENBECK, E.M. (Eds) (1991) *Endangered Languages*, Providence, RI: Berg.

ROCA, A. and LIPSKI, J.M. (Eds) (1993) *Spanish in the United States: Linguistic Contact and Diversity*, Studies in Anthropological Linguistics 6, Berlin: Mouton de Gruyter.

ROMAINE, S. (1988) *Pidgin and Creole Languages*, London: Longman.

ROMAINE, S. (1994) 'Hawai'i Creole English as a Literary Language', *Language in Society*, **23**, pp. 527–54.

ROSALDO, M. (1973) 'I have Nothing to Hide: The Language of Ilongot Oratory', *Language in Society*, **2**, pp. 193–223.

ROSEN, H. (1991) 'The Nationalisation of English', *International Journal of Applied Linguistics*, **1**, pp. 104–17.

ROUSSEAU, J.-J. (1756), *Discourse on the Origin and Foundations of Inequality Among Men*, in Masters, R.D. (Ed.) *The First and Second Discourses* (transl. MASTERS, R.D. and J.) New York: St. Martin's Press, 1964.

RUSHFORTH, S. (1981) 'Speaking to "Relatives-through-marriage" ': Aspects of Communication Among the Bear Lake Athapaskans. *Journal of Anthropological Research*, **37**, pp. 28–45.

RUSKIN, F. and VARENNE, H. (1983) 'The Production of Ethnic Discourse: American and Puerto Rican Patterns', in BAIN, B. (1983) *The Sociogenesis of Language and Human Conduct*, pp. 553–68.

SAHAGUN, B. DE (1956) [1840] *Historia general de las cosas de Nueva Espana*, edited by GARIBAY, A.M., 4 vols, Mexico: Porriva.

SALKIE, R. (1990) *The Chomsky Update: Linguistics and Politics*, London: Unwin Hyman Academic.

SAMARIN, W.J. (Ed.) (1976) *Language in Religious Practice*, Rowley, MA: Newbury House.

SANDERS, R. (Ed.) (1990/91) *Research on Language and Social Interaction*, **24**. [With section on ethnomethodology]

SAPIR, E. (1909), *Wishram Texts*, Publications of the American Ethnological Society, **2**, Leiden: E.J. Brill.

SAPIR, E. (1921) *Language*, New York: Henry Holt.

SAPIR, E. (1924) 'The Grammarian and his Language', *American Mercury*, **1**, pp. 149–55. Also in Mandelbaum (1949) *Selected Writings of Edward Sapir*, pp. 150–9.

SAPIR, E. (1927) 'The Unconscious Patterning of Behavior in Society', in Dummer, E.S. (Ed.) *The Unconscious: A Symposium*, New York: Knopf. Also in MANDELBAUM, D.G. (1949) *Selected Writings of Edward Sapir*, pp. 544–59.

SAPIR, E. (1933) 'Language', *Encyclopedia of Social Sciences*, **9**, New York: Macmillan, pp. 155–69. Also in Mandelbaum (1949) *Selected Writings of Edward Sapir*, pp. 7–32.

SAPIR, E. (1939) 'Psychiatric and Cultural Pitfalls in the Business of getting a Living', *Mental Health*, Publication No. 9, American Association for the Advancement of Science, pp. 237–44. Also in MANDELBAUM, D.G. (1949) *Selected Writings of Edward Sapir*, pp. 578–89.

SAPIR, E. and SWADESH, M. (1946) 'American Indian Grammatical Categories', *Word*, **2**, pp. 103–12.

SCHEGLOFF, E.A. (1968) 'Sequencing in Conversational Openings', *American Anthropologist*, **70**, 1075–95. Reprinted in GUMPERZ, J.J. and HYMES, D. (1972) *Directions in Sociolinguistics*, pp. 346–80.

SCHIEFFELIN, B.B. (1990) *The Give and Take of Everyday Life: Language Socialization of Kaluli Children*, Cambridge: Cambridge University Press.

SCHIEFFELIN, B. and Ochs, E. (1986) *Language Socialization Across Cultures*, Cambridge: Cambridge University Press.

SCHIFFRIN, D. (1994) *Approaches to Discourse*, Oxford: Blackwell.

SCHNEIDER, D.M. (1972) 'What is Kinship all about?', in Reining, P. (Ed.) *Kinship Studies in the Morgan Centennial Year*, Washington, DC: Anthropological Society of Washington, pp. 32–63.

SCHROYER, T. (1970) 'Toward a Critical Theory for Advanced Industrial Society', in Dreitzel, H.P. (Ed.) *Recent Sociology*, **2**, New York: Macmillan, pp. 209–34.

SCHROYER, T. (1971) 'A Reconceptualization of Critical Theory', in COLFAX, J.D. and ROACH, J.L. (Eds) *Radical Sociology*, New York: Basic Books.

SCHROYER, T. (1973) *The Critique of Domination: The Origins and Development of Critical Theory*, New York: Braziller. Paperback, Boston, MA: Beacon Press (1975).

SCOLLON, R. and SCOLLON, S.B.K. (1981) *Narrative, Literacy and Face in Interethnic Communication*, Norwood, NJ: Ablex.

SCOLLON, R. and SCOLLON, S.W. (1994) *Intercultural Communication*, Cambridge, MA: Blackwell.

SHERZER, J.F. (1973) 'Verbal and Nonverbal Deixis in San Blas Cuna', *Language in Society*, **2**, 1, pp. 117–32.

SHERZER, J.F. (1983) *Kuna Ways of Speaking: An Ethnographic Perspective*, Austin, TX: University of Texas Press.

SHERZER, J.F. (1990) *Verbal Art in San Blas*, Cambridge: Cambridge University Press.

SHERZER, J.F. and URBAN, G. (Eds) (1986) *Native South American Discourse*, Berlin: Mouton de Gruyter.

SHERZER, J.F. and WOODBURY, A.C. (Eds) (1987) *Native American Discourse: Poetics and Rhetoric*, Cambridge: Cambridge University Press.

SHUMAN, A. (1986) *Story Telling Nights*, Cambridge: Cambridge University Press.

SILVERSTEIN, M. (1981) 'The Limits of Awareness', *Sociolinguistic Working Paper* 84, Austin, TX: Southwest Educational Development Laboratory.

SINGER, P. (1974) Review of Clecak (1974), *New York Review of Books*, **21**, 12, pp. 20–4.

SLAMA-CAZACU, T. (1983) 'Theoretical Perspectives for a Contemporary Applied Linguistics', in Bain, B. *The Sociogenesis of Language and Human Conduct* (1983), pp. 257–71.

SLOTKIN, J.S. (1965) *Readings in Early Anthropology*, Viking Fund Publications in Anthropology, **40**, Chicago, IL: Aldine.

SMITH, J.S. and SCHMIDT, D.L. (1994 ms), 'Variability in written Japanese: Towards a sociolinguistics of script choice'.

SMITHERMAN, G. (1977) *Talkin' and Testifyin': The Language of Black America*, New York: Houghton, Mifflin. Second edition, Detroit: Wayne State University Press, 1986.

SNYDERS, G. (1965) *La Pédagogie en France aux XVII' et XVIII' Siècles*, Paris: Presses Universitaires de France.

SPRADLEY, J.P. and McCURDY, D.W. (Eds) (1972) *The Cultural Experience: Ethnography in Complex Society*, Chicago, IL: Science Research Associates.

STEIN, A. (1972) 'Educational Equality in the United States: The Emperor's Clothes', *Science and Society*, **36**, 4, pp. 469–76.

STEINER, G. (1971) *Extraterritorial*, New York: Atheneum.

STERN, T. (1957) 'Drum and Whistle Languages: An Analysis of Speech Surrogates', *American Anthropologist*, **59**, 487–506.

STUBBS, M. (1986) *Educational Linguistics*, Oxford: Basil Blackwell.

SWADESH, M. (1971) *Origin and Diversification of Languages*, Chicago, IL: Aldine.

SWANN, B. (Ed.) (1983) *Smoothing the Ground*, Berkeley and Los Angeles, CA: University of California Press.

SWANN, B. and KRUPAT, A. (Eds) (1987) *Recovering the Word: Essays on Native American Literature*, Berkeley and Los Angeles, CA: University of California Press.

SZWED, J. (1973) 'An American Anthropological Dilemmma: The Politics of Afro-American Culture', in Hymes, D. (1973b) *Reinventing Anthropology*, pp. 153–81.

TANNEN, D. (1989) *Talking Voices: Repetition, Dialogue and Imagery in Conversational Discourse*, Cambridge: Cambridge University Press.

TANNEN, D. (Ed.) (1993) *Gender and Conversational Interaction*, (Oxford Studies in Sociolinguistics), New York: Oxford University Press.

TANNEN, D. (1994) *Gender and Discourse*, New York: Oxford University Press.

TEDLOCK, D. (1972) *Finding the Center*, New York: Dial. Reprinted, Lincoln, NB: University of Nebraska Press, 1978.

TEDLOCK, D. (1983) *The Spoken Word and the Work of Interpretation*, Philadelphia, PA: University of Pennsylvania Press.

TENTCHOFF, D. (1975) 'Cajun French and French Creole: Their Speakers and the Question of Identities', in DESESTO, S. and GIBSON, J. (Eds) *The Culture of Acadiana: Tradition and Change in South Louisiana.* Lafayette, LA: University of Southern Louisiana.

THORNE, B., KRAMARAE, C. and HENLEY, N. (1983) *Language, Gender and Society*, Rowley, MA: Newbury House.

TITONE, R. (1983) 'Second Language Learning: An Integrated Pyscholinguistic Model', in Bain, B. *The Sociogenesis of Language and Human Conduct*, pp. 273–85.

TURNER, R. (Ed.) (1974a) *Ethnomethodology*, London: Penguin.

TURNER, R. (1974b) 'Words, Utterances and Activities', in TURNER, R., *Ethnomethodology*, pp. 197–215.

TWAY, P. (1975) 'Workplace Isoglosses: Lexical Variation and Change in a Factory Setting', *Language in Society*, **4**, 2, pp. 171–83.

ULDALL, H.J. (1944) 'Speech and Writing', *Acta Linguistica*, **4**, pp. 11–16.

URBAN, W.M. (1939) *Language and Reality: The Philosophy of Language and the Principles of Symbolism*, London: George Allen.

URBAN, G. (1991) *A Discourse-centered Approach to Culture: Native South American Myths and Rituals*, Austin, TX: University of Texas Press.

USEEM, E. and MICHAEL, L. (1974) *The Education Establishment*, Englewood Cliffs, NJ. Prentice Hall.

VACHEK, J. (1944–49) 'Some Remarks on Writing and Phonetic Transcription', *Acta Linguistica*, **5**, pp. 86–93.

VOEGELIN, C.F., VOEGELIN, F.M. and SCHUTZ, N.W., Jr (1967) 'The Language Situation in Arizona as Part of the Southwest Culture Area' in HYMES, D. (1967b) *Studies in Southwestern Ethnolinguistics*, pp. 403–51.

WADE, D. (1972) 'The Limits of the Electronic Media', *Times Literary Supplement Essays and Reviews*, **5** (May), pp. 515–16.

WAGGONER, D. (1981) 'Statistics on Language Use', in FERGUSON, C.A, and HEATH, S.B. (1981) *Language in the USA*, pp. 486–515.

WATSON, G. and SEILER, R.M. (Eds) (1992) *Text in Context: Contributions to Ethnomethodology*, Newbury Park, CA: Sage.

WERTSCH, J.V. (1983) 'The role of Semiosis in L.S. Vygotsky's Theory of Human Cognition', in Bain, B. (1983) *The Sociogenesis of Language and Human Conduct*, pp. 17–31.

WHATLEY, E. (1981) 'Language among Black Americans', in Ferguson, C.A. and Heath, S.B. (1981) *Language in the USA*, pp. 92–107.

WHITE, H. (1973a) 'Interpretation in History', *New Literary History*, **4**, 2, 281–314.

WHITE, H. (1973b) *Metahistory: The Historical Imagination in Nineteenth-century Europe*, Baltimore, MD: Johns Hopkins Press.

WHITING, B.B. (Ed.) (1963) *Six Cultures: Studies of Child Rearing*, New York: John Wiley.

WHORF, B.L. (1941) 'The Relation of Language to Habitual Thought and Behavior', in SPIER, L., HALLOWELL, A.I. and NEWMAN, S.S. (Eds), Menasha, WI: George Banta, pp. 75–93. Also in Carroll (1956), *Language, Thought and Reality*, pp. 134–59.

WHORF, B.L. (1942) 'Language, Mind and Reality', *Theosophist* (Madras), **63**, 1, pp. 281–91, 2, pp. 25–37. Also in Carroll (1956), *Language, Thought and Reality*, pp. 246–70.

WILLIAMS, C.H. (Ed.) (1991) *Linguistic Minorities, Society and Territory*, Clevedon and Philadelphia, PA: Multilingual Matters.

WILLIAMS, G. and ROBERTS, C. (1983) 'Language, Education and Reproduction in Wales', in BAIN, B. (1983) *The Sociogenesis of Language and Human Conduct*, pp. 497–515.

WILLIAMS, R. (1643) *A Key into the Language of America*, London: Gregory Dexter.

WILLIS, W.S. Jr (1973) 'Skeletons in the Anthropological Closet', in HYMES, D. (1973b) *Reinventing Anthropology*, pp. 121–52.

WOLFF, H. (1959) 'Intelligibility and Inter-ethnic Attitudes', *Anthropological Linguistics*, **1**, 3, pp. 34–41.

WOLFSON, N. (1976) 'Speech Events and Natural Speech: Some Implications for Sociolinguistic Methodology', *Language in Society*, **5**, 2, pp. 211–18.

WOLFSON, N. (1978) 'A Feature of Performed Narrative: The Conversational Historical Present', *Language in Society*, **7**, pp. 215–37.

WOLFSON, N. (1982) *The Conversational Historical Present in American English Narrative*, Topics in Sociolinguistics 1, Dordrecht: Foris.

WOLFSON, N. (1989) 'The Conversational Historical Present. Analyse de corpus oraux'. *LINX*, **21**, 1, pp. 135–50.

WORTH, S. (1972) *Through Navaho eyes*, Bloomington, IN: Indiana University Press.

WRIGHT, R. (1975) 'Black English (review article)', *Language in Society*, **4**, pp. 185–98.

ZENTELLA, A.C. (1981) 'Language Variety among Puerto Ricans', in FERGUSON, C.A. and HEATH, S.B. (1981) *Language in the USA*, pp. 218–38.

Subject Index

Name Index

Lichtheim   221
Lichman   138
Linguistic Society of
  America   208
Li Po   219
Longstreth (school)   19
Lousiana   72
Lucy   187, 212, 222
Luria   186

Macedonian   219
Madras   39, 40
Maesmann   79
Maine, Sir Henry   28
Malcolm   167
Mandelbaum   26, 27, 44

Maori   10
Marius Victorinus   42
Marx   52, 97, 99, 188,
  221
Marxism   52–3, 92, 101
Maryland   67
Mascall   42
Mayan Quiche   124
Maynard and Clayman
  91
McConnell-Ginet, Borker
  and Furman   74
McDavid   72
McDermott   14-5, 77,
  85
McLuhan   34
Mead   34, 84
Mehan   91
Merlan and Rumsey   90
Merleau-Ponty   45
Mescalero Apache   91
Metcalf, G.   28
Metcalf, P.   166
Mexicans   67
Michaels   140, 165,
  174–82, 183
Millar   16
Miller   163
Milroy and Milroy   73
Minami and McCabe
  163
Mitchell-Kernan   68, 70
Morgan, L.H.   5, 6, 11,
  18
Mt Hood   117
Mueller   113
Mühlhaüsler   191
  and Harré   212

Murray   36
Myers-Scotton   73

Nader   100
National Institute of
  Education   3
Native American   37, 66,
  72, 166, 193–4, 219
Native American
  (languages)   10, 75,
  78, 136
Navajo   213
Neo-Bloomfieldian   96–7
Neustupny   51, 78
New Guinea   19
Newmeyer   95
New World Spanish   68
New York   32, 71, 77, 82,
  86, 168, 191, 208;
  Brooklyn   86
New York Times   71
Nigeria   31
'Norris'   170–2
Northeast Philadelphia
  English   215
Nuyts and Verscheuren
  88

O'Barr   73
Ochs   90
Official English
  Movement   86
Old Testament   206
Olivares   68
Oregon   39, 75, 86, 131,
  193

Pacific Northwest   215
Parain   42, 45
Parker   83
Parsons   57, 94
Paultson   78, 79
Pearson   200
Petty   5, 15
Peynetsa, Andrew   126
Philadelphia   7–10, 18,
  19, 69, 203, 215–6
Philips   39, 75, 85, 111
Philips, Steele and Tanz
  74
Pierce   47
Pike   8, 9
Pima Indian   67
Plato   42
Plotinus   42

Pomerantz   91
Prague School   61
Prucha   95
Pueblo   213
Puerto Rico   67, 156

Quaker   58, 83
Quileute   28

Ramsey   42
Reading and Language
  Arts, University of
  Pennsylvania   147
Reich   34
Renaissance   28
Reynolds, Lloyd J.   40
Ricouer   45
Riesman   34
Robertson   16
Robins and Uhlenbeck
  86
Roca and Lipski   68
Romaine   71, 191
Rosaldo   47–8, 56
Rosen   210
Ross   166
Rossi-Landi   94
Rousseau, Jean Jaques
  25
Royal Society   15
Rushforth   56
Ruskin and Varnne   68
Russell   42

Sahagun, Father   4
Sahaptin   45
Salkie   95
Samarin   58
Samoa   84
Sanday   15
San Francisco   78
Sanders   91
Sapir,   26, 27, 28, 42, 43,
  44, 55, 60, 90, 96,
  103, 104, 137, 186,
  187, 208, 222
  and Swadesh   222
Sartre   45
Snyders   85
Schegloff   151
Schieffelin   90
  and Ochs   90
Schiffrin   88, 218
Schneider   11
Schroyer   51, 53, 62, 93